IMAGES
of America

GRAND CANYON PIONEER CEMETERY

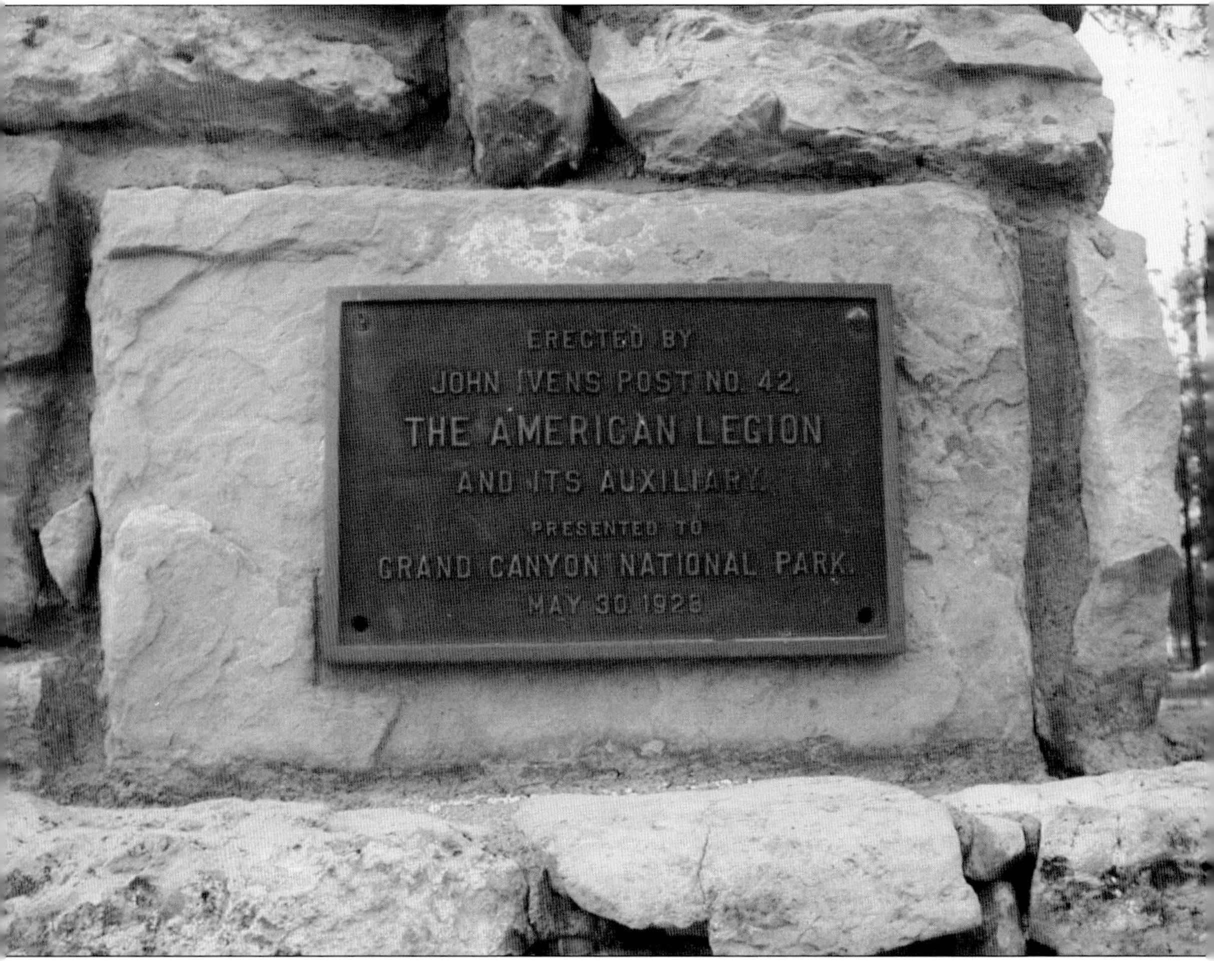

This plaque was erected on Memorial Day 1928 to officially establish the partnership of Grand Canyon National Park with the American Legion, John Ivens Post No. 42, in caring for the Grand Canyon Cemetery. This partnership remains intact today. (Lois Schmittinger.)

On the Cover: Members of the Masonic Lodge form a triangle image at the funeral of legendary Grand Canyon photographer Emery Kolb after Kolb's casket has been lowered into the ground. A military honor guard looks on. (Grand Canyon NP Museum Collection No. 06510.)

IMAGES
of America

Grand Canyon Pioneer Cemetery

Parker Anderson

ARCADIA
PUBLISHING

ISBN 978-1-4671-3223-7

Published by Arcadia Publishing
Charleston, South Carolina

Printed in the United States of America

Library of Congress Control Number: 2014933840

For all general information, please contact Arcadia Publishing:
Telephone 843-853-2070
Fax 843-853-0044
E-mail sales@arcadiapublishing.com
For customer service and orders:
Toll-Free 1-888-313-2665

Visit us on the Internet at www.arcadiapublishing.com

Dedicated to the men and women of the Grand Canyon, past and present, who have devoted their lives to preserving one of the greatest wonders of the world for generations to come

Contents

Acknowledgments

This book would not have been possible without the generous assistance and support of Colleen Hyde, museum specialist at the Grand Canyon National Park, as well as the American Legion, John Ivens Post No. 42, who submitted their early-day photographs of the Grand Canyon Pioneer Cemetery.

INTRODUCTION

It has often been said that the Grand Canyon is one of the very few national parks to have its own cemetery within its borders. In a broad scope, this is not entirely true. Many of the Civil War battlefields are in the national park system and contain the burial grounds of the fallen soldiers.

Perhaps the statement is more accurate if we rephrase it to say that the Grand Canyon is one of the very few national parks to have its own active cemetery—one that is still in use today.

The Grand Canyon Pioneer Cemetery began with the 1919 burial of John Hance, one of the first white settlers on the canyon rim. He was followed soon after by Ralph Berry, the son of canyon miner and businessman Pete Berry. The Grand Canyon attained national park status that same year, and as there came to be more deaths in the park, this cemetery in a quiet grove of pine trees started to grow. On Memorial Day 1928, the Grand Canyon American Legion, John Ivens Post No. 42, dedicated a plaque and entered into a partnership with the National Park Service to help maintain the cemetery.

Due to the obvious interest people would have in being buried at Grand Canyon, the National Park Service has had to enact strict regulations on who is eligible for interment. To be buried here, one has to have been a resident of the Grand Canyon for a minimum of three years. Indeed, there are many residents at the canyon. The park rangers, mule wranglers, concession employees, and other workers have to live at the canyon, often in communal housing, since the cities of Flagstaff and Williams, Arizona, are too far away to commute. Also, one cannot live at the Grand Canyon unless employed there, or without some other strong tie to the canyon.

The three-year residency requirement for interment in the cemetery can be waived if the deceased made a great contribution to the benefit and understanding of the canyon, as geologist Dr. John Maxson did. Also, immediate family members of canyon personnel are sometimes allowed to be buried here. The cemetery averages around four burials per year.

The graves represent the entire spectrum of Grand Canyon history, past and present. Buried in this beautiful, peaceful glade are park superintendents, rangers, miners, scientists, Fred Harvey girls, workers of all trades, and one murder victim—possibly two. The lure of the canyon is so strong that there are a number of cases of men and women who were returned here for burial, even though they had left the canyon many years earlier.

Visitors, tourists, and taphophiles who visit the Grand Canyon Pioneer Cemetery are often struck by how many of the park's legendary early settlers are buried here, together in the same resting place. It is difficult to name anyone significant in canyon history that does not rest here. Perhaps the only exceptions are Mary Colter, Burton and Niles J. Cameron, and members of the Fred Harvey family.

In 1970, after many years of plans and delays, a multipurpose center called the Shrine of the Ages was completed, with the purpose of hosting nondenominational religious events, private functions, lectures, and other presentations. It was built almost adjacent to the Grand Canyon

Pioneer Cemetery, and sometimes funerals for the deceased are held here. The National Park Service formally took over the Shrine of the Ages in 1975.

Many cemeteries in the United States are abandoned, in an advanced state of decay, or have vanished altogether, while others run the risk of suffering this fate. But the Grand Canyon Pioneer Cemetery, located within the boundaries of a national park, will never be in danger. It will be around long after we have passed from the scene, as a monument to those who helped make one of the Seven Wonders of the World what it is today.

One

Over the Years

When John Hance was buried in a secluded grove of ponderosa pines in 1919, it was not necessarily with the intent of starting a cemetery. But by the mid-1920s, there were more than a dozen graves here, and the National Park Service realized they had a bona fide burial ground in the park.

As time went on, the Grand Canyon American Legion, John Ivens Post No. 42, entered into an agreement with the National Park Service to care for the cemetery. Improvements were made, a gate was erected, and pathways were forged around the grounds by Civilian Conservation Corps (CCC) workers.

Millions of people have visited the Grand Canyon, and very few of them have ever realized there is a cemetery. While the location is beautiful, it is not on the rim, nor is it in view of the canyon itself, so it is difficult to just happen across it if one is not specifically looking for the site.

This chapter shows the cemetery as it appeared over the years and the work that was done on it. It is a part of Grand Canyon history that has seldom been written about or discussed.

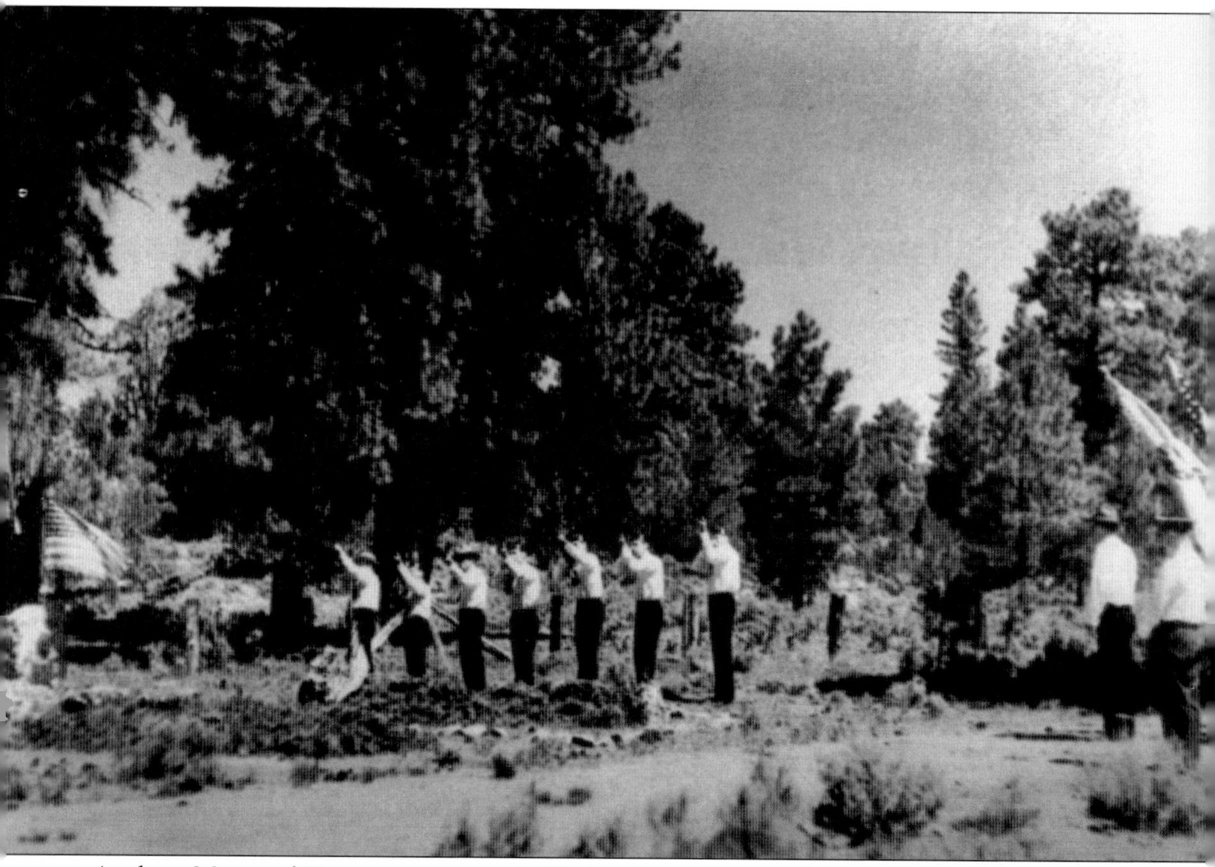

At these Memorial Day ceremonies in 1928, the Grand Canyon American Legion, John Ivens Post No. 42, officially took stewardship of the cemetery along with the National Park Service. This partnership remains in effect today, and in fact, the burial ground is more formally known as the Grand Canyon American Legion Cemetery. (American Legion, John Ivens Post No. 42.)

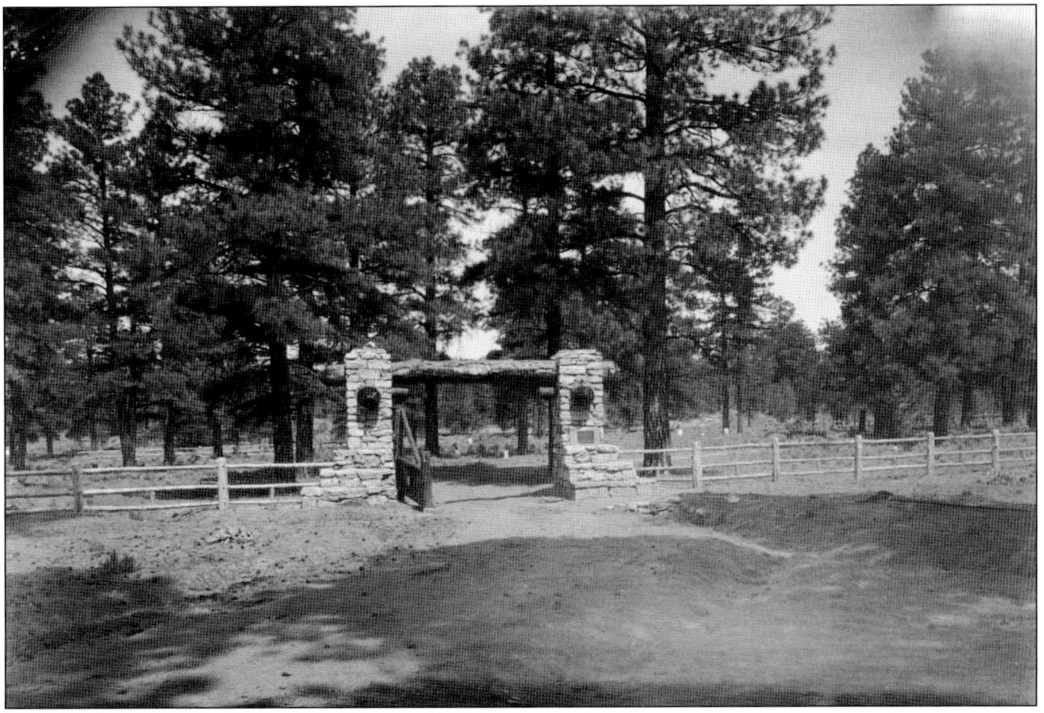

This is the entrance to the Grand Canyon Pioneer Cemetery in 1935. It looks much the same today as it did then. (Grand Canyon NP Museum Collection No. 00569a.)

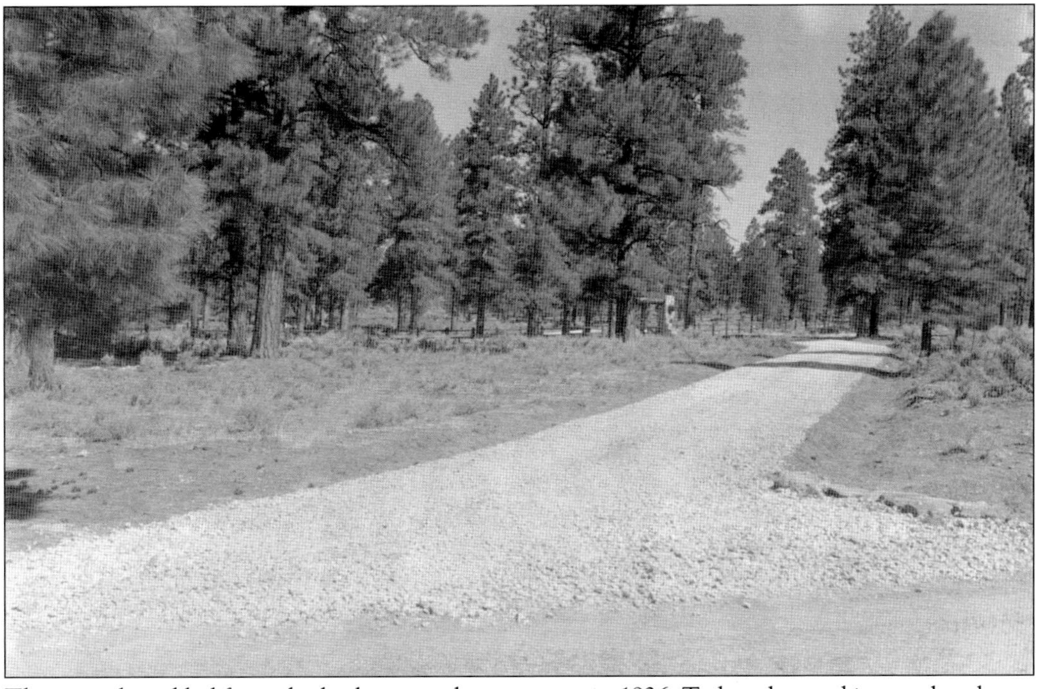

This gravel road led from the highway to the cemetery in 1936. Today, the road is paved and near Market Plaza, where the main general store, post office, and bank are located for canyon residents and tourists. (Grand Canyon NP Museum Collection No. 00296.)

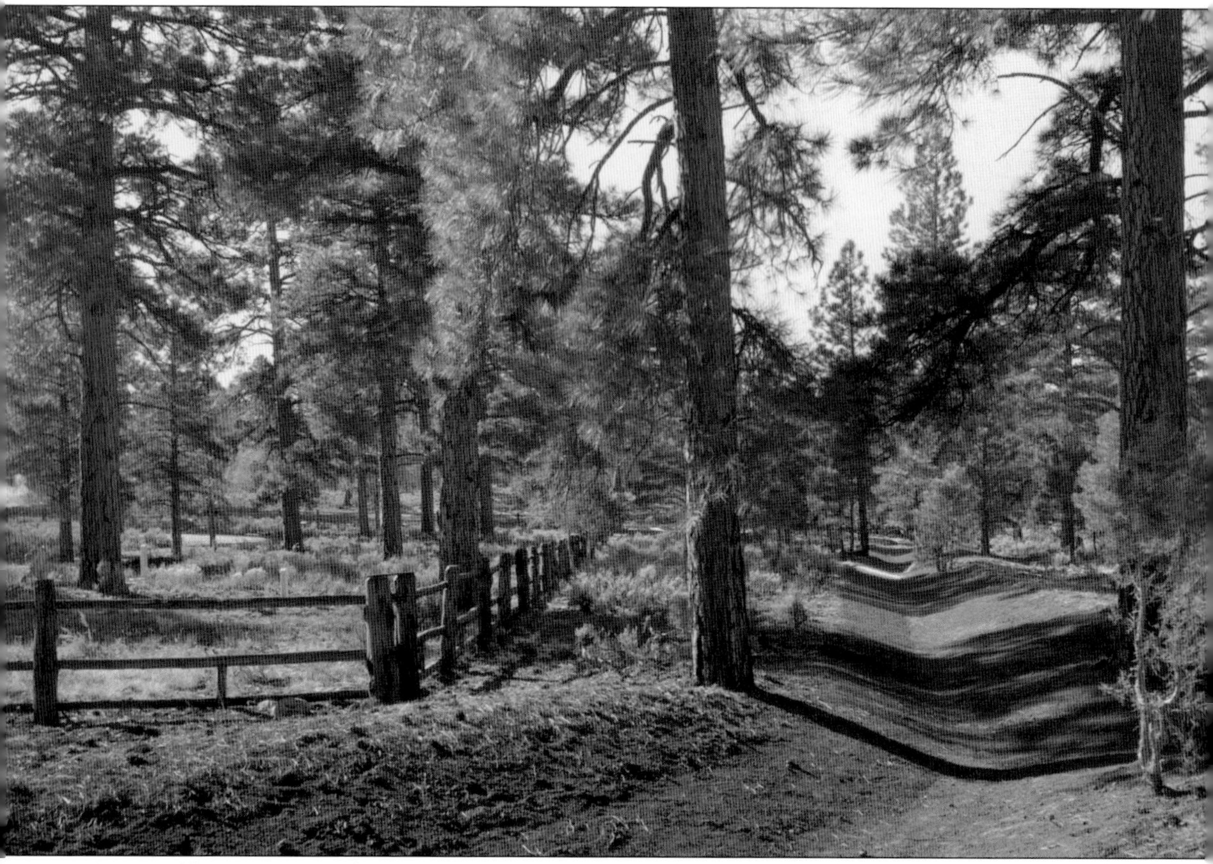
Pictured here on December 12, 1936, is a culvert and a water drainage ditch with the cemetery fence to the left. (Grand Canyon NP Museum Collection No. 00295.)

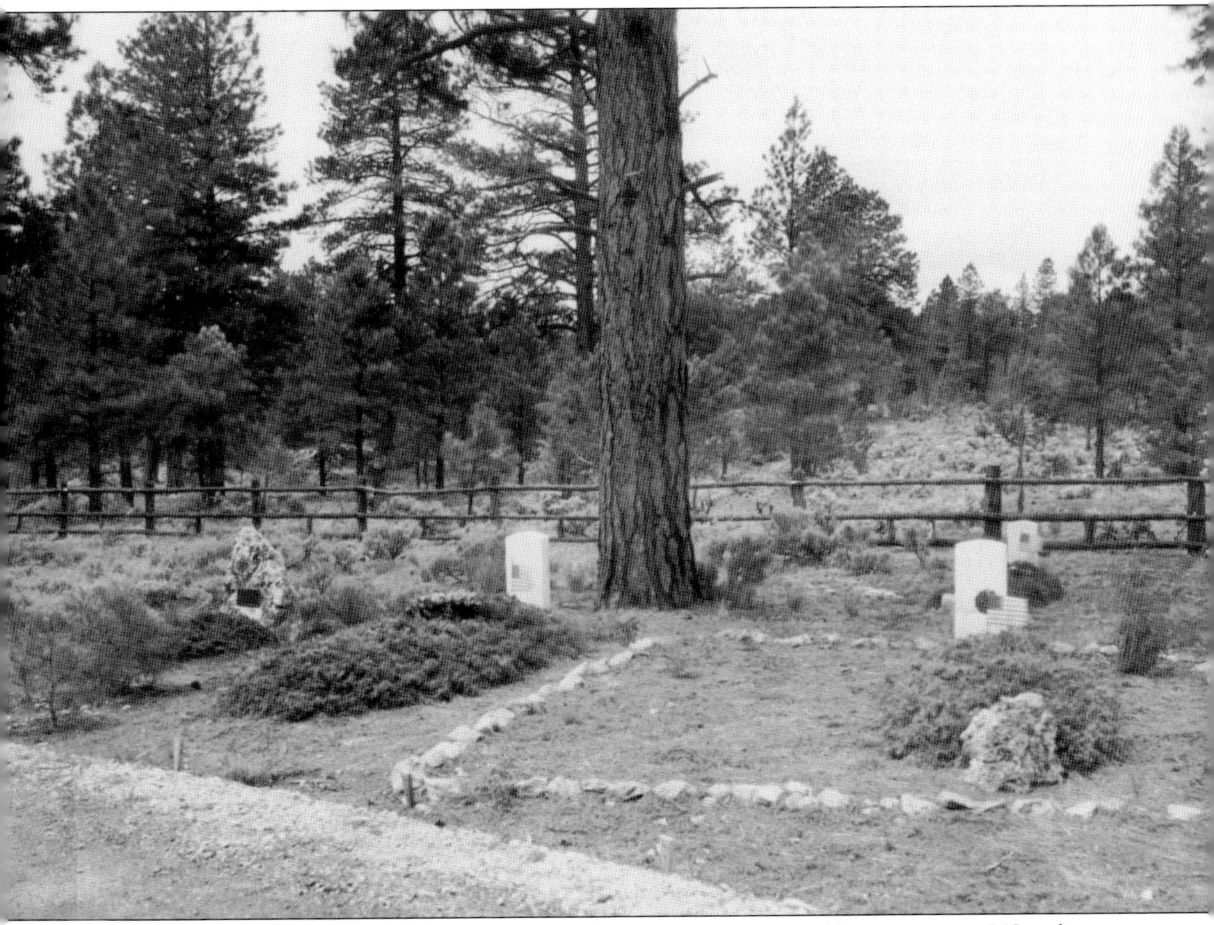

Pictured here in 1937 is the veterans' section of the cemetery, so named because many US military veterans are interred together in the southwest corner of the burial ground. (Grand Canyon NP Museum Collection No. 01406.)

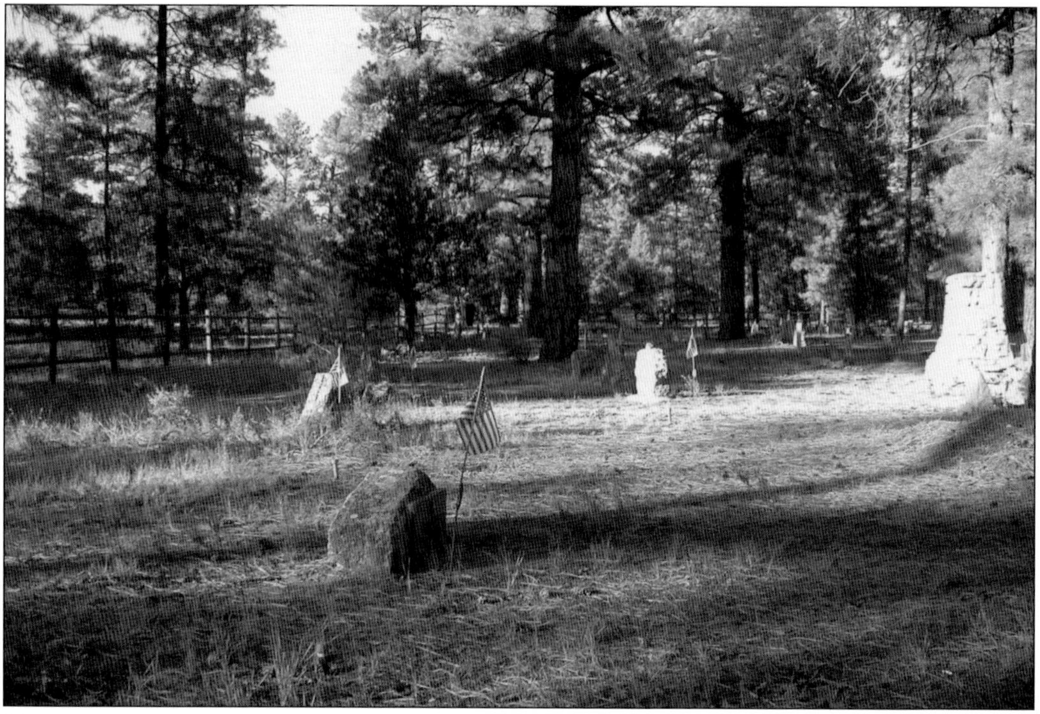

This is the veterans' section as seen today, with considerably more burials over the years. (David Schmittinger.)

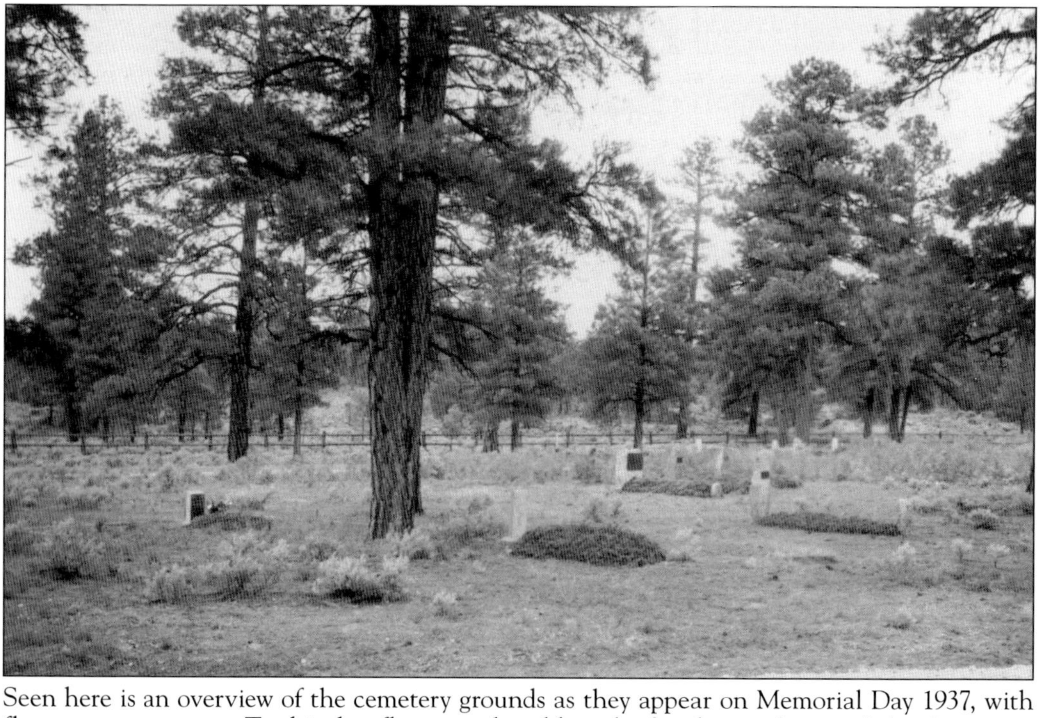

Seen here is an overview of the cemetery grounds as they appear on Memorial Day 1937, with flags on many graves. To this day, flags are placed here by family members and the American Legion. (Grand Canyon NP Museum Collection No. 01408.)

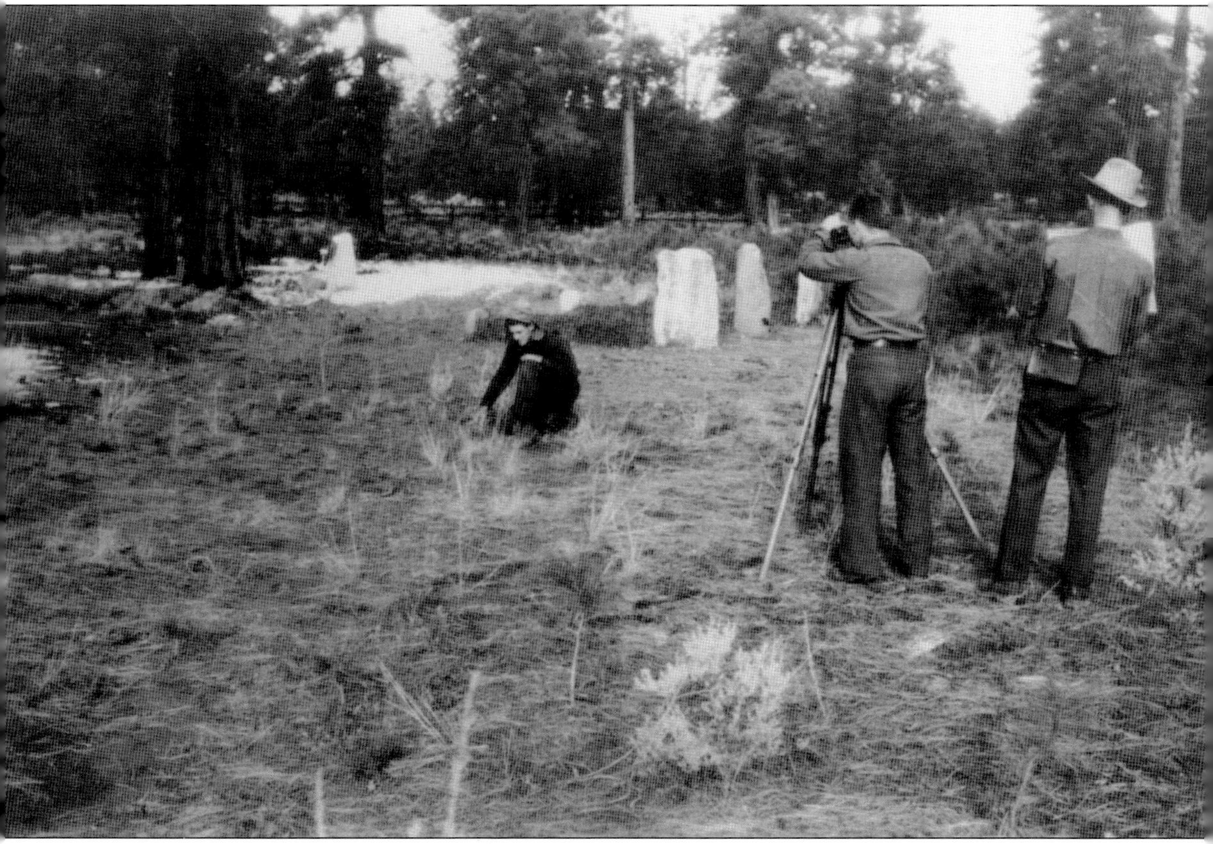

On January 28, 1938, a survey was made of the cemetery by Civilian Conservation Corps (CCC) workers to establish the corners of future burial lots. They did so by placing lead pipes at each of the corners of the new lots. (Grand Canyon NP Museum Collection No. 03853.)

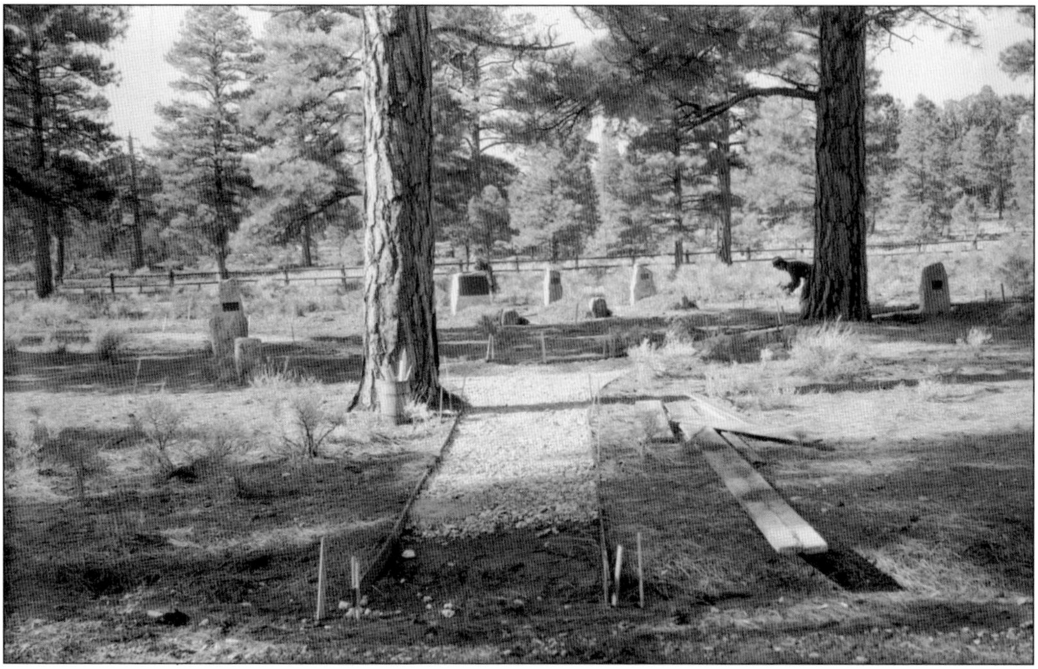

Another CCC project was to construct sidewalks and pathways through the cemetery to make it easier for visitors to navigate. The two photographs on this page, taken January 17, 1938, show this early effort to beautify the cemetery. In the above image, the grave of John Hance can be seen to the far left, while in the image below, the tall white marker for Lizzie Clawson is seen at far left, with the stone for Dr. David White on the far right. (Above, Grand Canyon NP Museum Collection No. 06153; below, Grand Canyon NP Museum Collection No. 06154.)

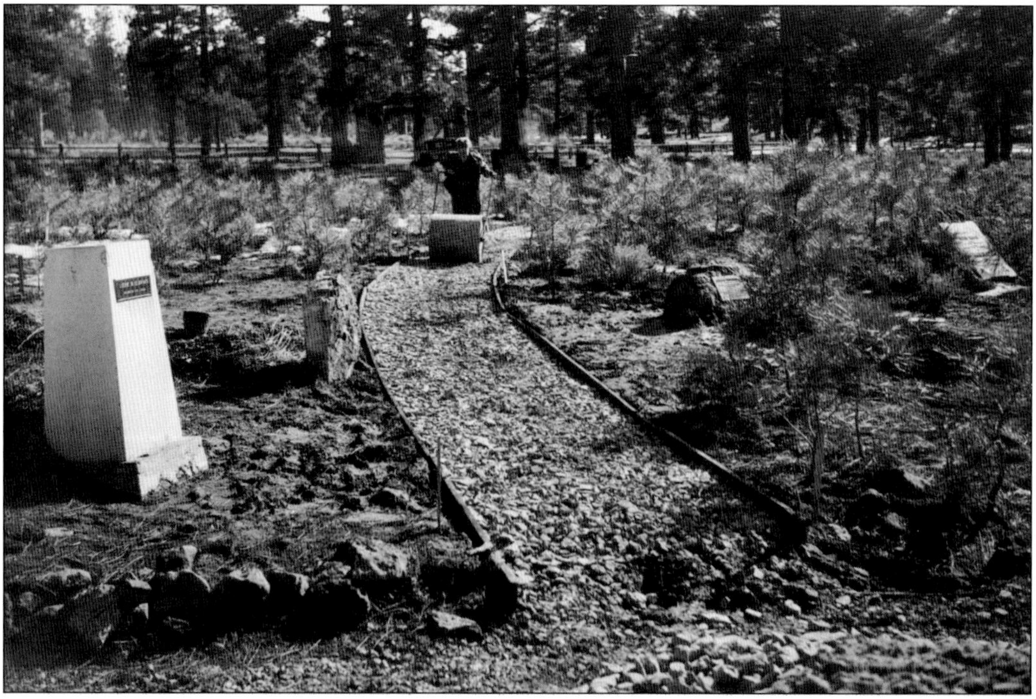

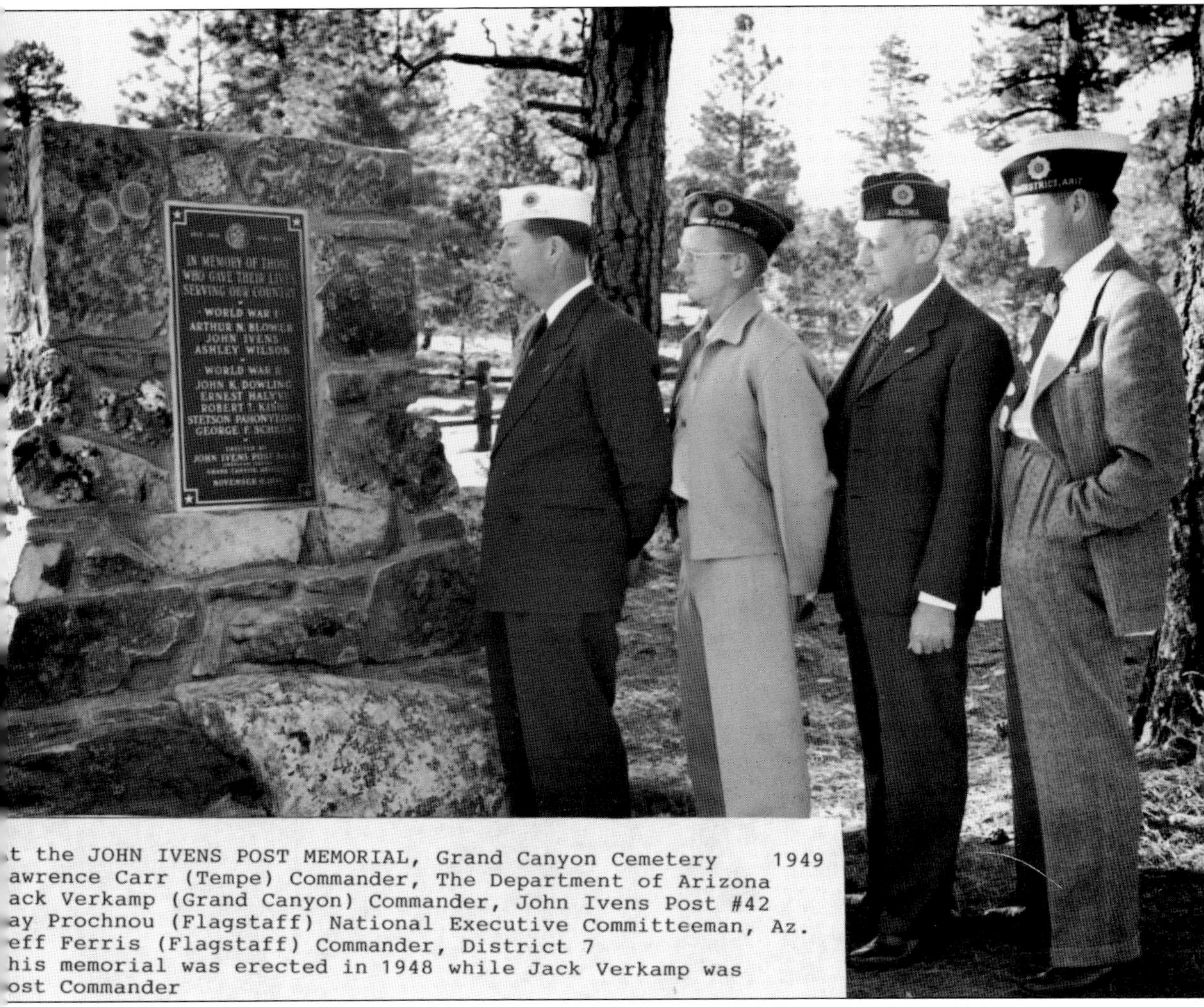

In 1948, the American Legion celebrated the 20th anniversary of its stewardship of the cemetery. At the Memorial Day ceremonies that year, a plaque was erected to honor this milestone. This 1949 photograph shows dignitaries from the John Ivens Post No. 42 posing at the memorial. Jack Verkamp (second from left) was post commander at the time, and he was the son of John Verkamp, the owner of the Grand Canyon's first novelty store. Jack Verkamp, who died in 2001, is buried in the cemetery. (American Legion, John Ivens Post No. 42.)

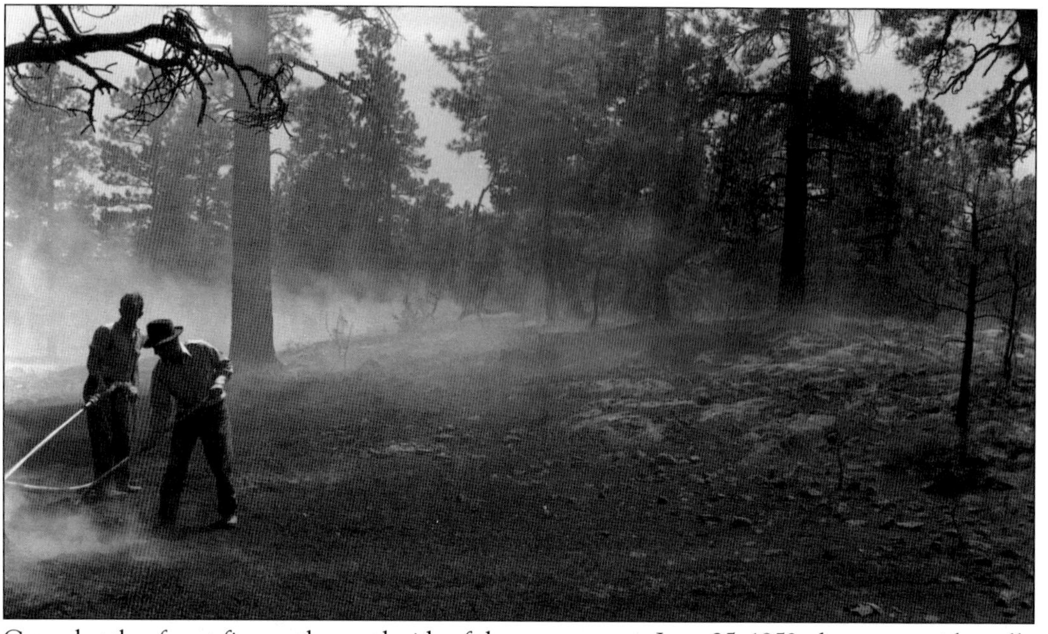

Crews battle a forest fire on the south side of the cemetery on June 25, 1953, that was accidentally set by a Fisher Construction unit during a slash burn. (Photograph by Steve Leding; Grand Canyon NP Museum Collection No. 02500.)

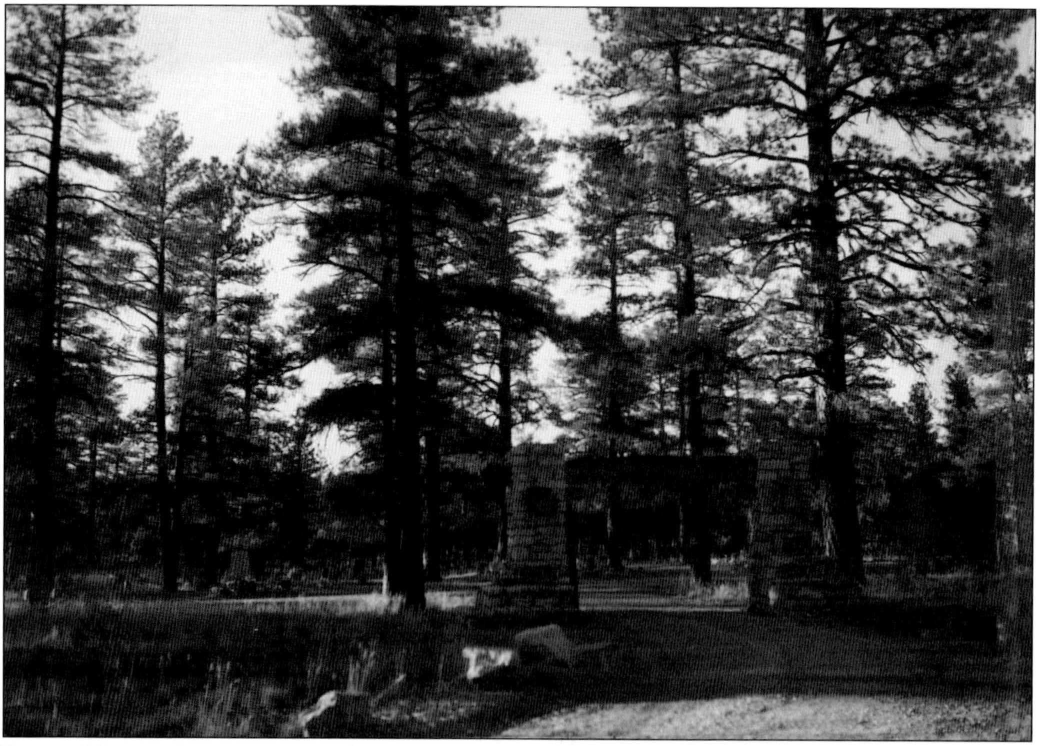

Pictured here is the entrance to the cemetery as seen in 1965. Once again, little has changed over the years; compare this photograph with the entrance photograph from around 1935 on page 11. (Grand Canyon NP Museum Collection No. 04791A.)

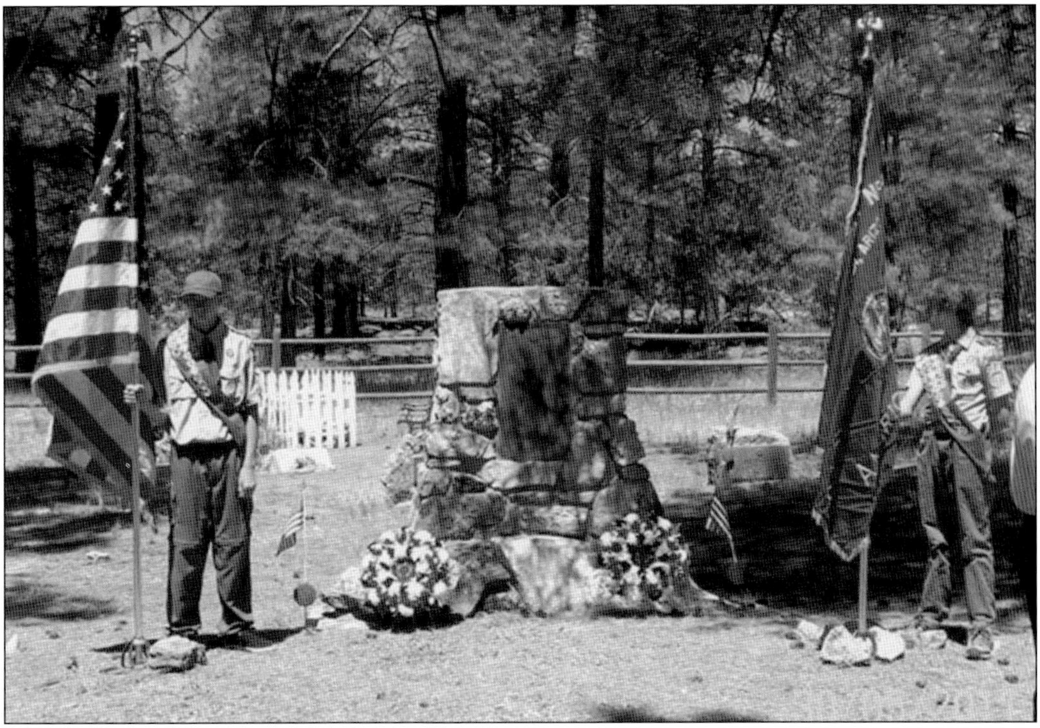

Boy Scouts and an honor guard participate in Memorial Day ceremonies at the cemetery in 2011 in these two photographs. These ceremonies are a tradition at the Grand Canyon Pioneer Cemetery. (Both, American Legion, John Ivens Post No. 42.)

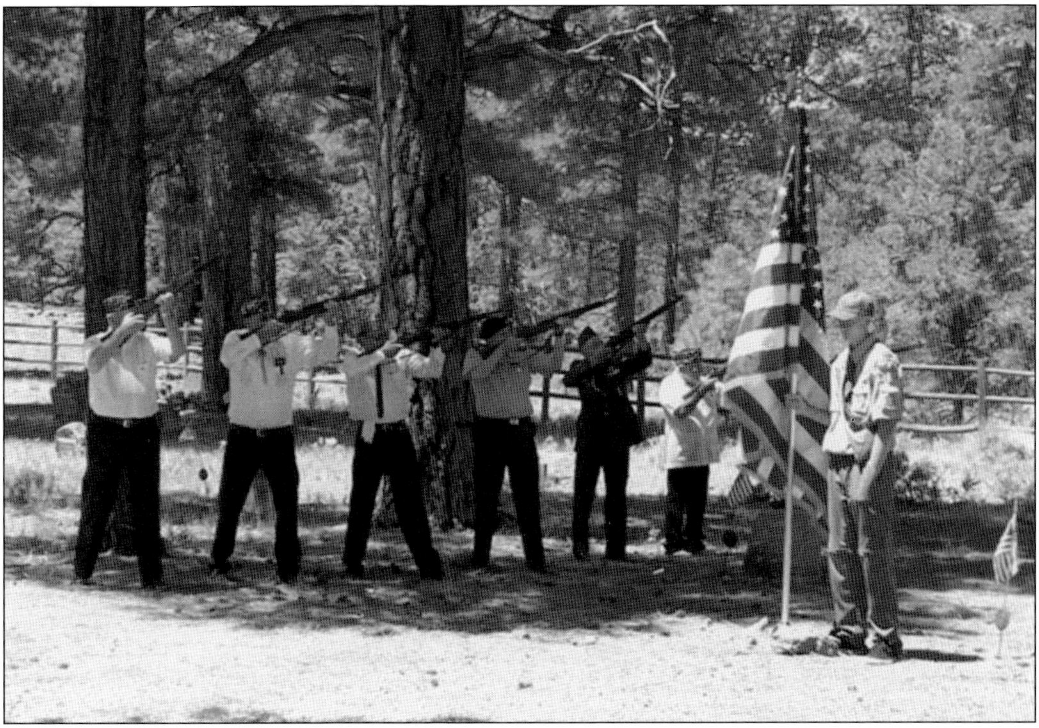

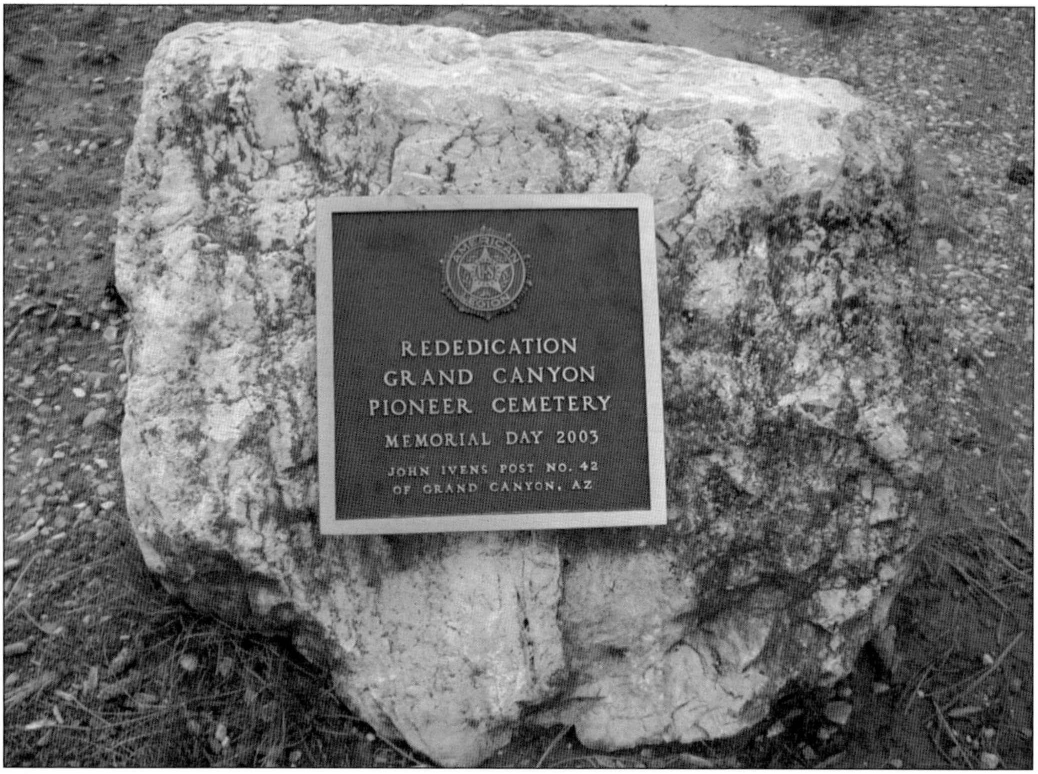

This plaque was erected at the American Legion cemetery rededication ceremonies on Memorial Day 2003 to mark the 75th anniversary of the John Ivens Post No. 42's stewardship. (Lois Schmittinger.)

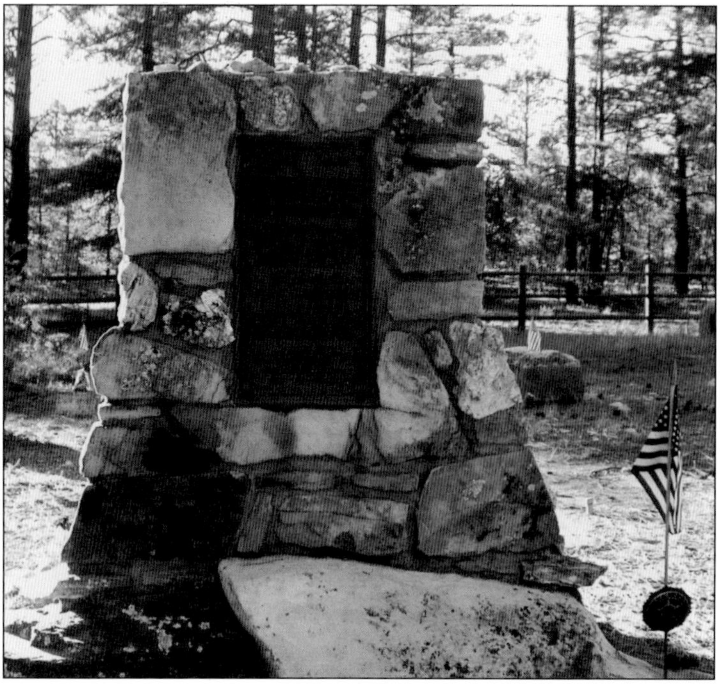

This memorial to the veterans of World War II, erected in 1948, commemorates the sacrifice that many Grand Canyon residents made during that conflict. (David Schmittinger.)

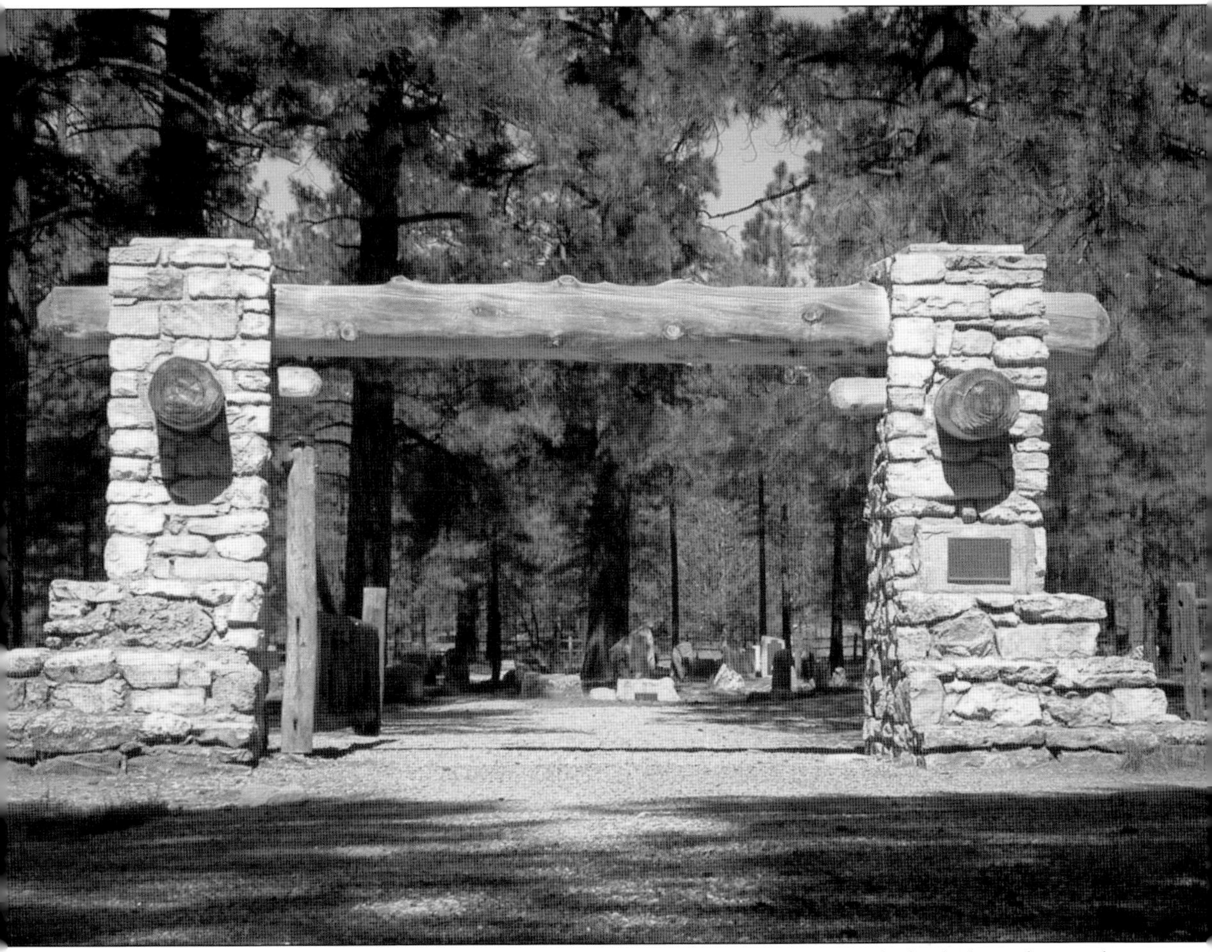

Pictured here is the entrance to the cemetery as seen today. Surprisingly little has changed to the entrance over the years, but the number of graves has increased to nearly 400. (Lois Schmittinger.)

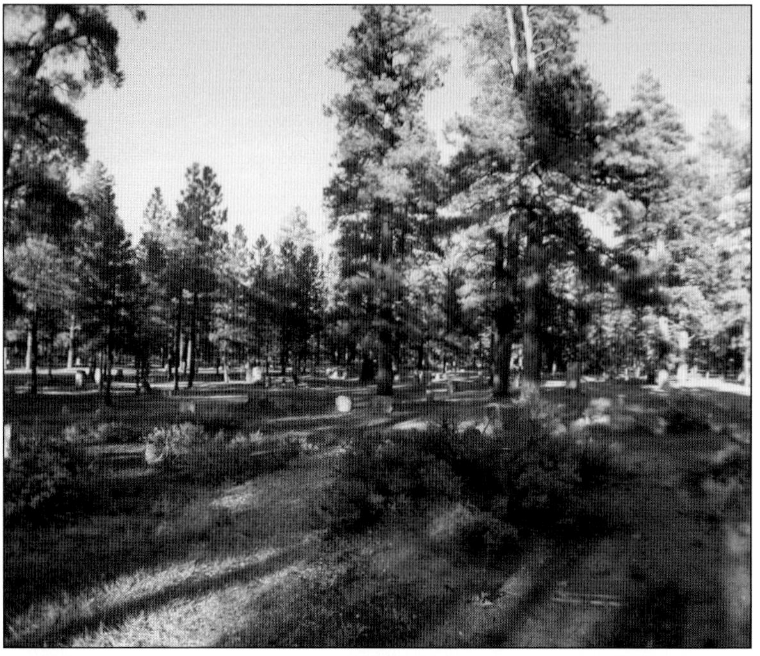

This is an overview of the cemetery, facing north, in 2014. As it is still an active burial ground, the boundaries may well expand in the coming years. (David Schmittinger.)

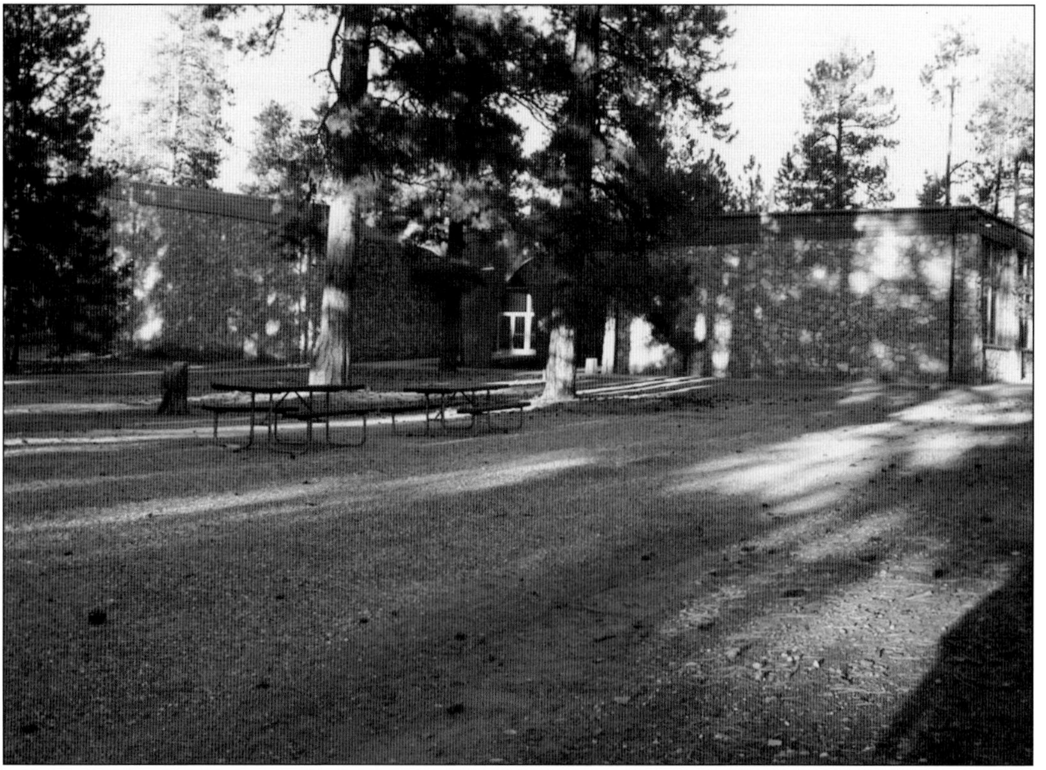

The Shrine of the Ages, a multipurpose building used for religious services, meetings, presentations, and sometimes funerals, was completed in 1970 and acquired by the National Park Service in 1975. It sits nearly adjacent to the Grand Canyon Pioneer Cemetery on its east side. (David Schmittinger.)

Two

JOHN HANCE

John Hance is regarded by Grand Canyon historians as the first white settler on the canyon rim (although William Wallace Bass would later make the same claim). Little is known about Hance's background beyond what he revealed himself, which is tainted by his well-known penchant for spinning tall tales to entertain his visitors. He claimed to have been born in Tennessee and served in the Confederate army during the Civil War, hence his "Captain" nickname, but definitive proof is lacking.

Still, Hance was the first man to court the potential tourist trade, advertising tours of this giant hole in the ground. He forged the Old Hance Trail as well as the New Hance Trail, near what is now Grandview Point, in the 1890s. He reportedly charged $2 to ride down his trails and $10 if he provided the mules and his services as a tour guide. As other canyon entrepreneurs came along, Hance would associate with Pete Berry and Ralph Cameron, but he later switched sides and went to work as a tour guide for the Fred Harvey Company when it moved into the canyon to compete fiercely with the men who owned small businesses in the area.

From the ramshackle cabin he lived in, John Hance's tours became so popular that when important men like Theodore Roosevelt visited the Grand Canyon, they would specifically ask for him. The colorful old man never disappointed them, spinning his fanciful stories.

As John Hance was the first white settler at the Grand Canyon, it is somehow fitting that upon his death in 1919, he would become the first burial in what is now the Grand Canyon Pioneer Cemetery. His footstone is eight feet away from his headstone as a nod to his tall tales.

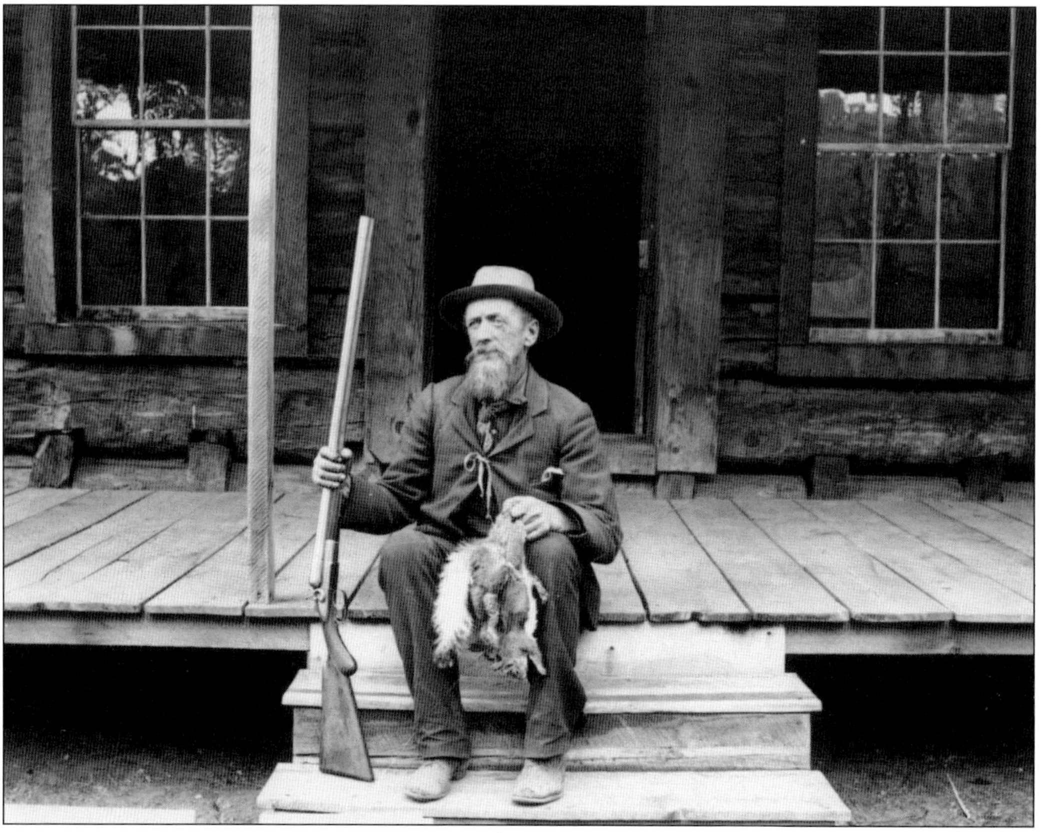

John Hance sits on the porch of his cabin, posing with his rifle and a number of squirrel pelts in this June 1899 photograph. Like many pioneer men of his day, Hance was an avid hunter. With food and supplies so far away, hunting was essential. (Grand Canyon NP Museum Collection No. 00825.)

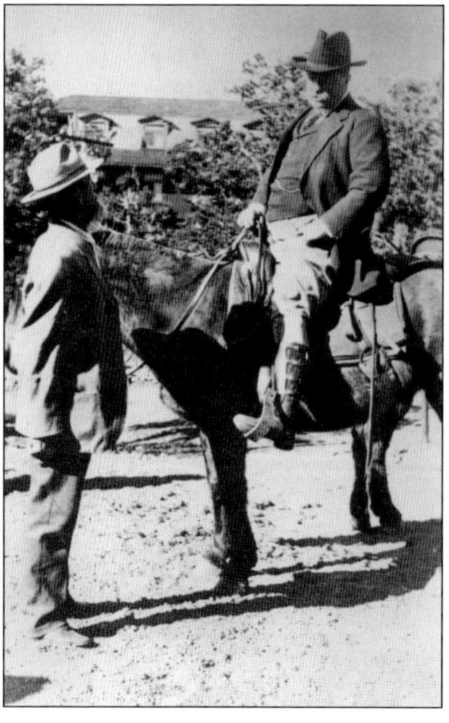

In this photograph, John Hance chats with former president Theodore Roosevelt, who is astride one of the canyon's mules. Roosevelt had specifically asked for Hance as a tour guide during his visit to the canyon. The El Tovar Hotel is in the background. (Grand Canyon NP Museum Collection No. 01573.)

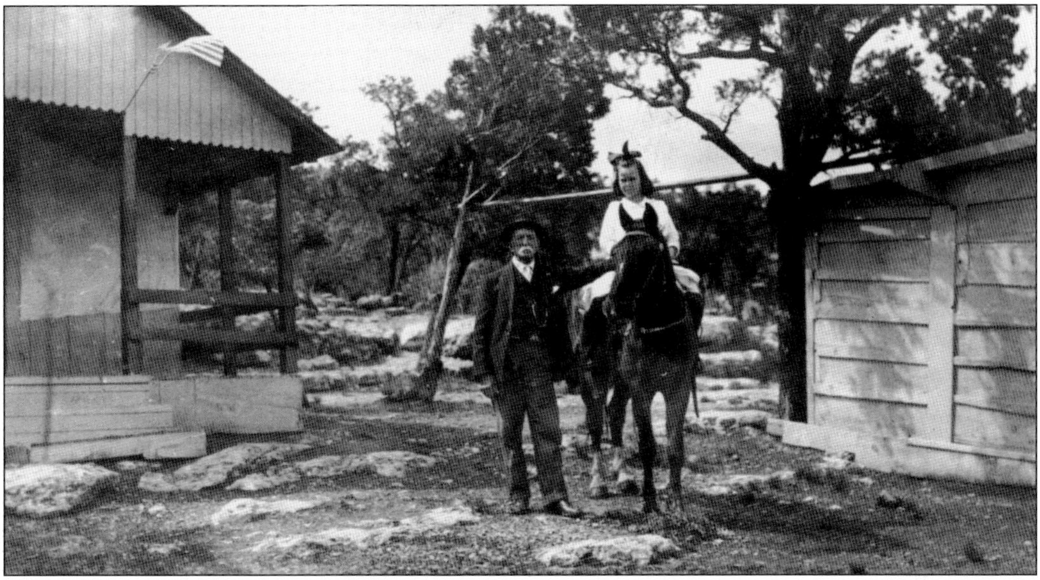

Hance poses for a photograph with Edith Kolb (daughter of photographer Emery Kolb, who is discussed in chapter 5) in 1915. The location is reportedly Ralph Cameron's Bright Angel Camp. (Grand Canyon NP Museum Collection No. 01567.)

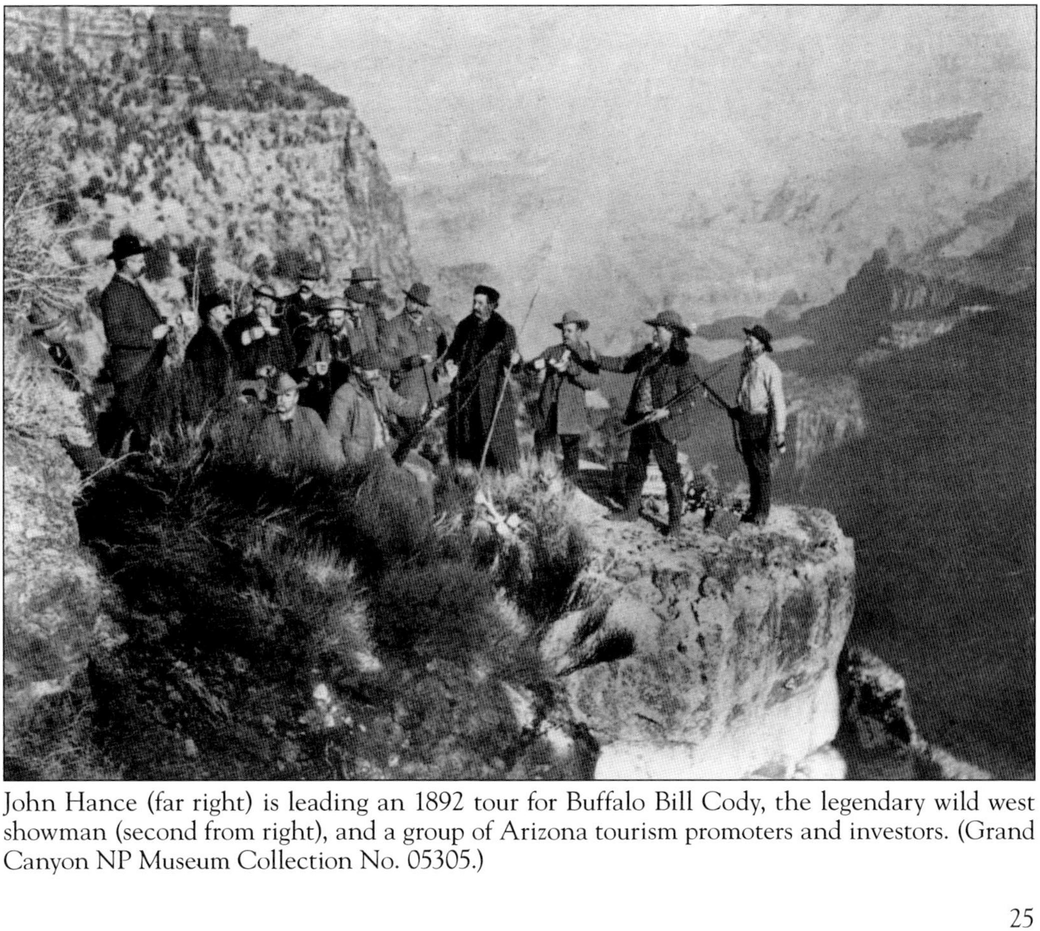

John Hance (far right) is leading an 1892 tour for Buffalo Bill Cody, the legendary wild west showman (second from right), and a group of Arizona tourism promoters and investors. (Grand Canyon NP Museum Collection No. 05305.)

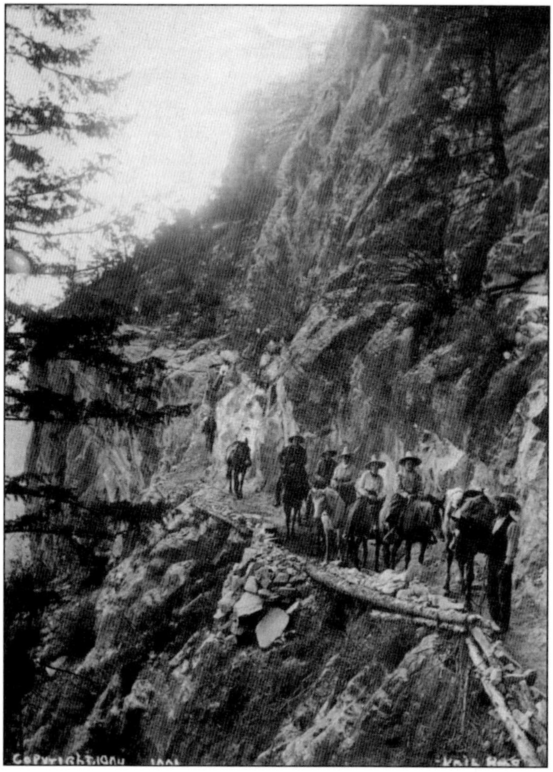

Hance leads a tour for former presidential candidate William Jennings Bryan down the Bright Angel Trail in 1904, with Bryan himself the last in the party in this photograph. Bryan was a beloved figure in America at this time, but his memory has been tainted by history for his participation in the 1925 Scopes evolution trial. (Photograph by Emery Kolb; Grand Canyon NP Museum Collection No. 05431.)

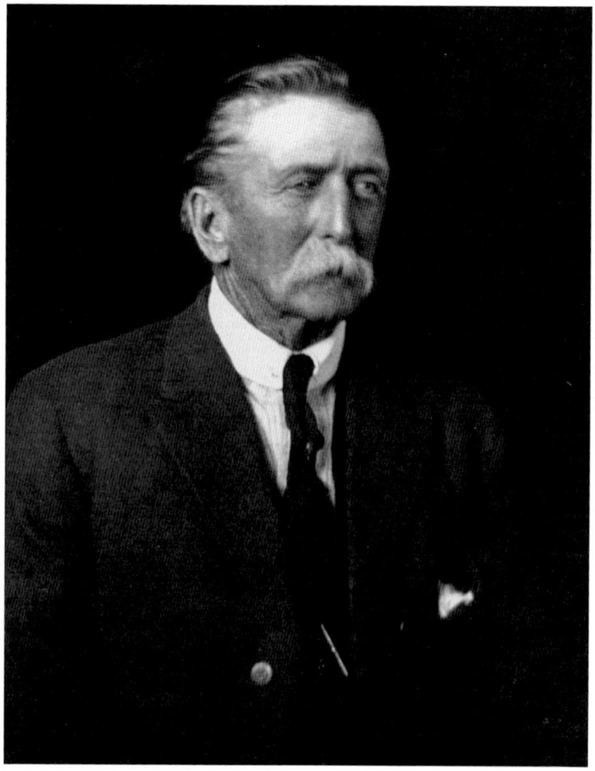

In 1918, the Fred Harvey Company took this formal portrait of then employee John Hance. Hance was 80 years old at the time and apparently had shaved off his trademark long beard for the occasion. (Grand Canyon NP Museum Collection No. 03676.)

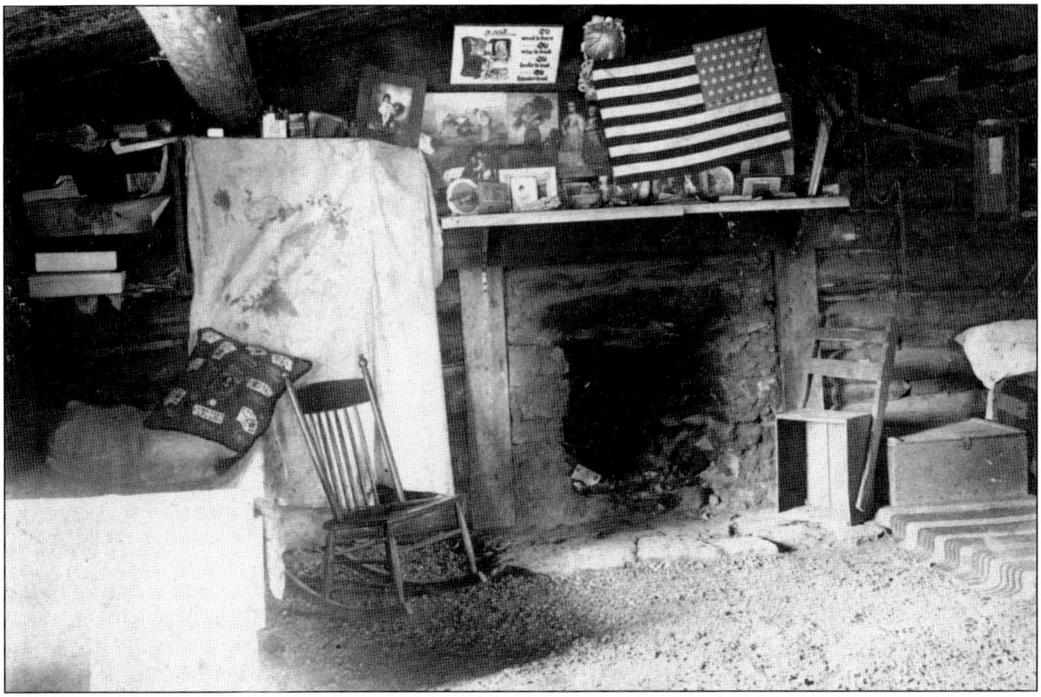

These two photographs taken by Emery Kolb show the interior of John Hance's cabin on October 10, 1903. Hance lived simply, and he reputedly built this cabin himself. (Above, Grand Canyon NP Museum Collection No. 04465A; below, Grand Canyon NP Museum Collection No. 04465B.)

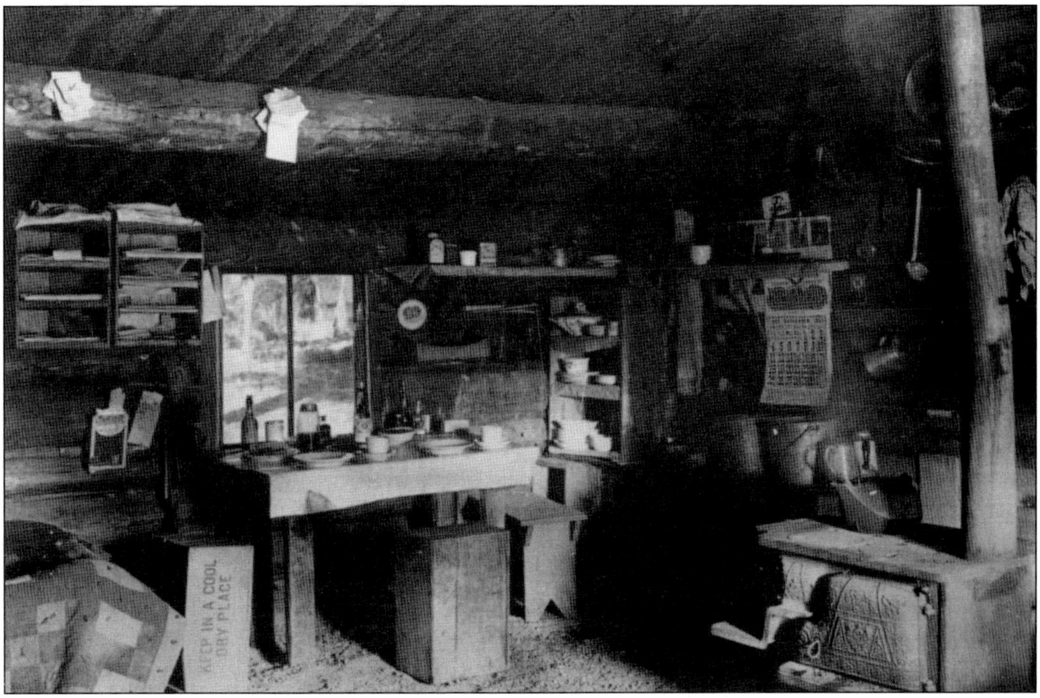

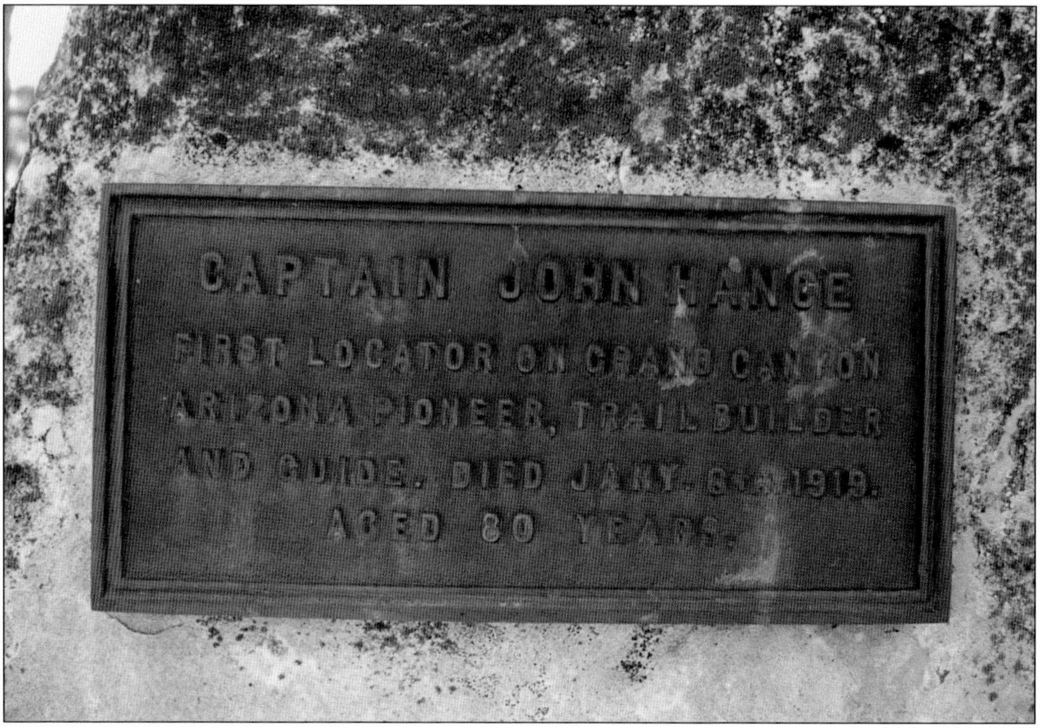

John Hance was the first to be buried in what is now the Grand Canyon Pioneer Cemetery on January 6, 1919. This is his grave as seen today. The footstone, seen in the foreground, is eight feet from the headstone as a nod to his very tall tales. (Both, David Schmittinger.)

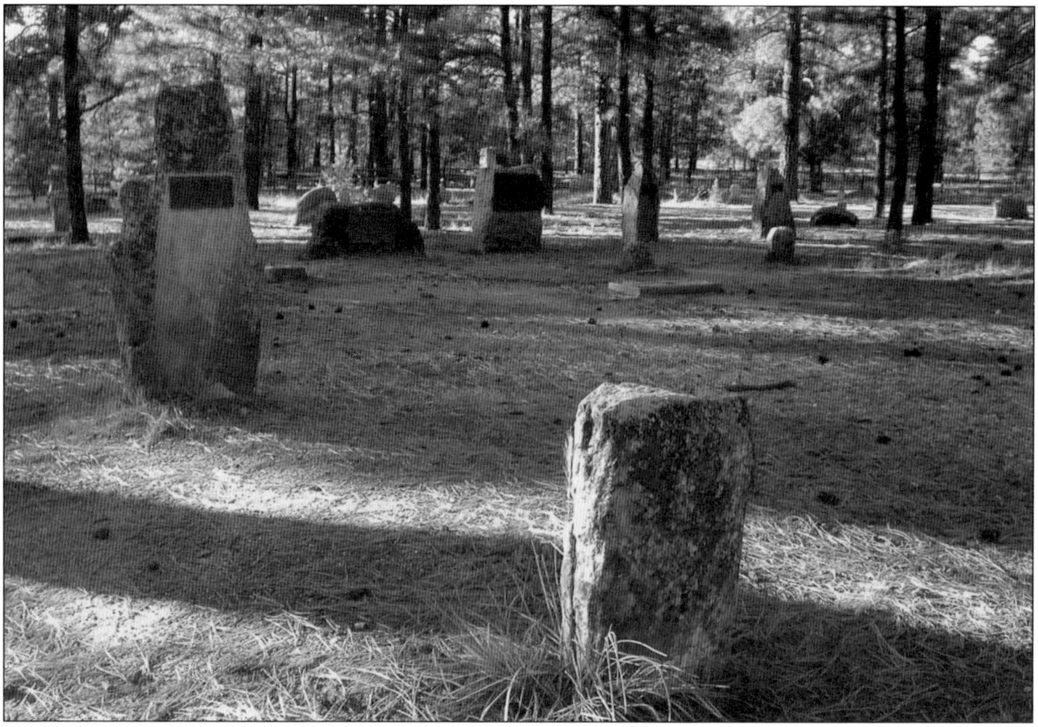

Three

Pete Berry

Pete Berry was one of the early miners and business entrepreneurs in the Grand Canyon. He and his business partners located the extremely profitable Grandview and Last Chance mining claims, and it was he and his work crew that forged the Grandview Trail. He had originally arrived in the area from Pitcairn, Colorado, around 1887, reportedly to settle the affairs of his brother John, a Flagstaff saloon owner who had been shot to death trying to break up a barroom brawl.

The Grand Canyon Copper Company was organized by Berry and his prospecting partners, the brothers Niles, Burton, and Ralph Cameron, locating claims near Horseshoe Mesa, near what is today known as the Grandview Lookout, a popular hiking trail. Not much ore was found overall, but these mining claims helped the partners control the land and tourism.

Berry opened one of the first hotels at the canyon, the Grandview. Tourist business was very profitable for him until the Fred Harvey Company and the Santa Fe Railroad moved in and fought to get a monopoly on the tourist trade. The railroad had enough pull to get the US Forest Service to terminate the water rights to the Grandview Hotel. Unable to compete or fight back, Pete Berry eventually sold his properties.

Pete Berry lived on the South Rim with his second wife, Martha, and his son from his first marriage, Ralph (named after his good friend and business partner Ralph Cameron). Young Ralph died during the Spanish influenza epidemic that decimated the nation in 1919. Pete himself lived on until 1932, long after he had been run out of business.

It has been said that history is always written by the victors, and there may be some truth to that. Grand Canyon historians tend to depict men like Pete Berry as villains and scoundrels for trying to make money off the tourists. Simultaneously, history regards Fred Harvey and the Santa Fe Railroad as heroes of the canyon for doing virtually the same thing.

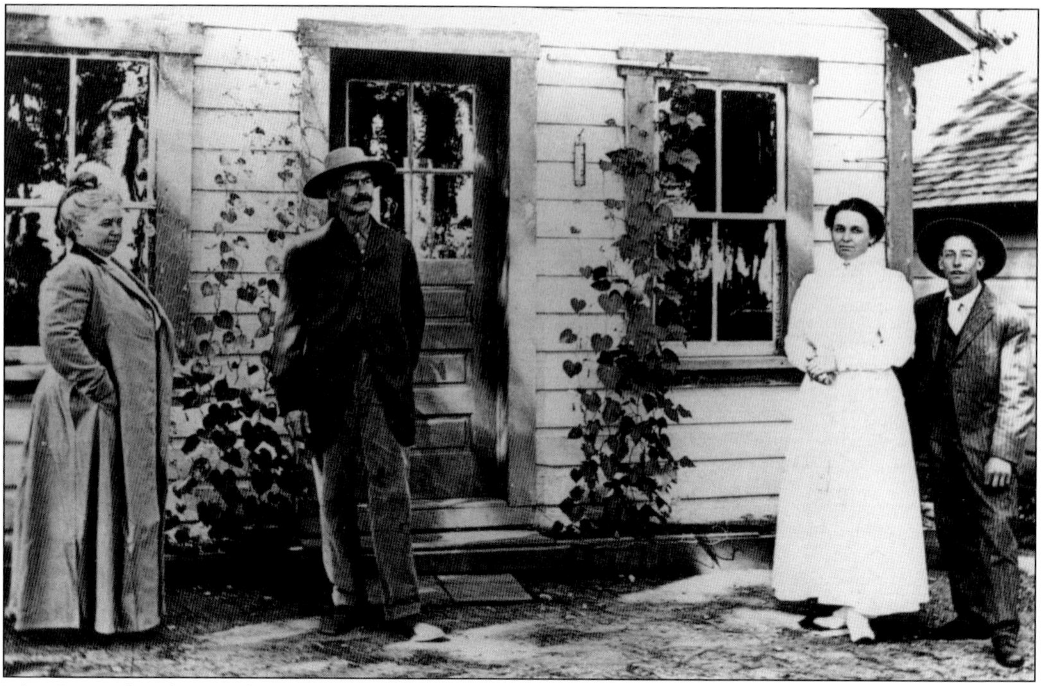

The Berry family stands in front of their home around 1895. Pictured here from left to right are Martha Berry (Pete's wife), Pete Berry, Martha's sister (name unknown), and Ralph Berry (Pete's son). (Grand Canyon NP Museum Collection No. 06935.)

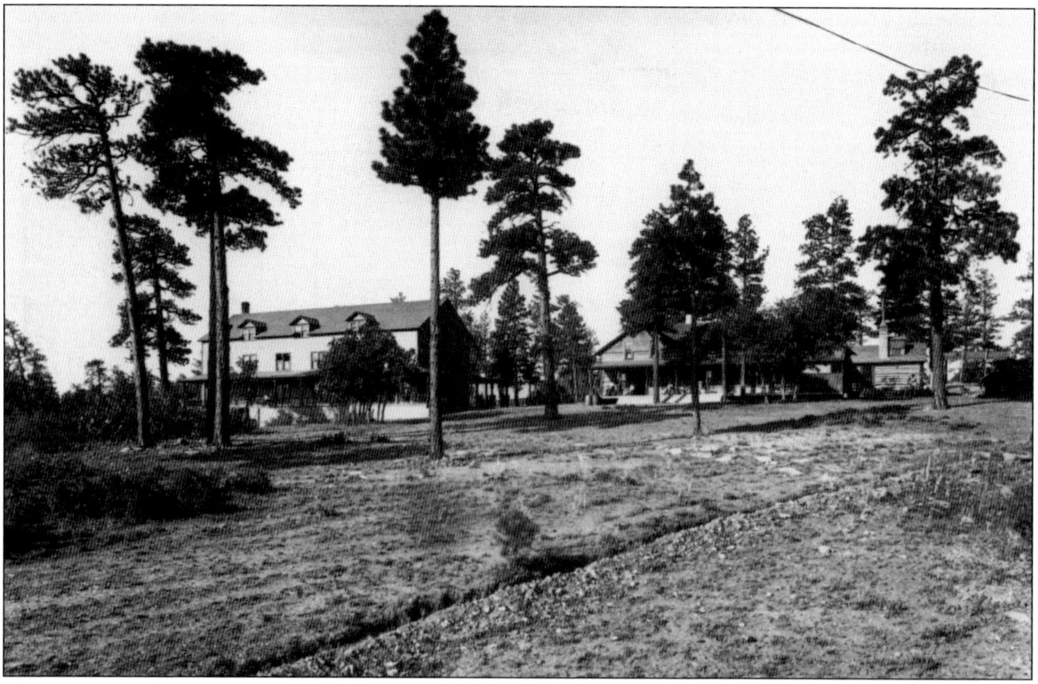

This is an undated photograph of the grounds of Pete Berry's Grandview Hotel. It was later demolished after Berry was forced out of business by the unbeatable competition from the Fred Harvey Company. (Grand Canyon NP Museum Collection No. 12089.)

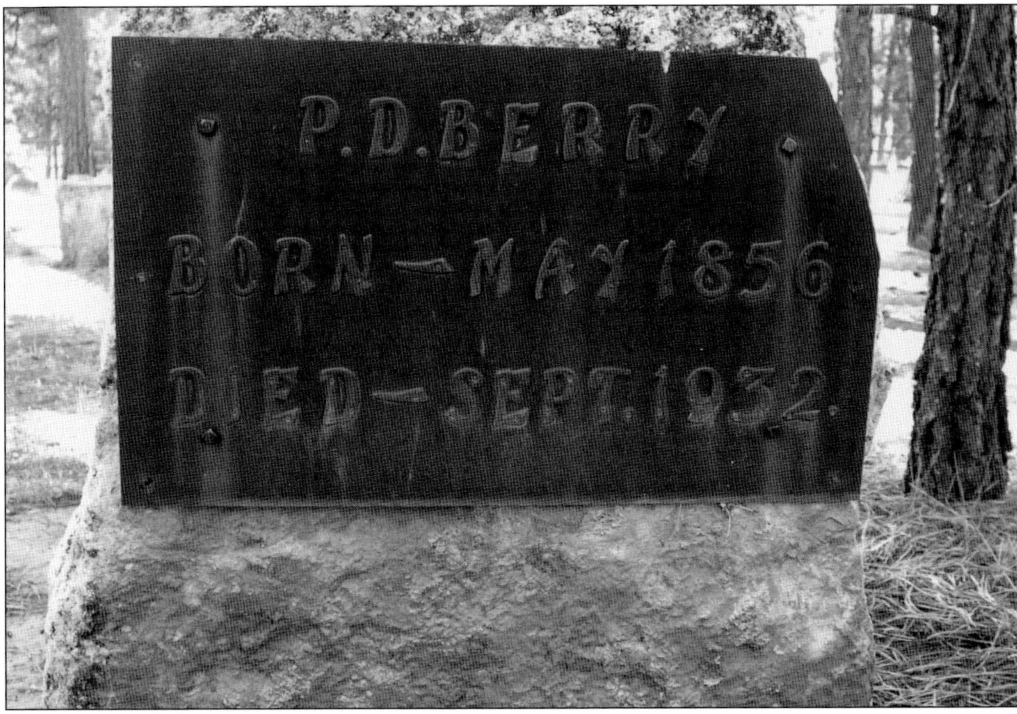

Seen here is the grave of Pete Berry, who died in 1932 at the age of 76. He continued to live at the canyon after closing his hotels. (David Schmittinger.)

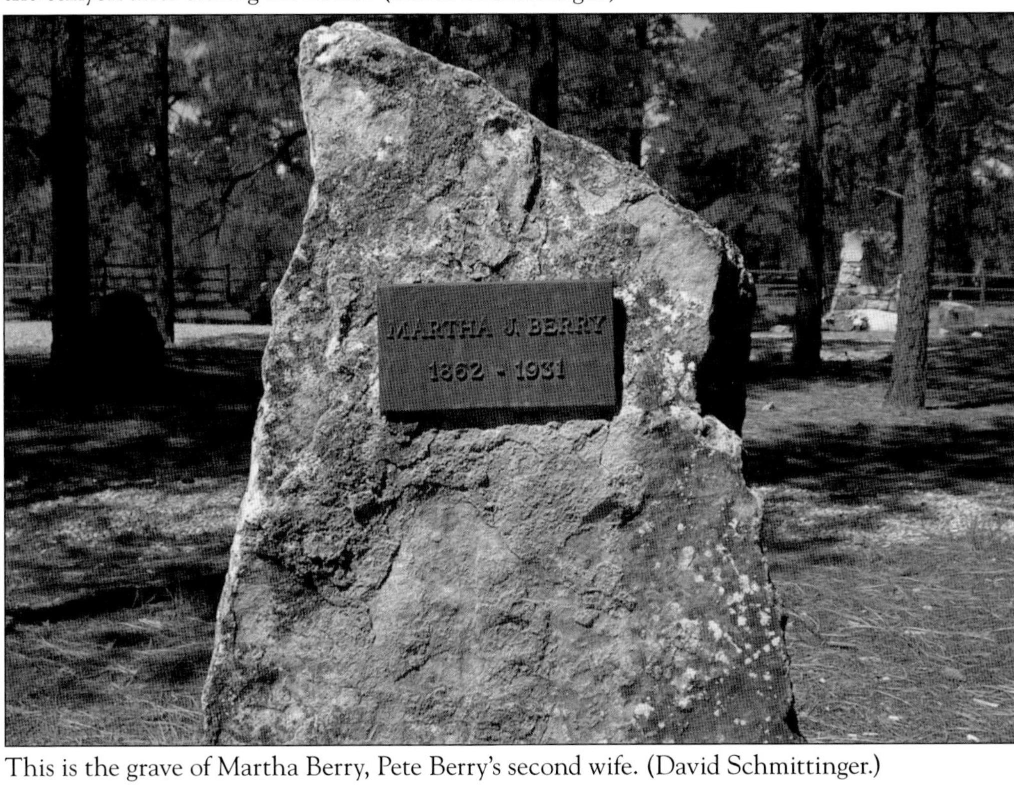

This is the grave of Martha Berry, Pete Berry's second wife. (David Schmittinger.)

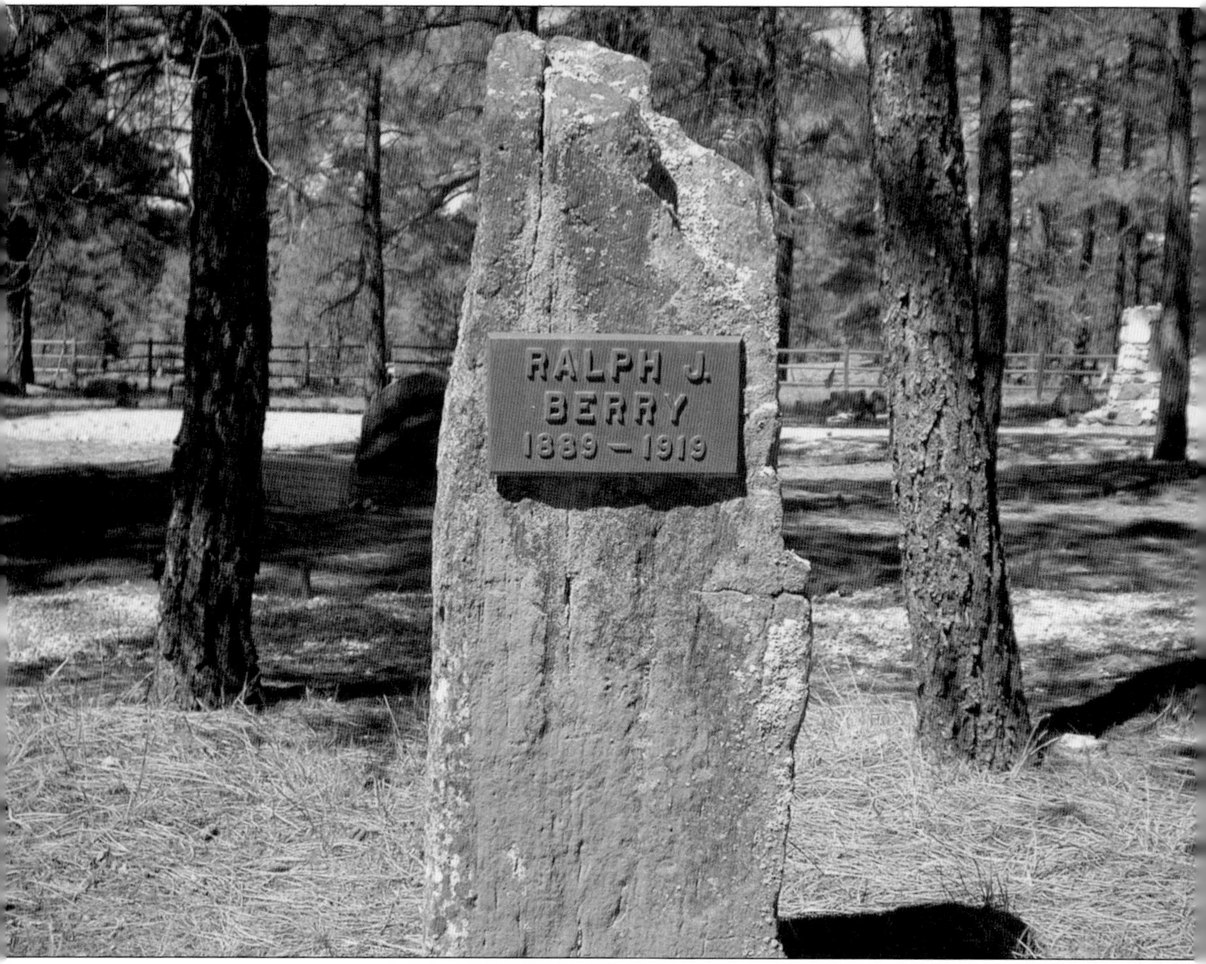

Ralph Berry, Pete's son from his first marriage, died during the Spanish flu pandemic that followed World War I. There is an unverifiable canyon legend that, after his divorce from his first wife, Pete asked his friend Ralph Cameron to send some professionals to Phoenix, Arizona, and kidnap his child, Ralph Berry, from his ex-wife and return him to the canyon. (David Schmittinger.)

Four

Ralph Henry Cameron

Ralph Cameron was one of the major figures on the South Rim in the early days of Grand Canyon development. He held many profitable mining claims, operated a successful tourist camp, served as territorial delegate to the US House of Representatives at the time of Arizona statehood, and was a household name in Arizona, with many friends. It was he and his work crew that forged the Bright Angel Trail, which remains the most popular trail in the Grand Canyon.

Yet today, Grand Canyon historians go out of their way to avoid talking about him. Most books on the history of the canyon do not even mention the name of Ralph Henry Cameron. He is forgotten today, his name erased from the history books, and the few times it is mentioned, it is always with loathing. This is because Cameron kept the government tied up in court for many years with lawsuits and counter-suits, desperately trying to prevent the Grand Canyon from becoming a national park. He knew that park status would invalidate the mining claims and businesses of the men on the rim, particularly himself. It was a classic David versus Goliath situation, and if it had been any land other than the Grand Canyon, Cameron might be remembered as a hero instead of a malevolent villain. But it was the Grand Canyon.

After years of court battles, Cameron finally got his day in the US Supreme Court in 1920, the year after the Department of the Interior finally succeeded in declaring the Grand Canyon a national park. The court ruled that Cameron was a trespasser in the park and ordered him to vacate forthwith.

However, that same year, in a nationwide Republican sweep, Ralph Cameron had gotten himself elected to the US Senate from Arizona. From there, an embittered Cameron spent his six-year term trying to use his power as senator to seek revenge on the Department of the Interior for what it had done to him. Shocked by his vindictiveness, the Arizona voters turned him out after a single, polarizing term.

After that, Ralph Cameron eventually left Arizona and died many years later in Washington, DC, on February 12, 1953, at the age of 89. In a final gesture of defiance against his enemies, his family arranged for him to be buried in the Grand Canyon Pioneer Cemetery next to his old friend Pete Berry. However, because of his sinister reputation, be it justified or unjustified, his grave has very few visitors and is one of the few at which no one leaves flowers or memorials.

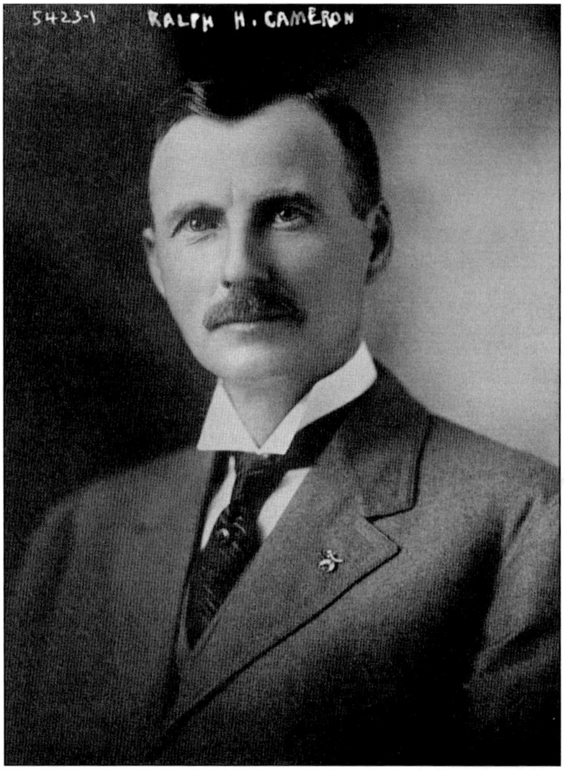

This is a formal portrait of Ralph Cameron, taken in the early 20th century. (Library of Congress.)

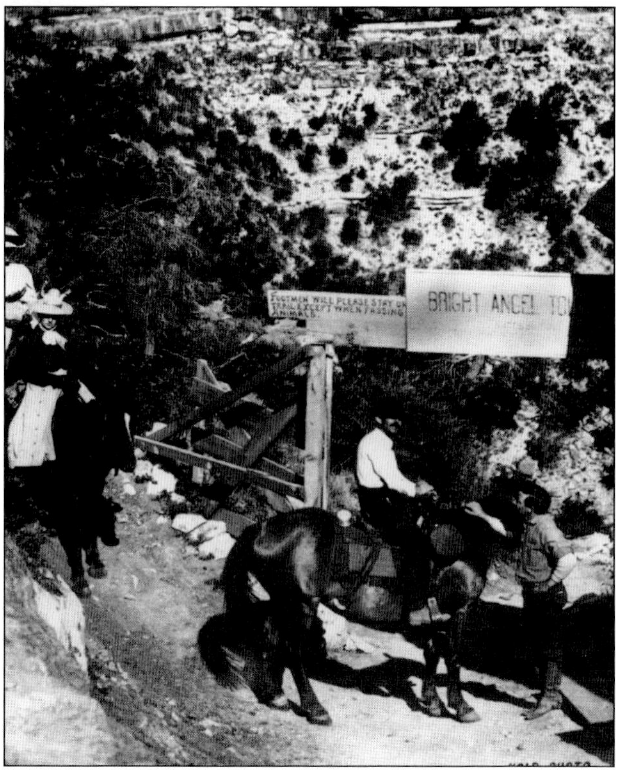

This is Ralph Cameron's infamous toll gate at the Bright Angel trailhead, where he charged tourists $1 each to hike into the canyon. Historians have reviled Cameron for this, even though it was not illegal and not much different from various canyon fees today. (Photograph by Emery Kolb; Grand Canyon NP Museum Collection No. 04744.)

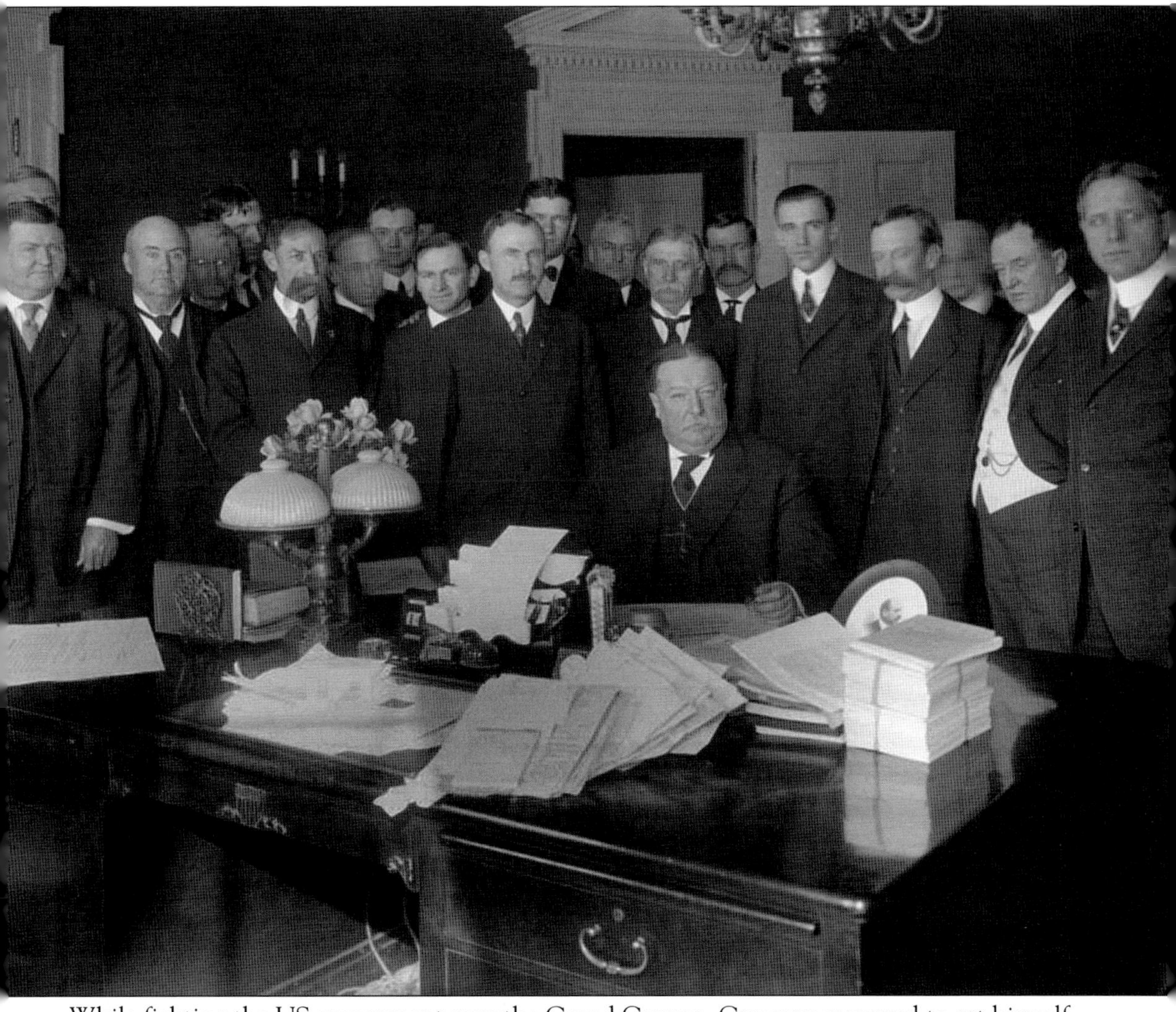

While fighting the US government over the Grand Canyon, Cameron managed to get himself elected as territorial delegate to the US House of Representatives in 1908 on a promise to fight for and deliver statehood for Arizona. Statehood did come for Arizona in 1912 while Cameron was in office, and many at the time believed it was due to his influence. Today, however, historians dismiss the claim, and Cameron's name is almost never mentioned in connection with statehood. Cameron's name has been erased from the history books on Arizona statehood as it has been with Grand Canyon history. Yet that is indeed Ralph Cameron standing to the immediate left of Pres. William Howard Taft at the signing of the Arizona Statehood Bill. (Library of Congress.)

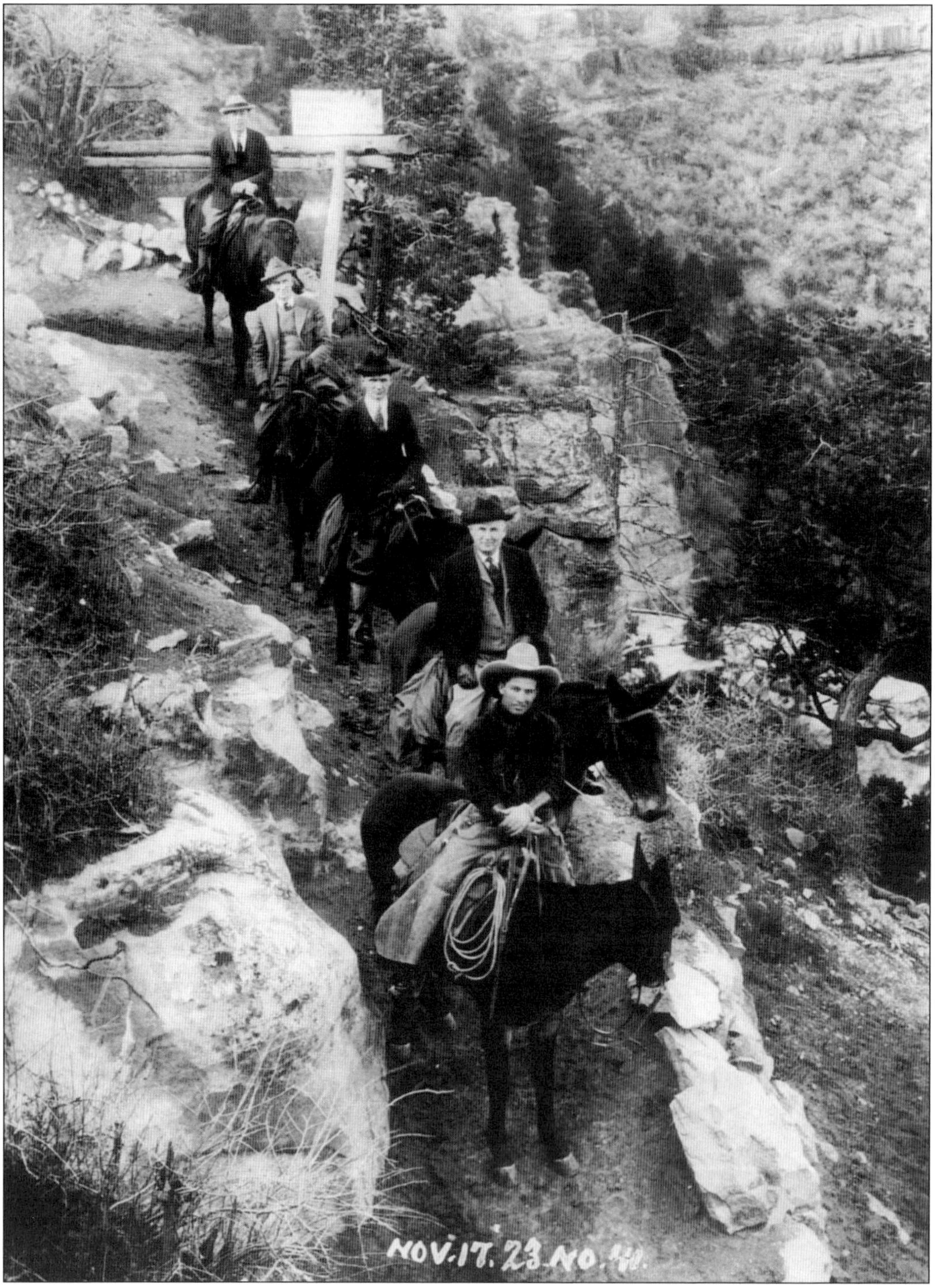

US senator Ralph Cameron (second from front) audaciously leads a VIP party down the Bright Angel Trail in 1923. He is clean-shaven, gray-haired, much older, and hardly looks like the same man who had been a popular name in Arizona 20 years earlier. Tour guide George Cravey (also noted on page 87) is at the head of the party. (Sharlot Hall Museum; No. 2008.117.)

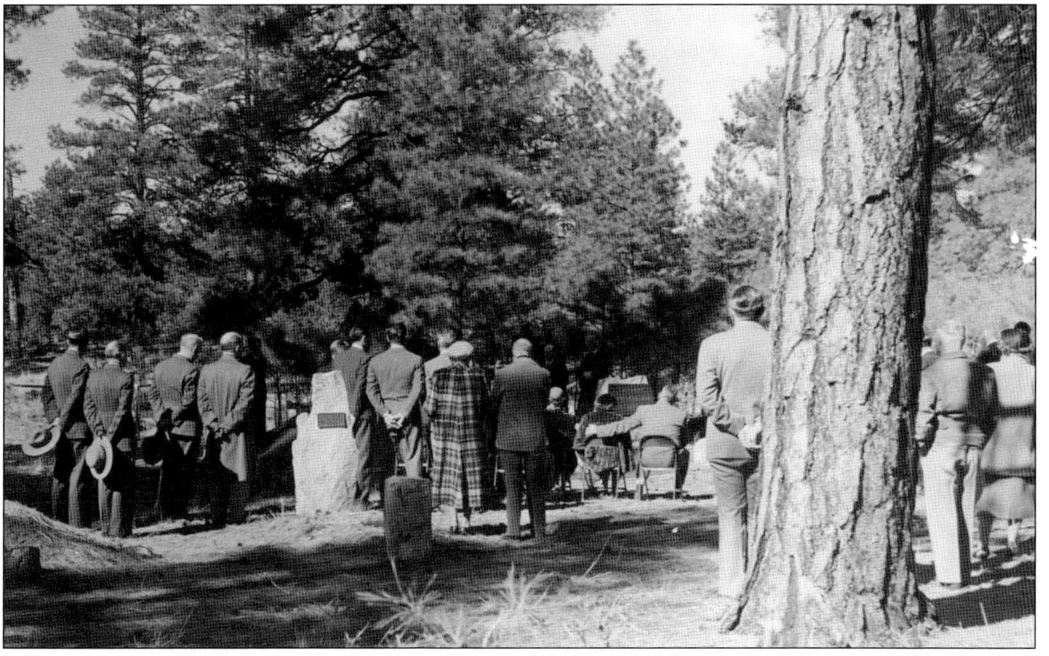

Pictured here is the graveside funeral service held for Ralph Cameron on February 16, 1953, in the Grand Canyon Pioneer Cemetery. Arizona governor Howard Pyle was in attendance. Cameron's family is seated center in this photograph, and the grave of John Hance is in the foreground. (Photograph by Steve Leding; Grand Canyon NP Museum Collection No. 02418.)

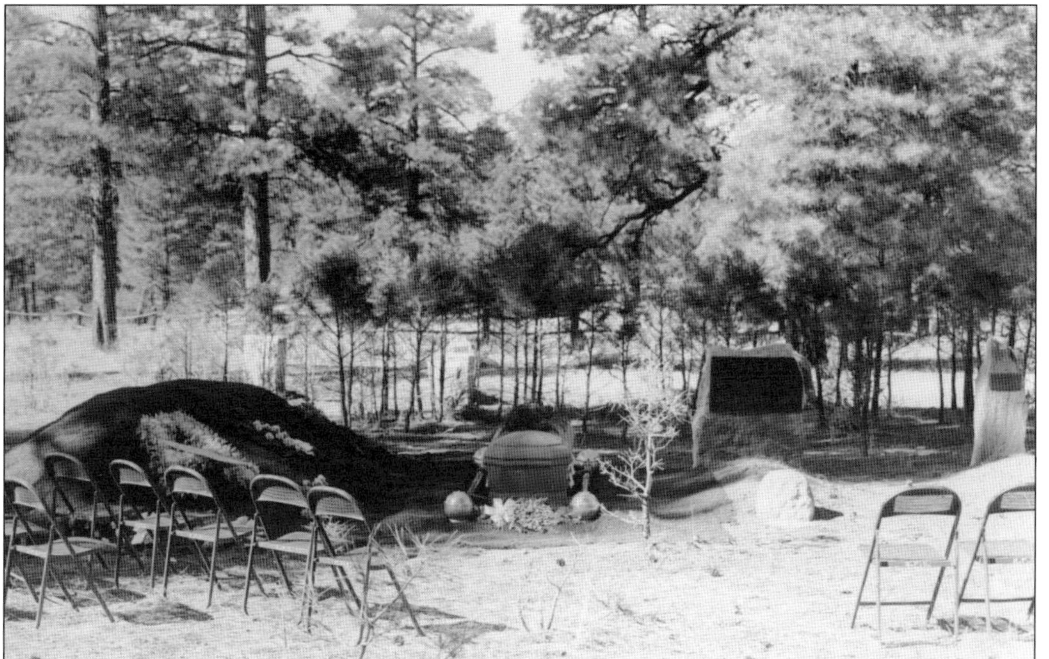

In this photograph, the casket of Ralph Henry Cameron is about to be lowered into the ground immediately following his funeral, next to the grave of his old friend Pete Berry. (Photograph by Steve Leding; Grand Canyon NP Museum Collection No. 02416.)

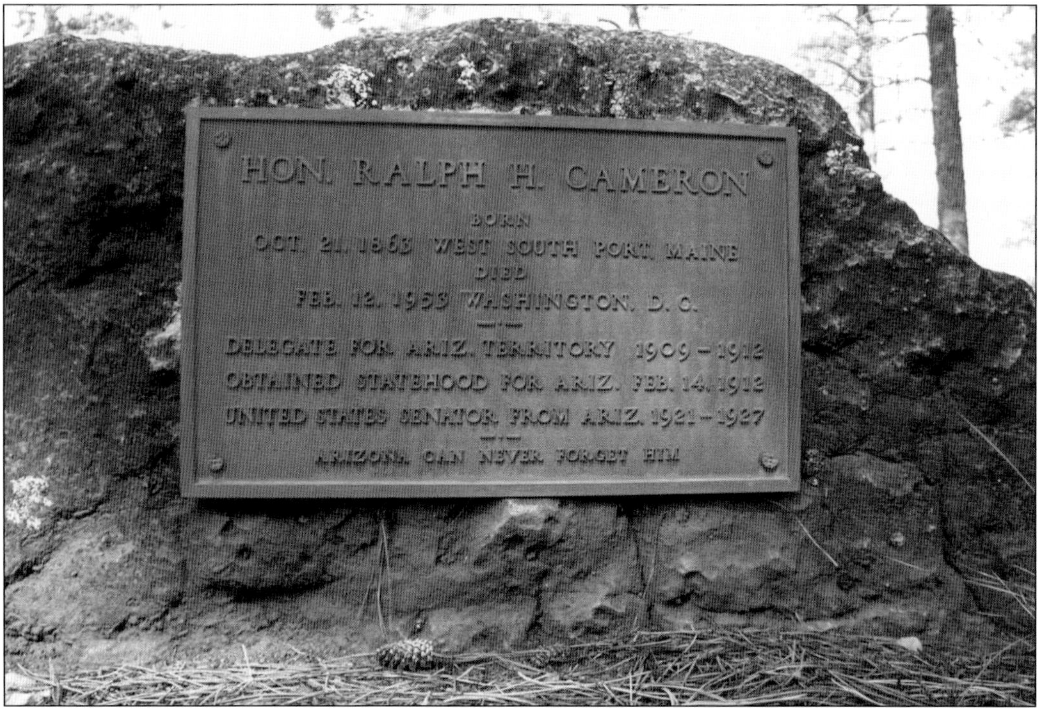

Pictured here is Ralph Cameron's tombstone, with inscriptions reminding people that he "obtained Statehood for Arizona" and "Arizona Can Never Forget Him." But Arizona has indeed forgotten Ralph Henry Cameron. His grave is almost always bare, with no flags or flowers. (Lois Schmittinger.)

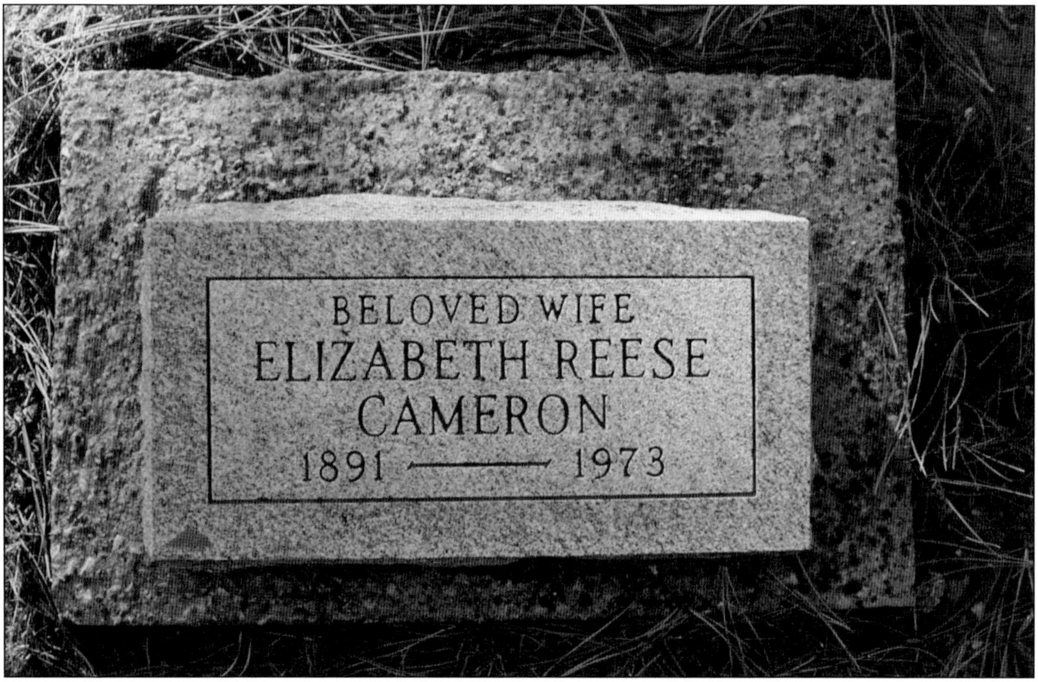

Pictured here is the grave of Ralph's second wife, Elizabeth. Very little is known about her at this time, as they married after he left the public eye. (David Schmittinger.)

Five

The Kolb Family

Brothers Ellsworth and Emery Kolb arrived at the Grand Canyon from Pittsburgh, Pennsylvania, around 1901. They opened a photography studio at the Bright Angel trailhead on land they leased from Ralph Cameron, and from there, they took hundreds of photographs of the canyon and surrounding areas for tourists. Their photographs, as well as their 1911 boating trip down the Colorado River, which they captured on movie film (titled *Grand Canyon Film Show*), have become the stuff of Grand Canyon legend. This film can still be seen in their studio on the rim of Grand Canyon or at the Cline Library on the campus of Northern Arizona University in Flagstaff, Arizona.

When the Grand Canyon became a national park in 1919, the Department of the Interior awarded all of the concession contracts (hotels, restaurants, etc.) to the Fred Harvey Company. The Kolb brothers were allowed to stay so it would not look like the US government had given the Fred Harvey Company a complete monopoly. Still, the Fred Harvey Company and the Santa Fe Railroad constructed the Lookout Studio on the rim not far from the Kolb Studio (a building designed by Mary Colter) in 1914 to compete with the Kolbs and drive them from the canyon. The brothers survived.

As the years went on, the relationship between the two brothers became strained, and Ellsworth left the canyon in 1924, returning only in death in 1960 to the Grand Canyon Pioneer Cemetery. Emery stayed on at the Kolb Studio for the rest of his life with his wife, Blanche, and daughter Edith. He continued to take photographs.

The relationship between Emery Kolb and the National Park Service (NPS) was acrimonious and largely unfriendly, even though they let him stay on the rim. The NPS finally agreed to let him stay until his death, conditional that he not sell his business to anyone else and that it would die with him. As it turned out, Emery Kolb lived far longer than expected. When he died in 1976 at the age of 95, the park shut down the Kolb Studio, and the building sat empty, unused, and boarded up for many years.

By the 1990s, a new generation of National Park Service officials had taken over, and they recognized the historic value of the Kolbs' contribution to the Grand Canyon. They refurbished the old studio and reopened it to tourists, where it is once again frequented by visitors learning the fascinating history of Ellsworth and Emery Kolb.

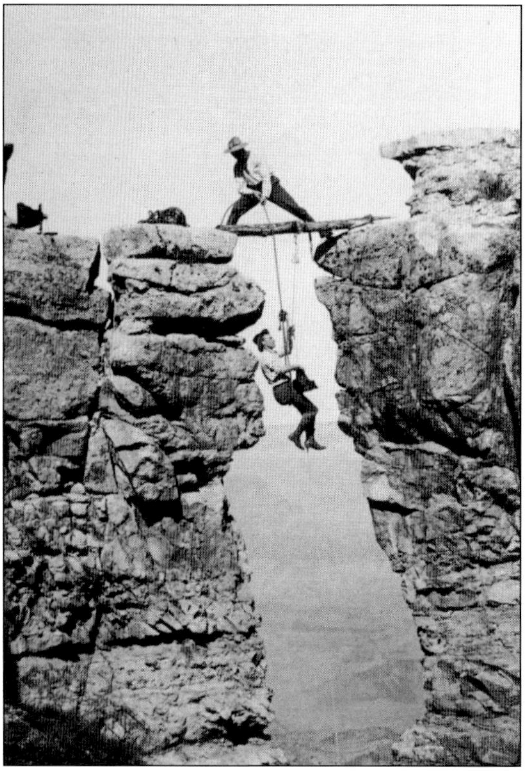

Pictured is a famous publicity photograph of the Kolb brothers, taken around 1913 and used to promote their photography studio. Emery is on top, with Ellsworth hanging on the rope. Many historians believe this is a trick shot, and they were not as high up as it appears. (Grand Canyon NP Museum Collection No. 17185B.)

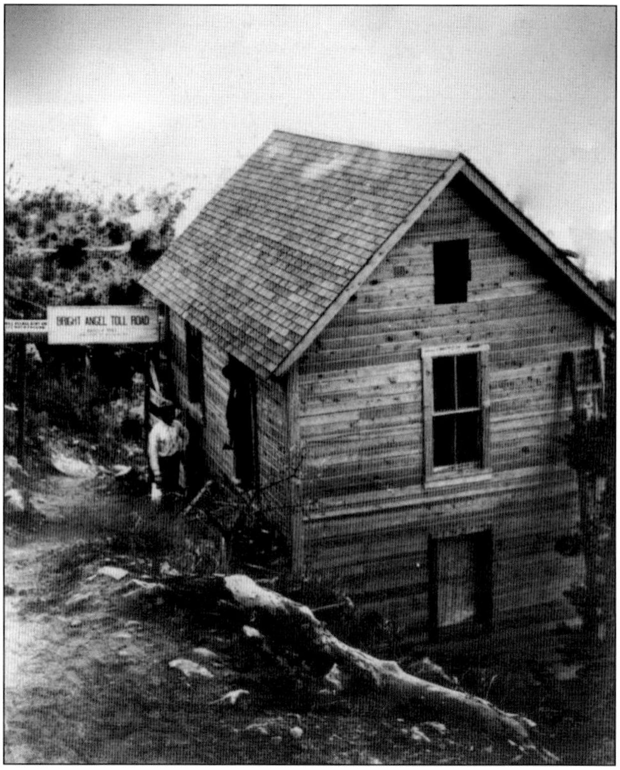

Here is a view of the Kolb Studio in 1904 next to Ralph Cameron's toll gate at the Bright Angel trailhead. Until Cameron was driven from the canyon, the brothers' name was sullied a bit for their association with him. (Grand Canyon NP Museum Collection No. 07729.)

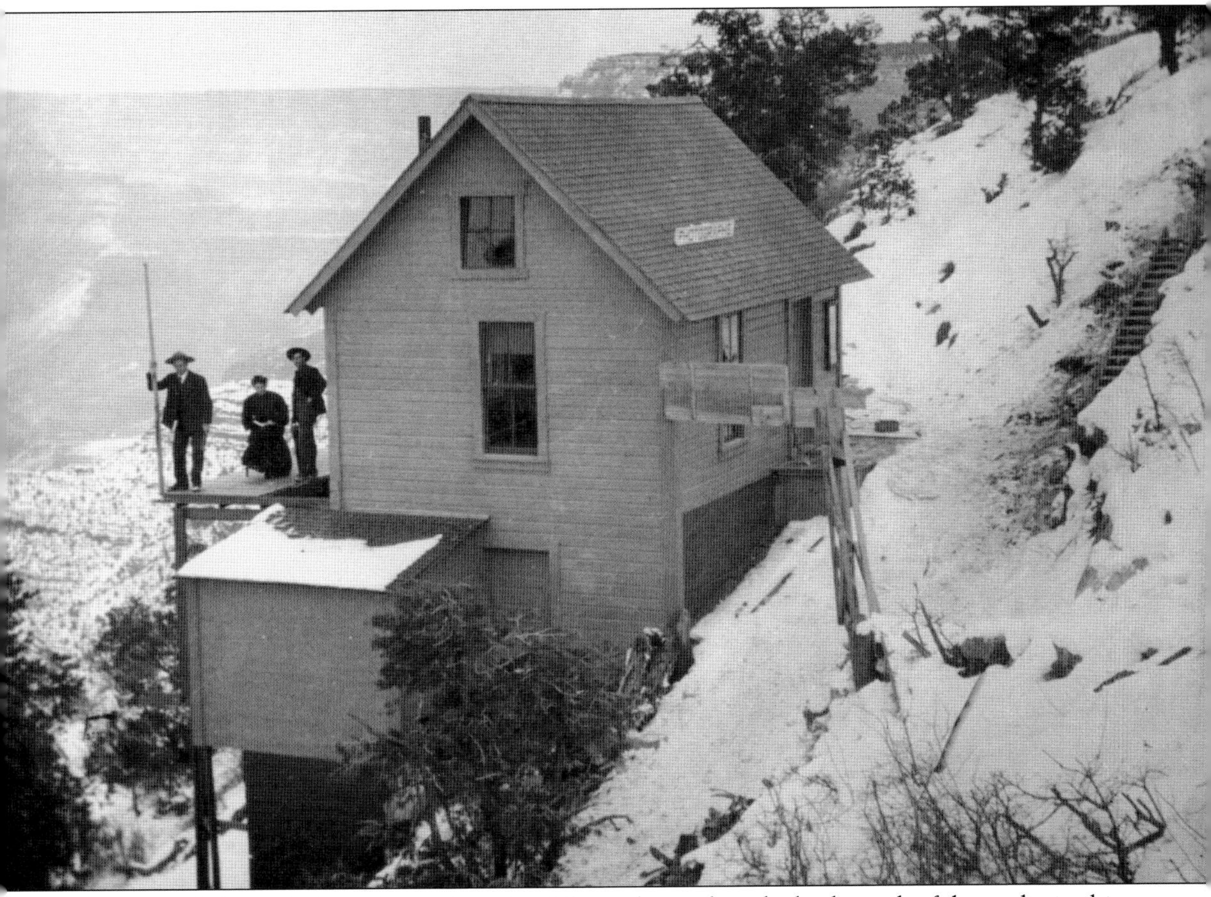

Emery Kolb; his wife, Blanche; and brother Ellsworth stand on the back porch of the studio in this 1904 winter photograph. They would later construct some additions on to the building. (Grand Canyon NP Museum Collection No. 04896.)

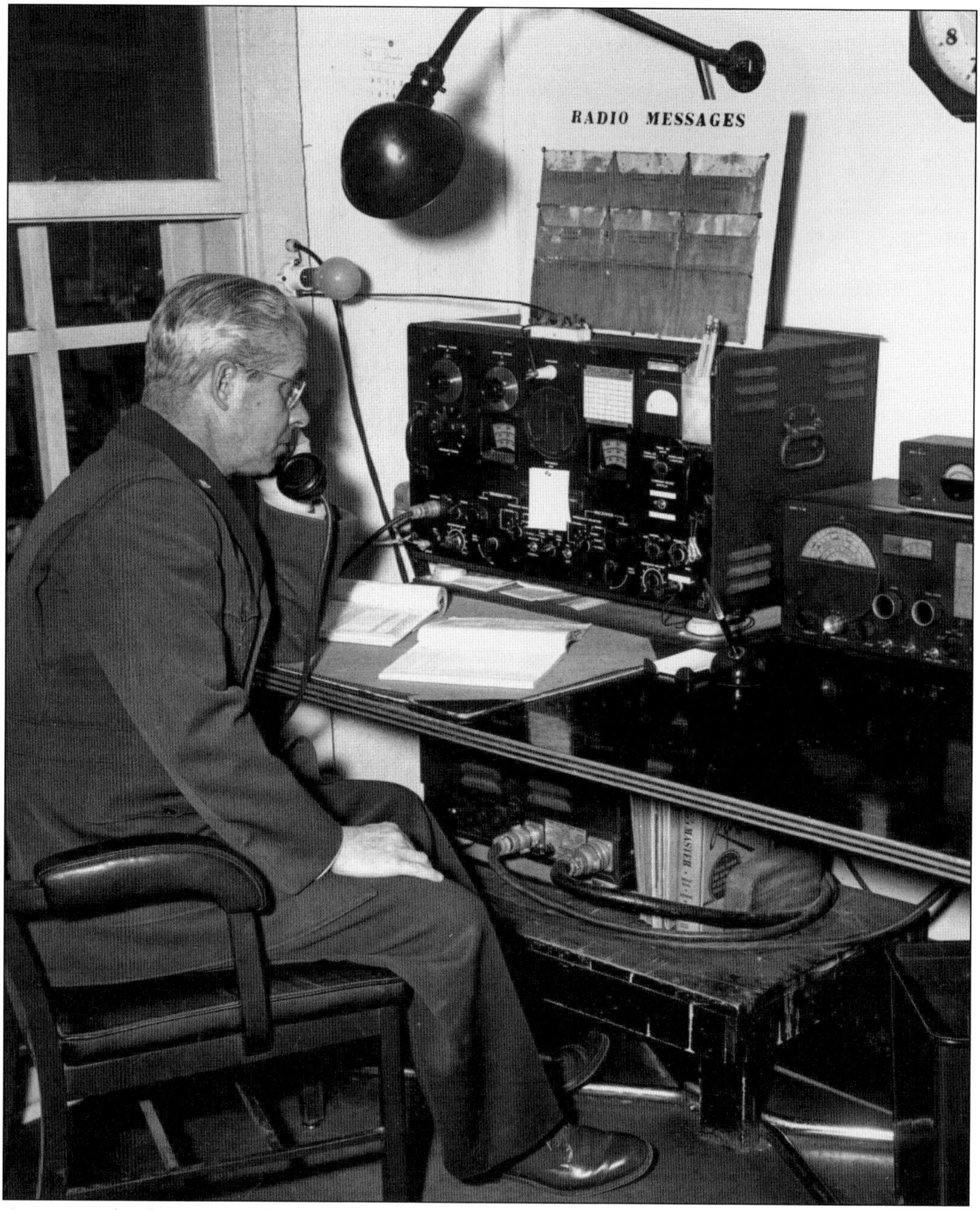

Assistant chief ranger Carl Lehnert is seen here operating a radio dispatch unit in 1955. Lehnert became Emery Kolb's son-in-law when he married Kolb's daughter Edith. (Photograph by Steve Leding; Grand Canyon NP Museum Collection No. 02736.)

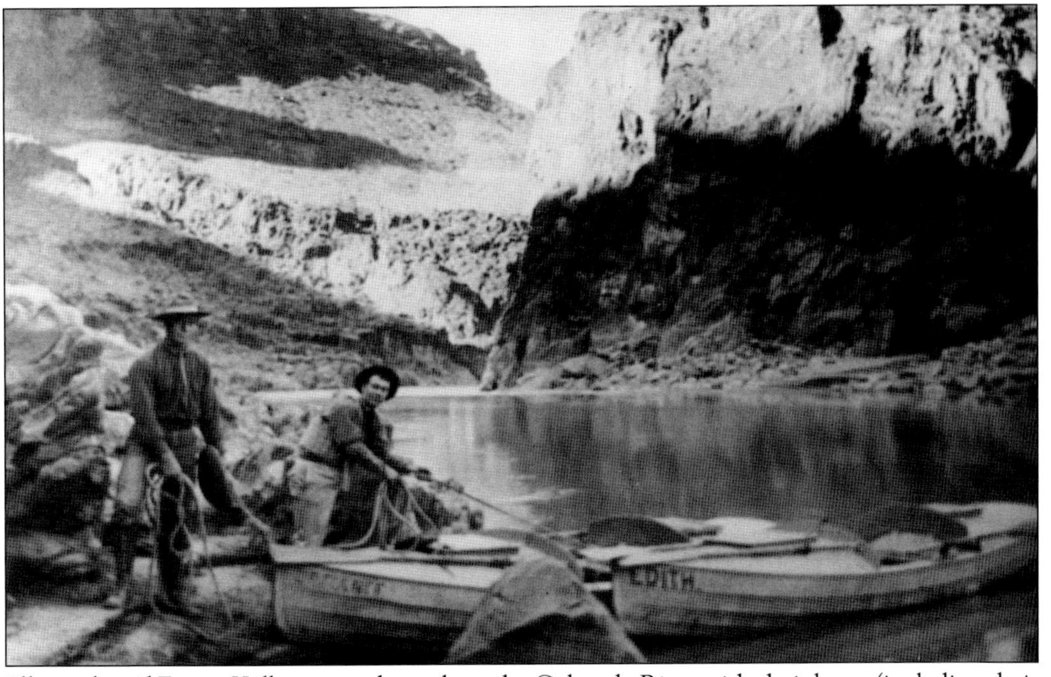

Ellsworth and Emery Kolb are seen here along the Colorado River with their boats (including their famous exploring boat *Edith*, named for Emery's daughter) in this undated photograph, probably taken in the early 1920s before Ellsworth left the canyon. (Sharlot Hall Museum, po0123P.)

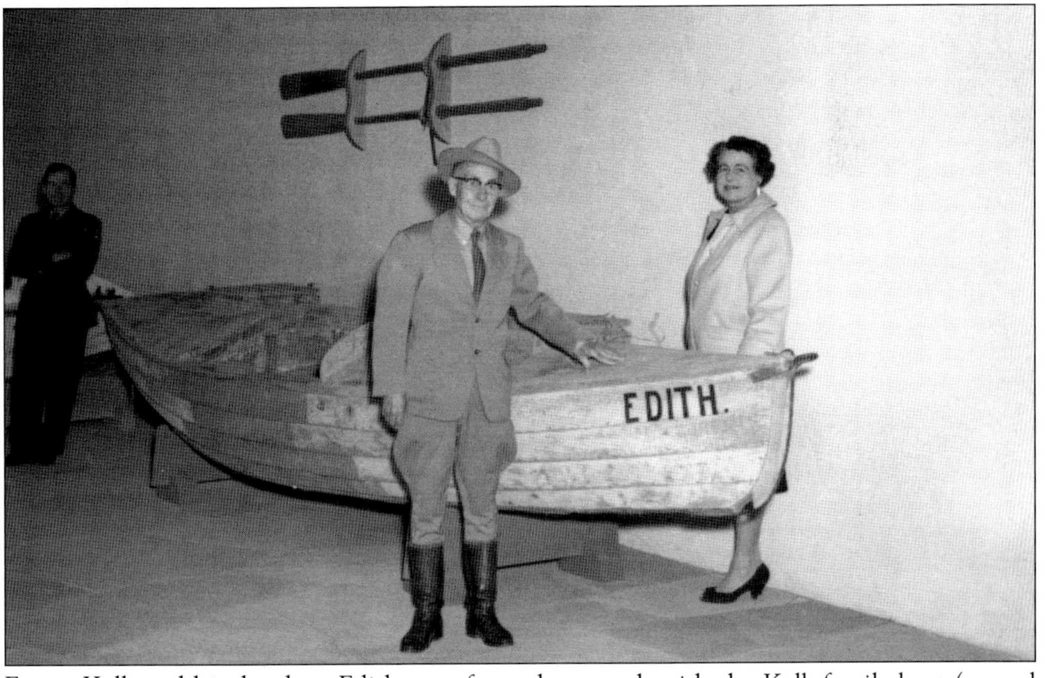

Emery Kolb and his daughter Edith pose for a photograph with the Kolb family boat (named *Edith*), which was used in the brothers' famous 1911 Colorado River trip. This photograph, taken in May 1959, was on the occasion of the boat being moved to the Grand Canyon Visitors' Center. (Photograph by Steve Leding; Grand Canyon NP Museum Collection No. 03424.)

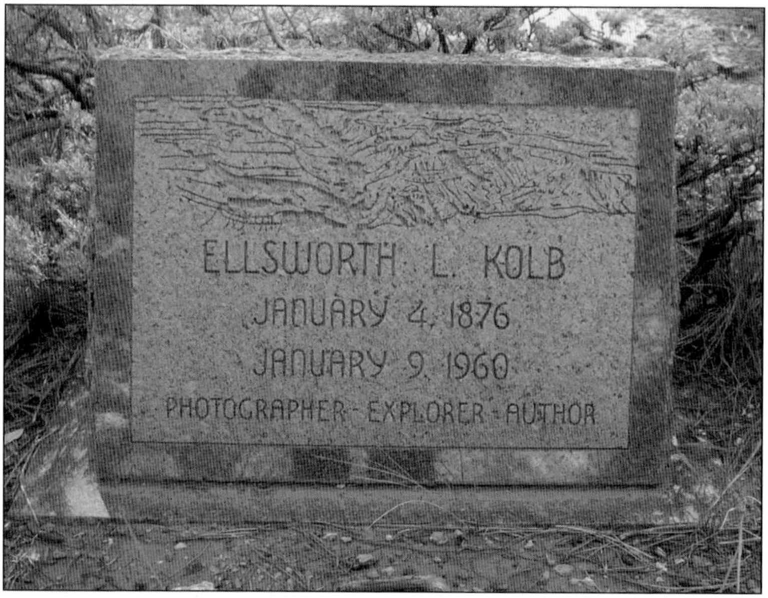

Pictured here is the grave of Ellsworth Kolb in the Grand Canyon Pioneer Cemetery. Time had not healed the broken relationship between the two brothers, and when Ellsworth was returned here for burial, Emery reportedly made sure his brother would not be interred anywhere near his own reserved plot. (David Schmittinger.)

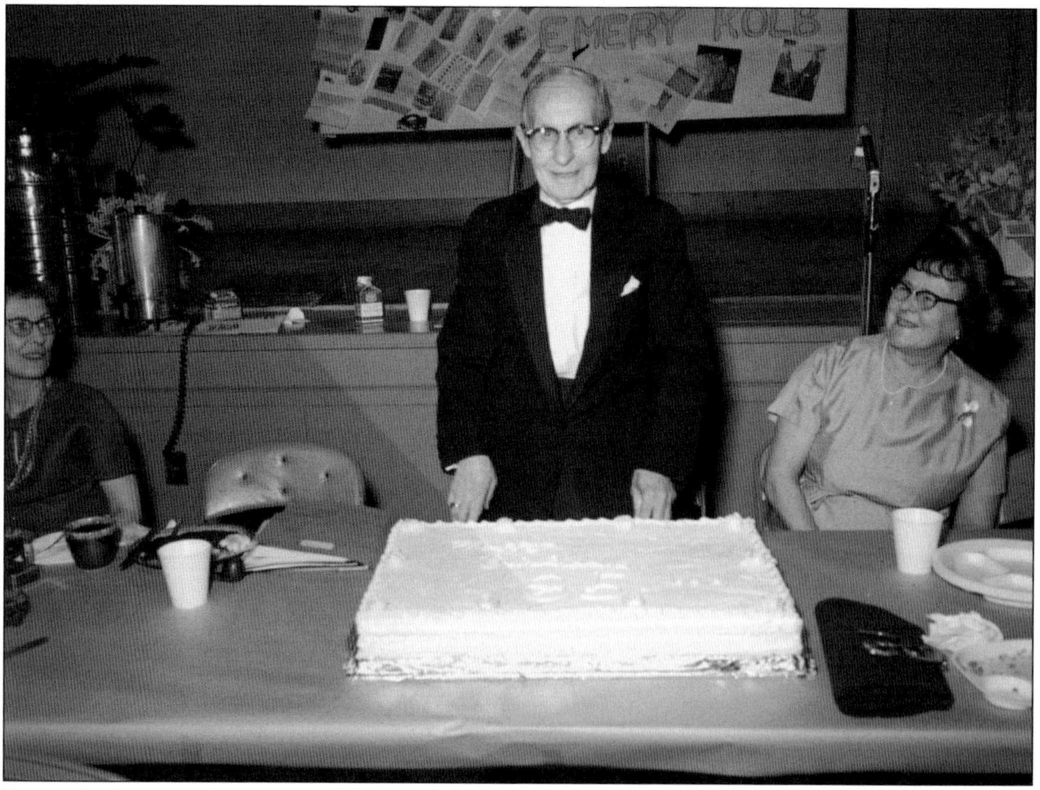

Emery Kolb is seen here at his 85th birthday party on February 15, 1966, at the Grand Canyon Community Building. To the continuing chagrin of the National Park Service, he would live for 10 more years. (Photograph by Merrill D. Beal; Grand Canyon NP Museum Collection No. 04814A.)

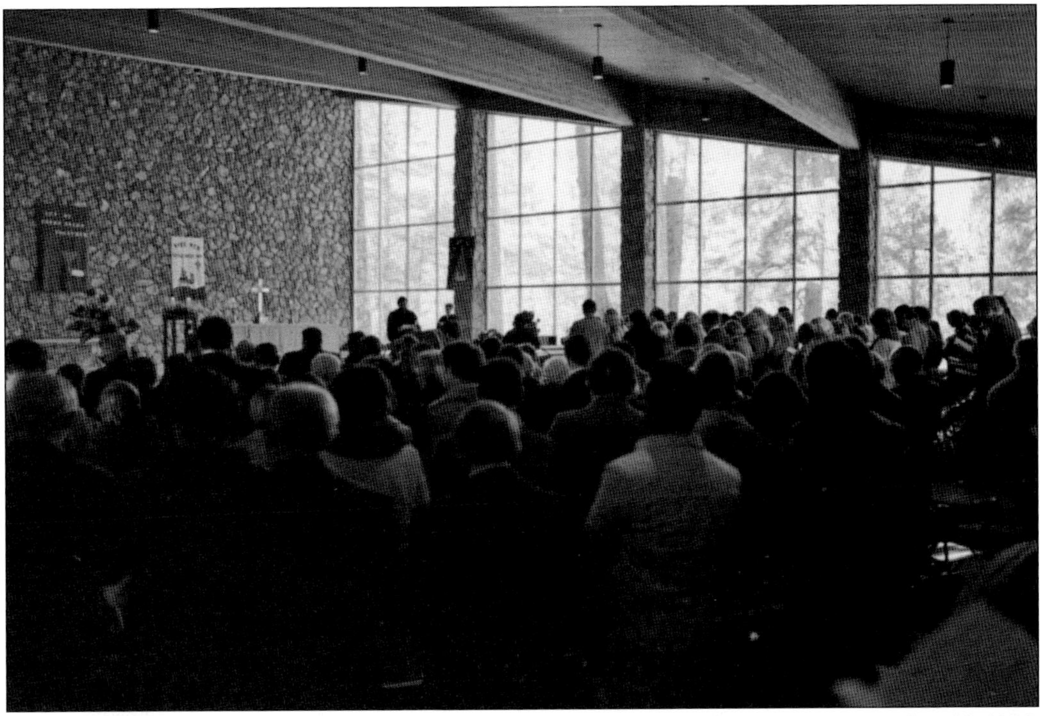

Here a scene from the funeral of Emery Kolb inside the Shrine of the Ages on December 16, 1976. Pastor Fred Doidge is presiding. (Grand Canyon NP Museum Collection No. 06458.)

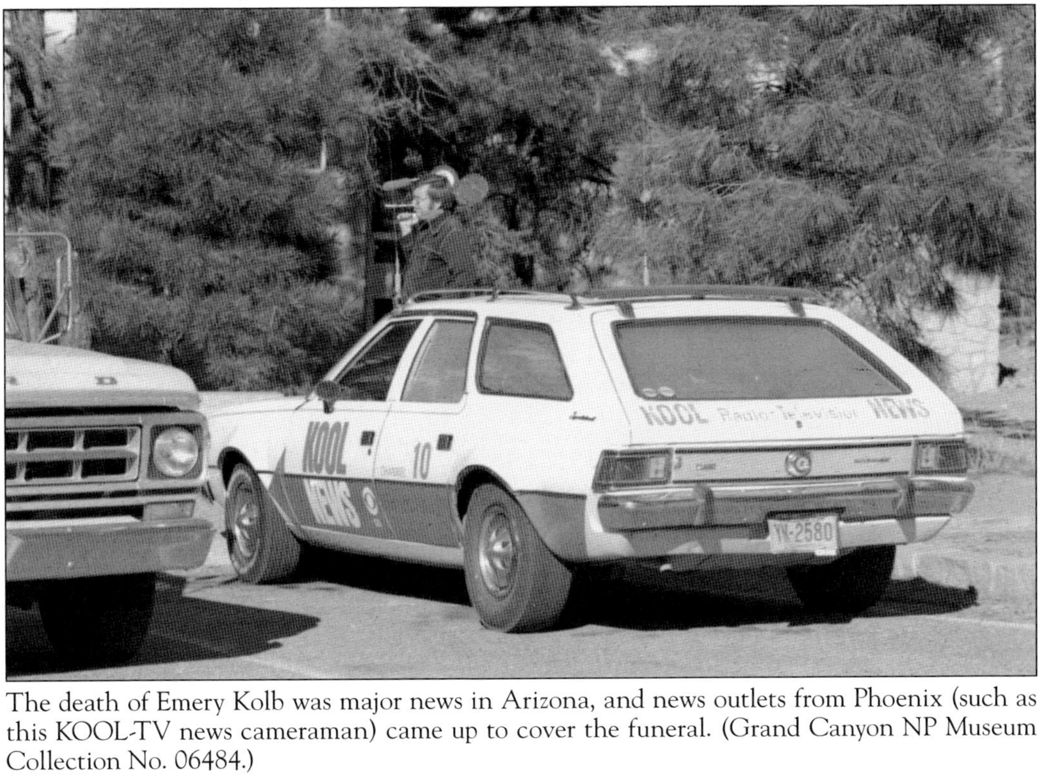

The death of Emery Kolb was major news in Arizona, and news outlets from Phoenix (such as this KOOL-TV news cameraman) came up to cover the funeral. (Grand Canyon NP Museum Collection No. 06484.)

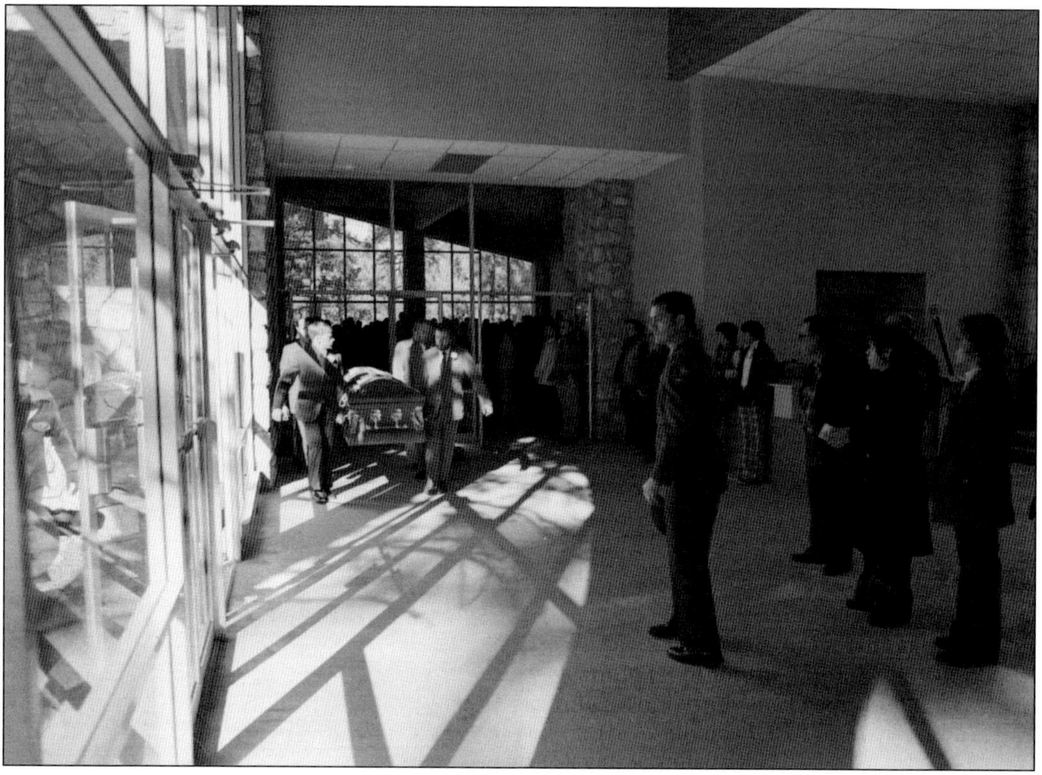

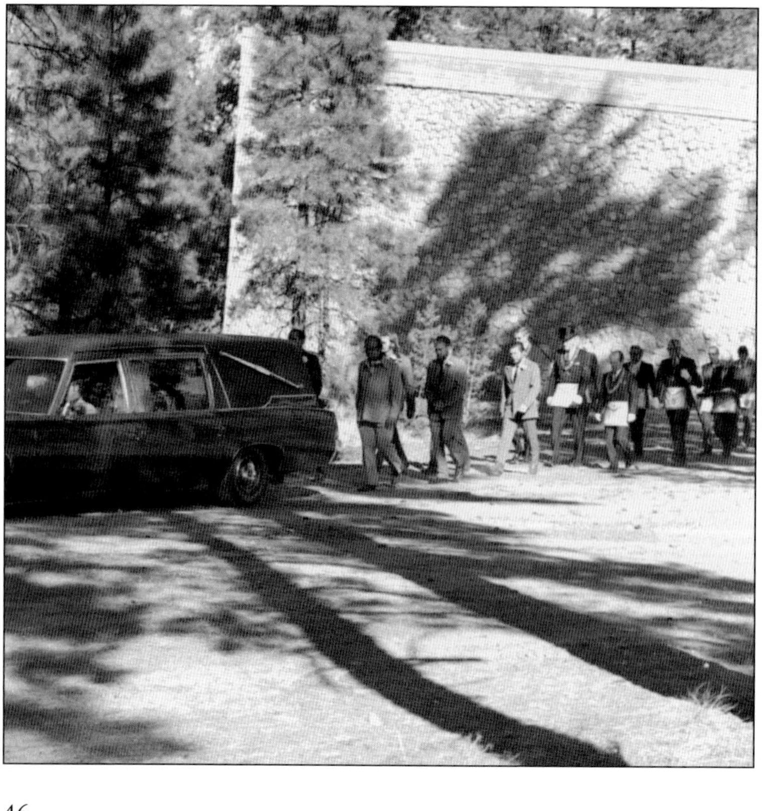

Pallbearers with the casket of Emery Kolb exit the Shrine of the Ages following the funeral service. (Grand Canyon NP Museum Collection No. 06463.)

Emery Kolb was a member of the Masonic Lodge, and the Masons were out in force at his funeral on December 16, 1976. Their procession is seen here leaving the Shrine of the Ages. (Grand Canyon NP Museum Collection No. 06495.)

The Emery Kolb funeral procession enters the Grand Canyon Pioneer Cemetery. (Grand Canyon NP Museum Collection No. 06493.)

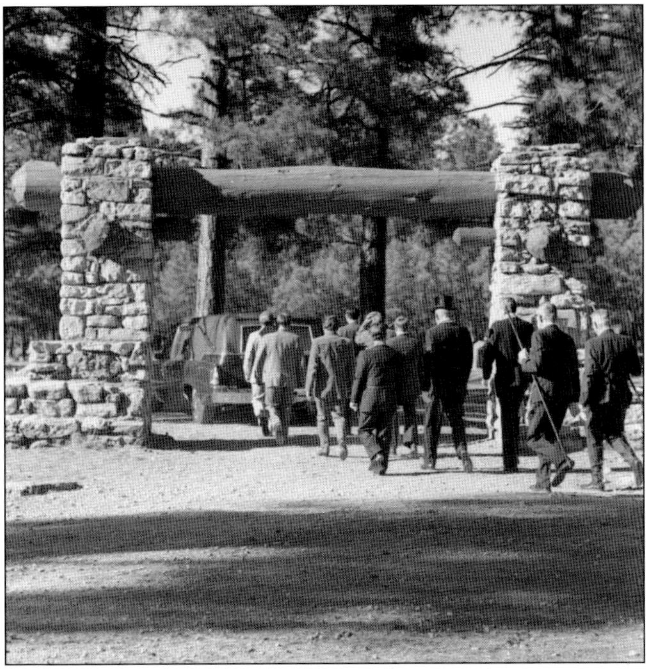

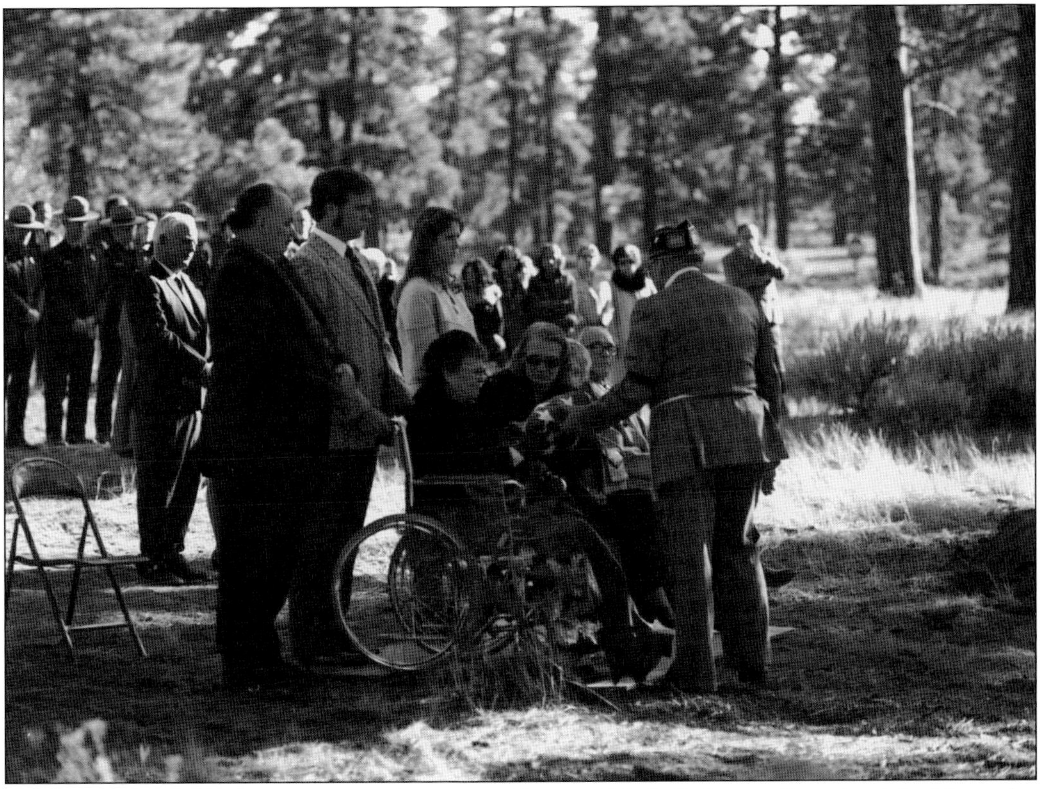

A group of veterans present an American flag to Edith Lehnert (in wheelchair) at the graveside service for her father. Her husband, Carl, died in 1962. (Grand Canyon NP Museum Collection No. 06481.)

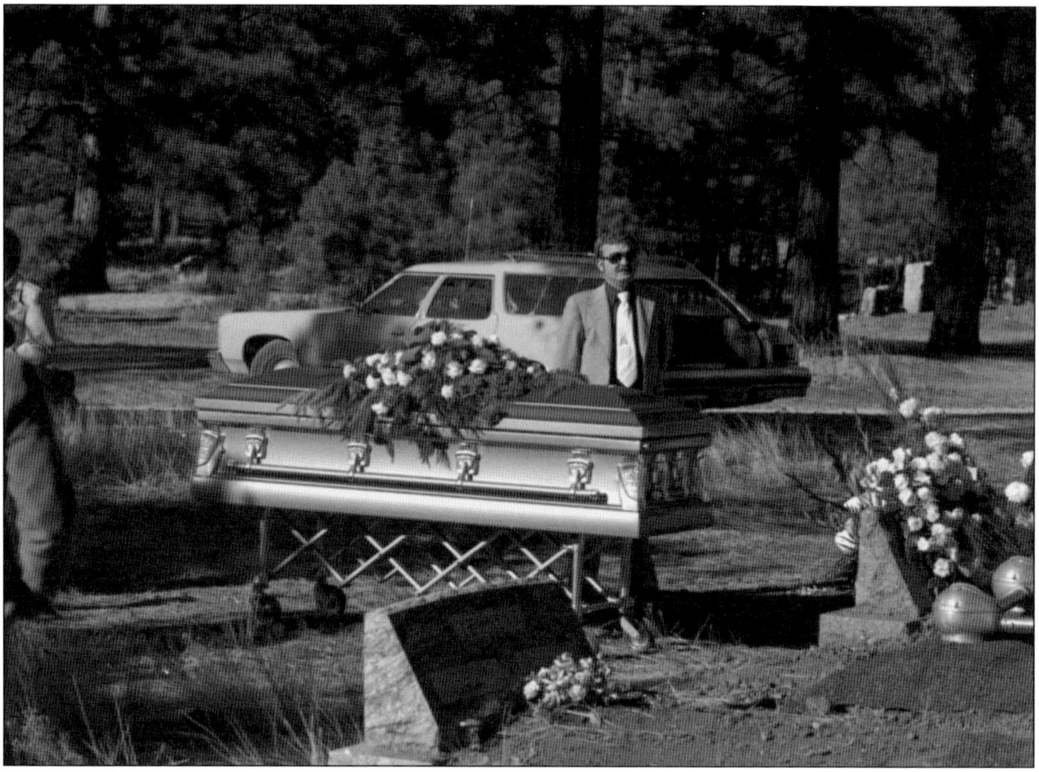

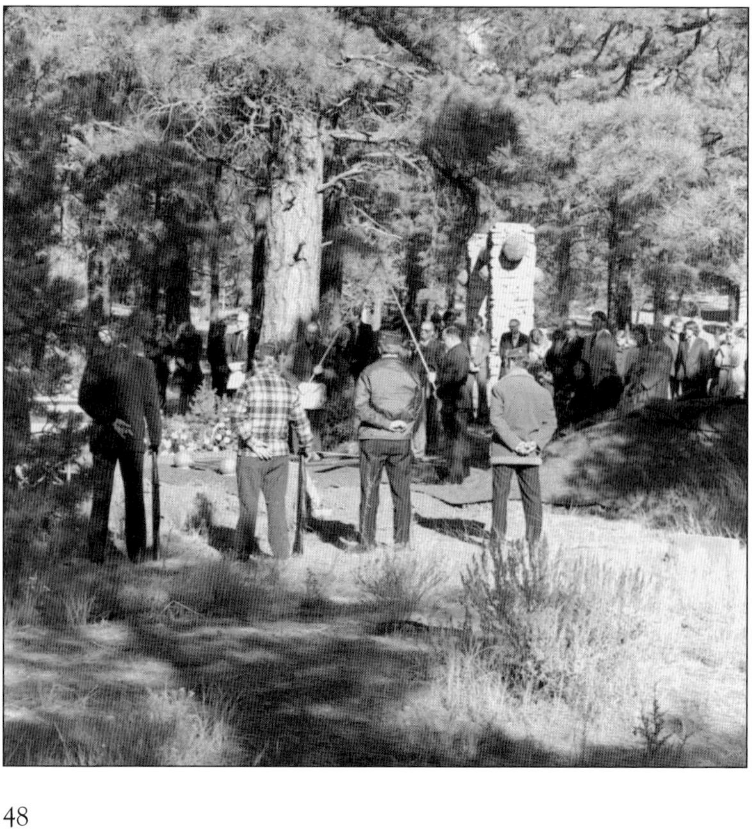

Pictured here is Emery Kolb's casket at graveside, just before it was lowered into the ground. The grave of his son-in-law Carl Lehnert is in the foreground. (Grand Canyon NP Museum Collection No. 06472.)

Members of the Masonic Lodge make a triangle figure, while a military honor guard looks on, as Emery Kolb's casket is lowered into the ground. (Grand Canyon NP Museum Collection No. 06510.)

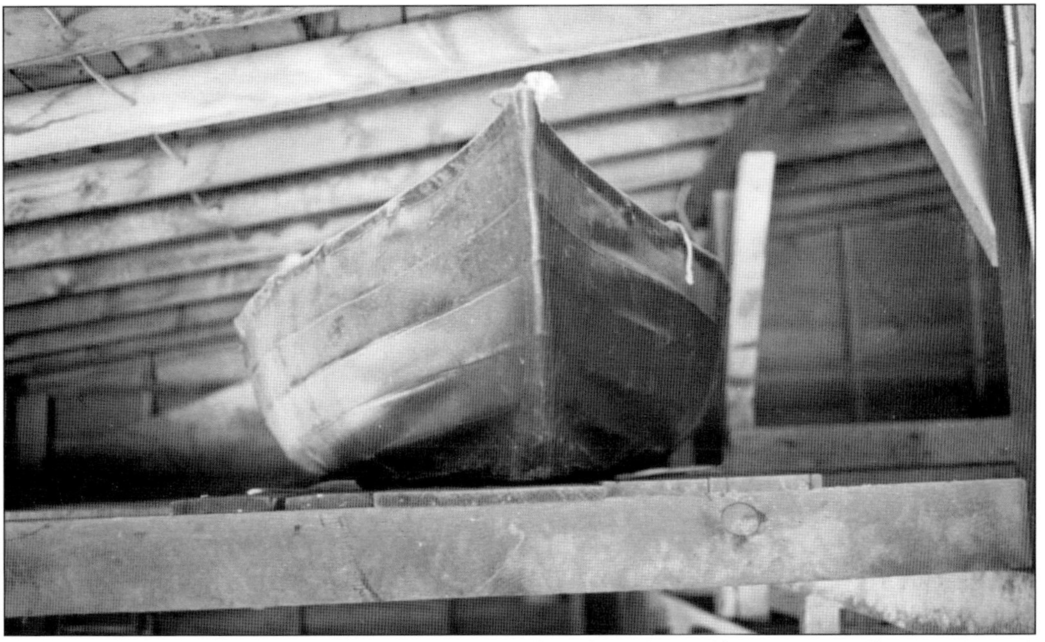

This boat belonged to Emery Kolb and was stored in the rafters of his garage. Following Emery's death, a skeleton was discovered in the boat. Rumors and speculation were rampant, but investigators ultimately concluded that the skeleton was that of an unidentified man found in the canyon in 1933. Kolb, as a member of the coroner's inquest on the skeleton, used his influence to get it donated to a medical school in Flagstaff. They gave it back to him later, and he had simply stored it in his garage. This photograph was taken on July 10, 1984. (Grand Canyon NP Museum Collection No. 13626.)

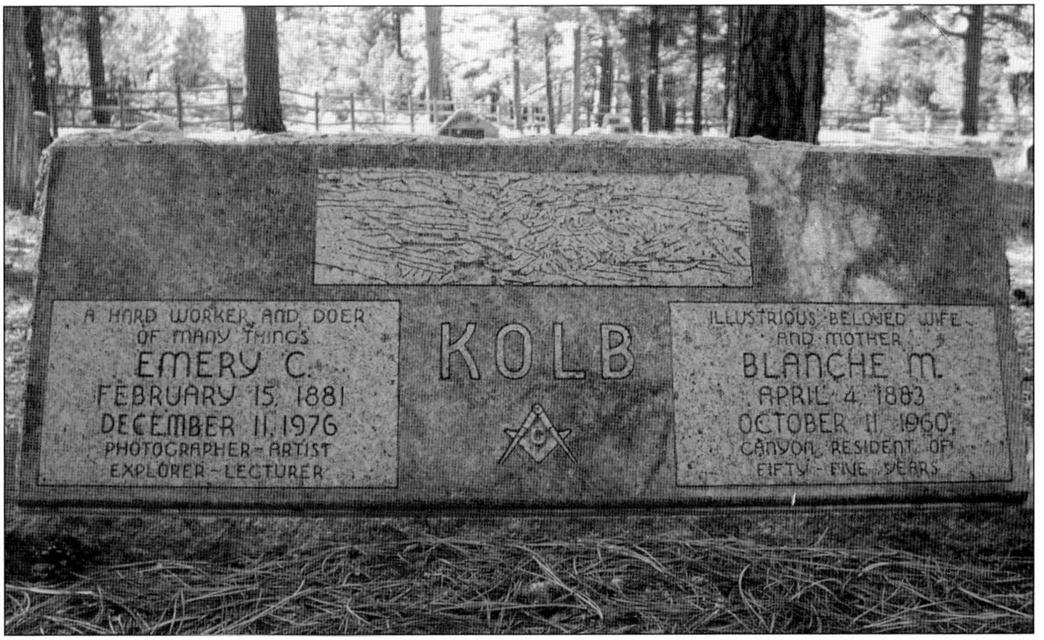

Seen here are the graves of Emery Kolb and his wife, Blanche. Their deaths were 16 years apart, and Emery never remarried. (David Schmittinger.)

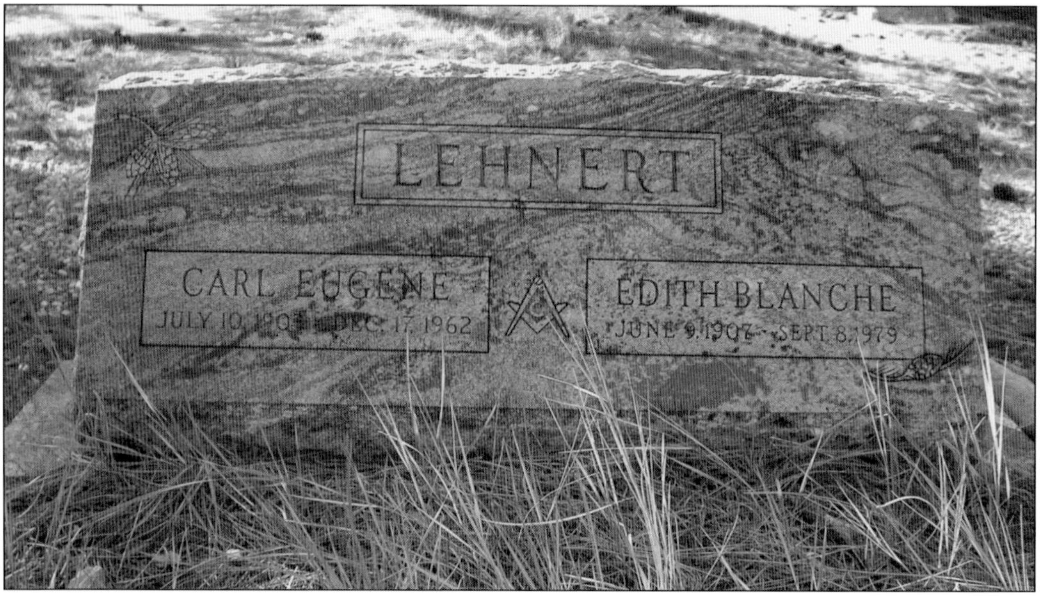

These are the graves of Edith and Carl Lehnert, Kolb's daughter and son-in-law. Note the Masonic symbol on the tombstone, which would seem to indicate that Emery made sure his daughter's husband became a member of the lodge. Edith and Carl's son Emery (named after his grandfather) died in 2012 and is buried in the cemetery, but his grave thus far is unmarked. (David Schmittinger.)

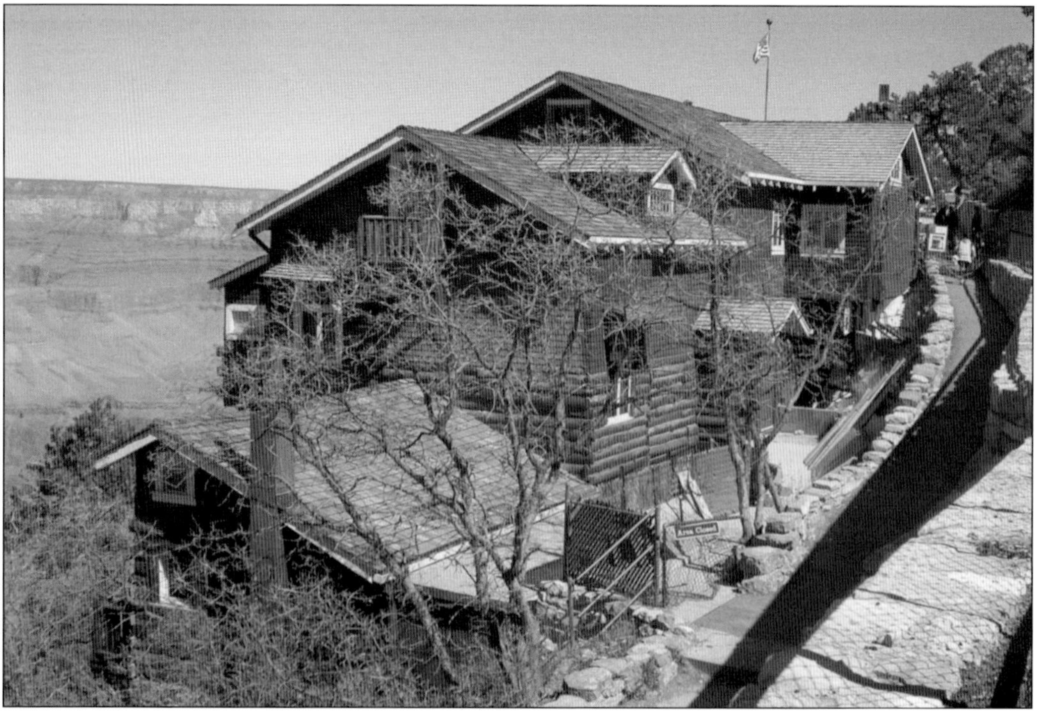

Pictured here is the Kolb Studio as seen today, restored by the National Park Service in the 1990s after nearly 20 years of being boarded up and ignored. It is now open to visitors and tourists who appreciate the rich photographic history of Ellsworth and Emery Kolb. (Lois Schmittinger.)

Six

The Bass-Lauzon Family

William Wallace Bass arrived at the Grand Canyon in the early 1880s, and along with John Hance, was one of the first white settlers on the rim. Bass would later claim he had arrived there before Hance, but most canyon historians are not convinced.

Bass set up mining operations and is credited with forging 50 miles of early canyon trails, including the first trail to the North Rim. When the tourist trade started, he opened his own hotel. In 1892, he married a much younger woman, Ada (a music teacher from the town of Prescott, Arizona), and they became the first white couple to raise children at the Grand Canyon.

William and Ada's daughter Edith married Hubert Lauzon, a wagon driver for her father. They had several children, but she died in 1924 after an appendix operation at the age of 28. Hubert later married a woman named Rosa White and became a national park ranger at the Grand Canyon.

As it was with Pete Berry and Ralph Cameron and their businesses, the Bass Hotel was put out of business by the unbeatable competition of the Fred Harvey Company and the Santa Fe Railroad. After the Grand Canyon was declared a national park, William and Ada Bass moved to Wickenburg, Arizona, and opened a motel there.

Like so many early Grand Canyon inhabitants, William and Ada Bass returned to the canyon in death. Their descendants, along with Lauzon descendants, have been buried here also.

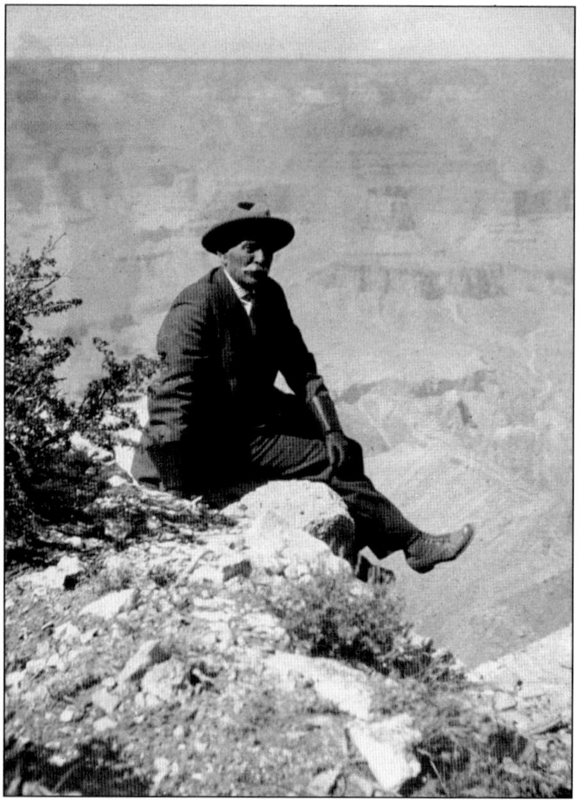

William Wallace Bass is seen here sitting on the canyon edge around 1910. (Grand Canyon NP Museum Collection No. 03635.)

William Wallace Bass poses for a tourist photograph in 1899 with his burro Joe and his dog Shep at the edge of the canyon. (Grand Canyon NP Museum Collection No. 00833.)

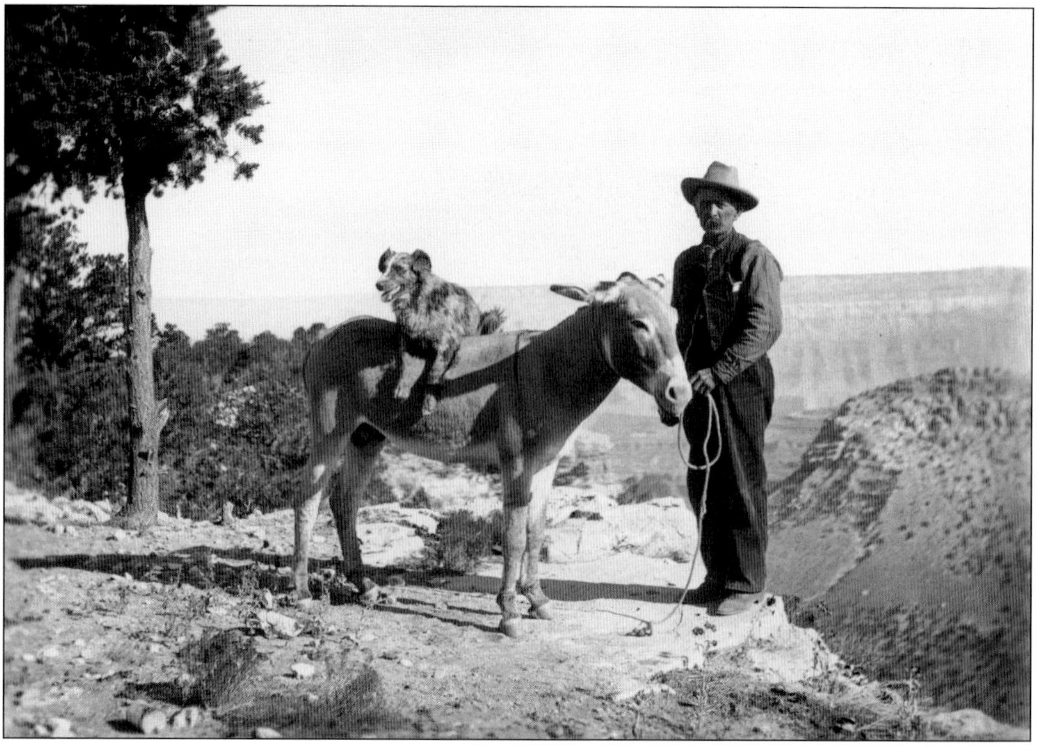

This is a late 1800s portrait of Ada Diefendorf Bass, likely taken in Prescott, Arizona, where she worked as a music teacher before marrying William. (Grand Canyon NP Museum Collection No. 17796.)

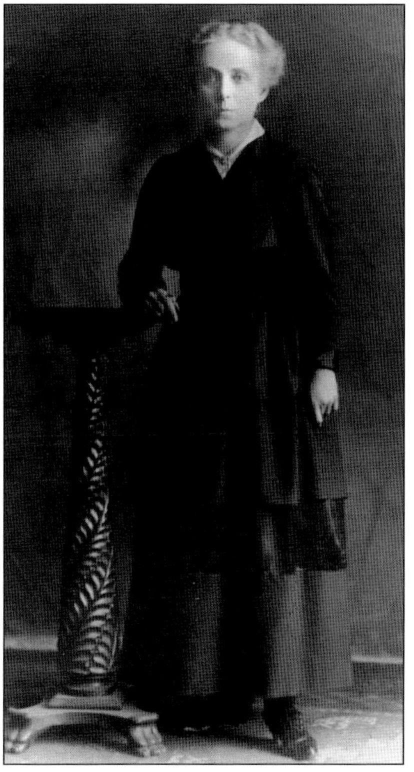

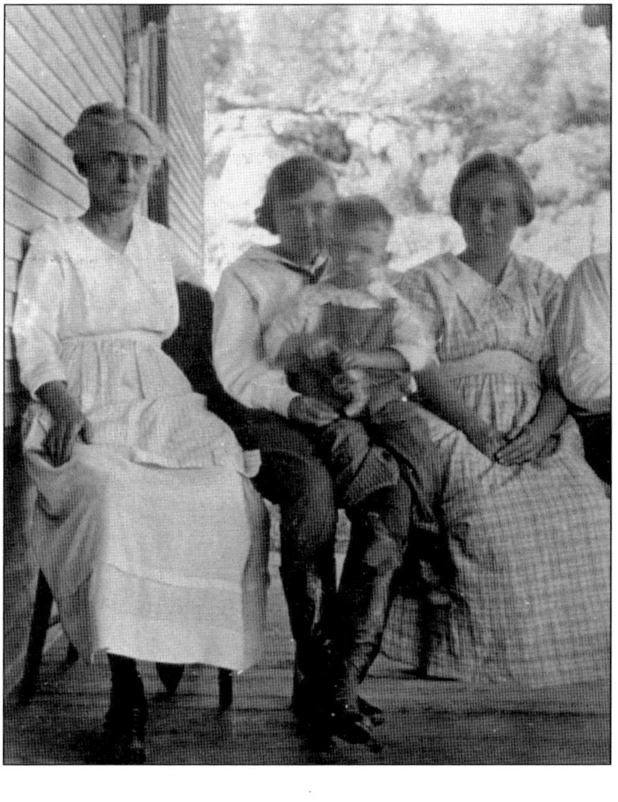

Pictured here in 1917 are, from left to right, Ada Bass; her daughter Mabel, holding Edith's son Hubert Jr.); and Edith, who is pregnant with her son Loren. (Grand Canyon NP Museum Collection No. 17797.)

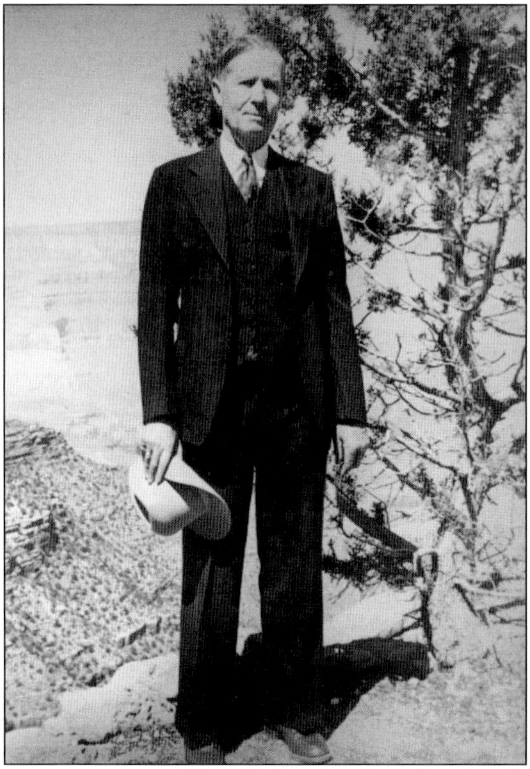

Hubert Lauzon was a Grand Canyon park ranger from 1929 to 1951. He had lived at the canyon even earlier, when married to Edith Bass, who died in 1924. This photograph was taken in 1951, shortly before his death on November 3. (Grand Canyon NP Museum Collection No. 02103.)

When William Wallace Bass died in 1933 at the age of 84, he was cremated and his ashes were scattered over a section of the canyon that was subsequently named Bass Tomb. Cremation, though not unheard of, was far less common in those days than it is today. In 1980, a group of Grand Canyon historians and Arizona governor Bruce Babbitt had this plaque erected beside Ada Bass's grave. (David Schmittinger.)

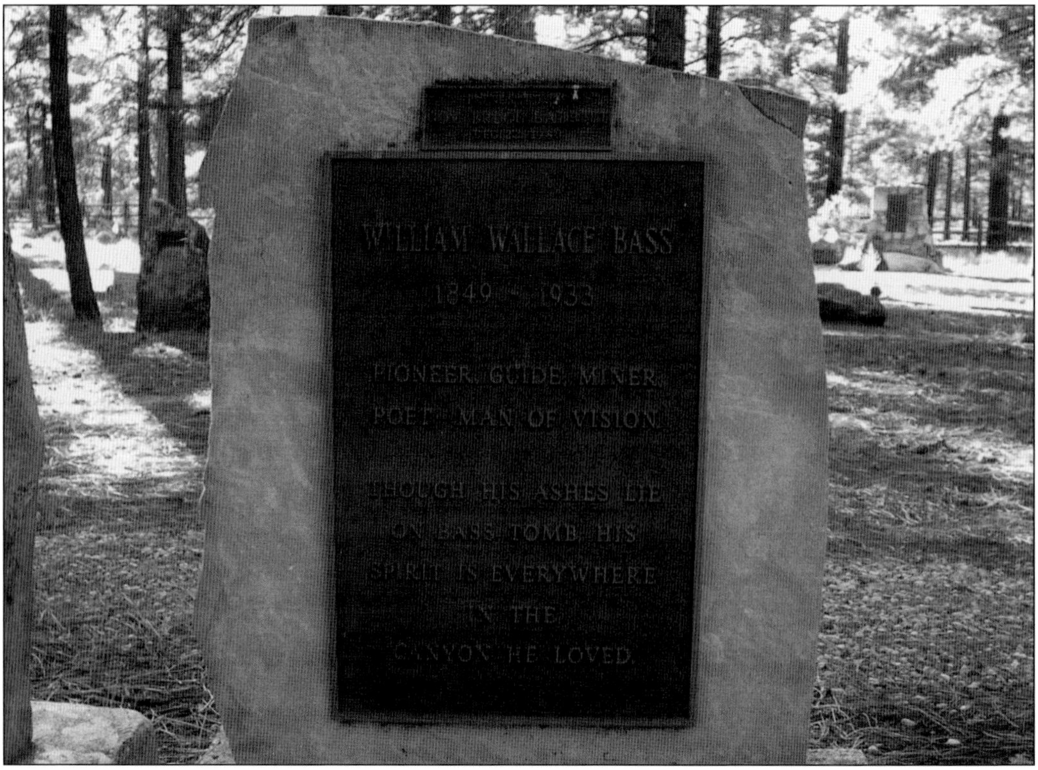

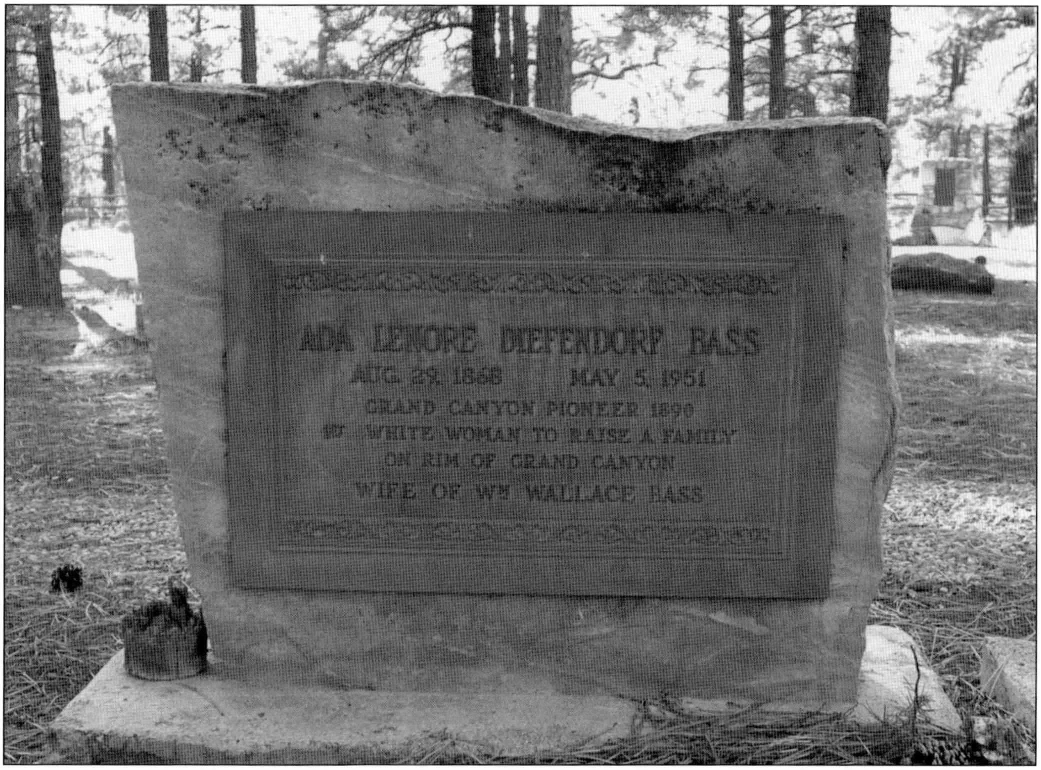

Ada Bass outlived her husband by 18 years. She died on May 5, 1951, at the age of 83. (David Schmittinger.)

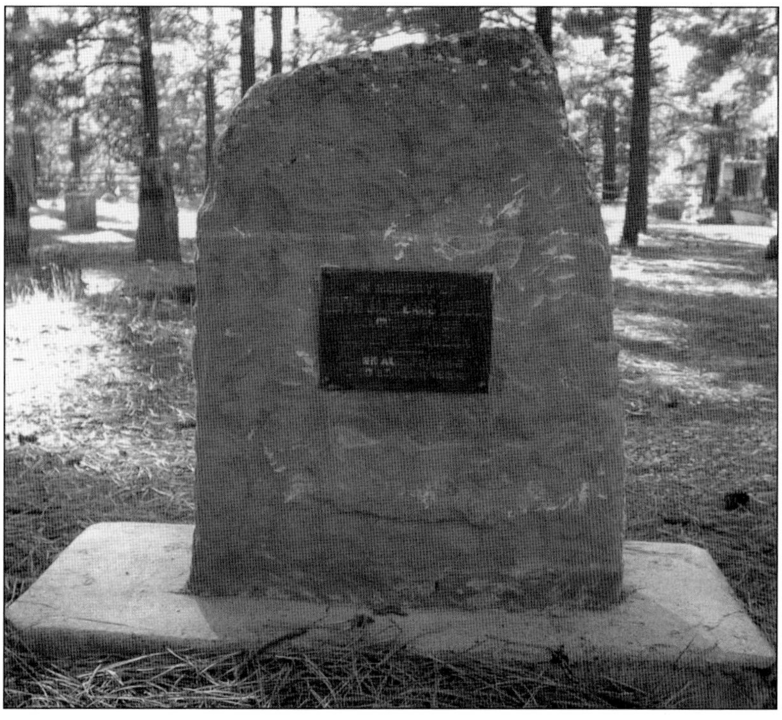

Edith Bass Lauzon, daughter of William and Ada and wife of Hubert Lauzon, died after an appendix operation at the age of 28, leaving behind her husband and young children. (David Schmittinger.)

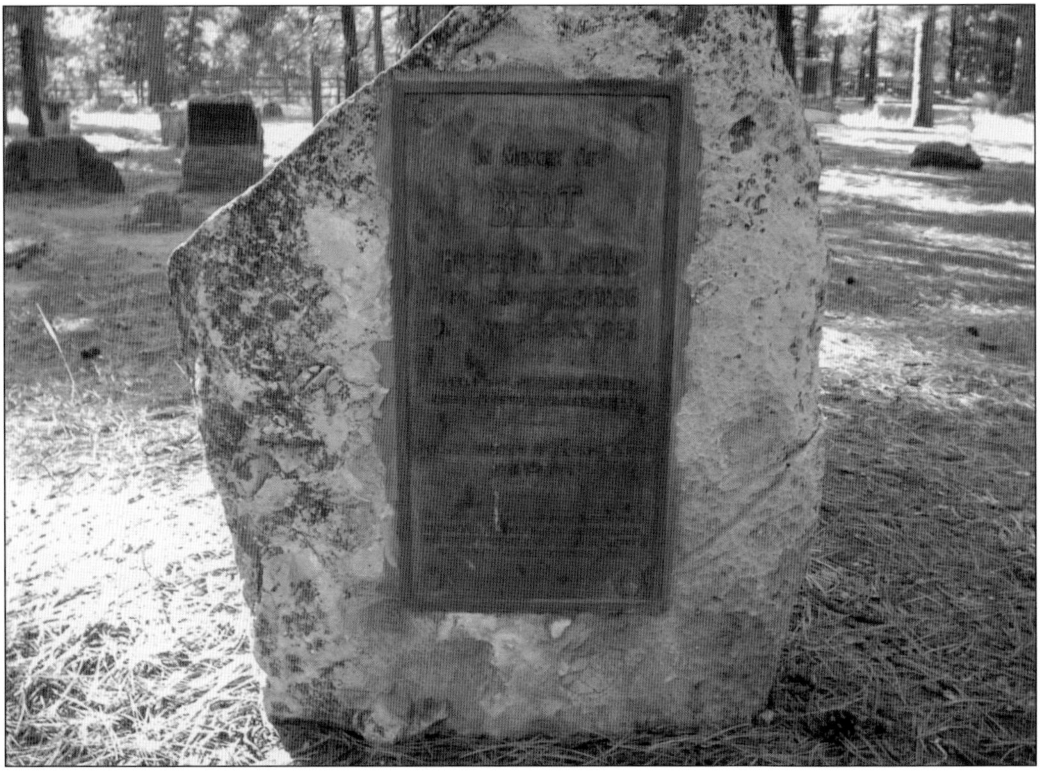

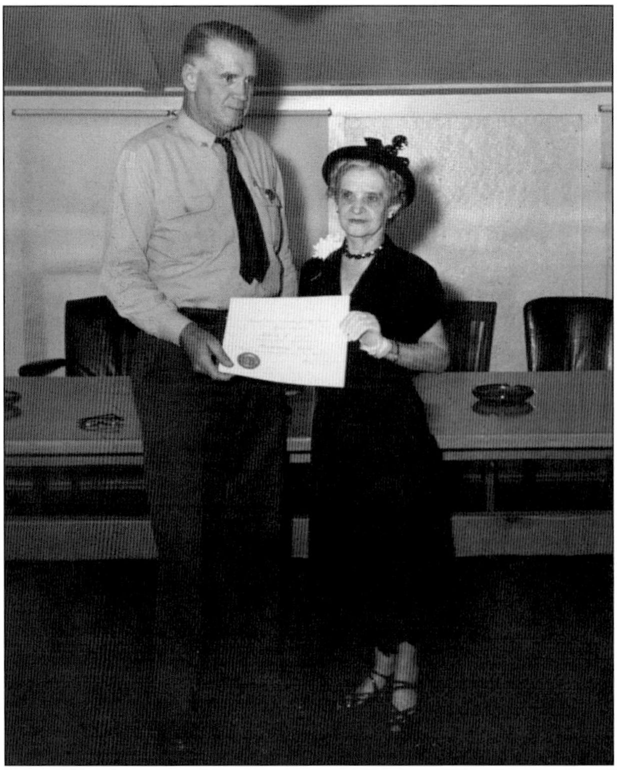

Hubert Lauzon remarried, continued to live at the Grand Canyon, and worked as a forest ranger until his death on November 3, 1951, at the age of 65. (David Schmittinger.)

Grand Canyon assistant superintendent Lon Garrison (also noted on page 95) presents a service medal and certificate for Hubert Lauzon to Lauzon's widow, Rosa, in this 1952 ceremony. (Photograph by Steve Leding; Grand Canyon NP Museum Collection No. 02314.)

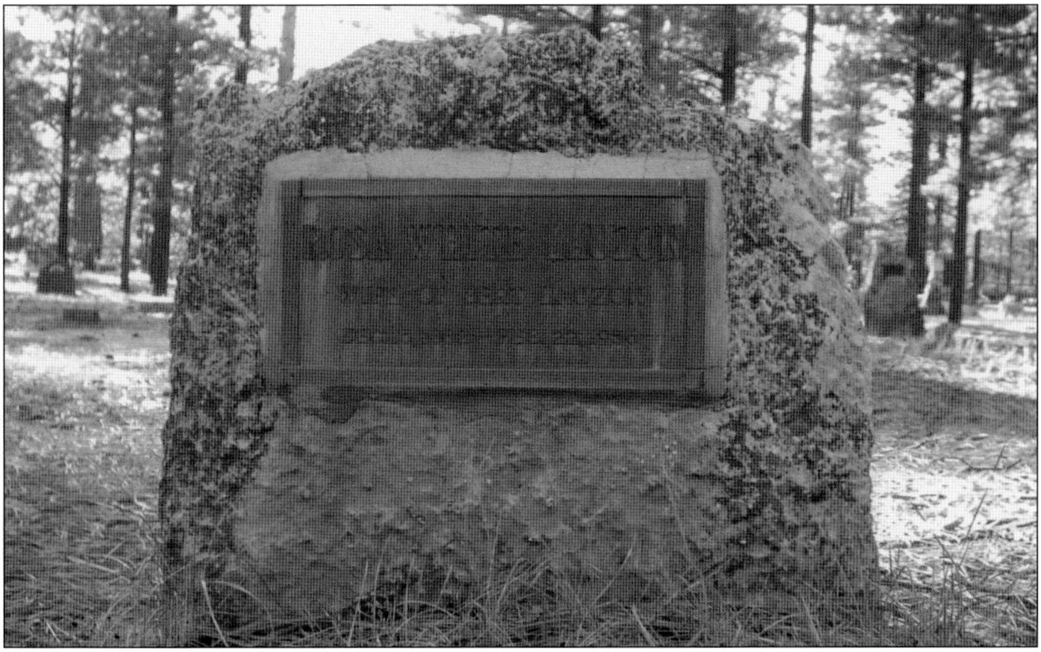

Rosa Lauzon (1882–1956), Hubert's second wife, is buried here. It is interesting to note that Hubert Lauzon and both of his wives are buried in the same family row together. (David Schmittinger.)

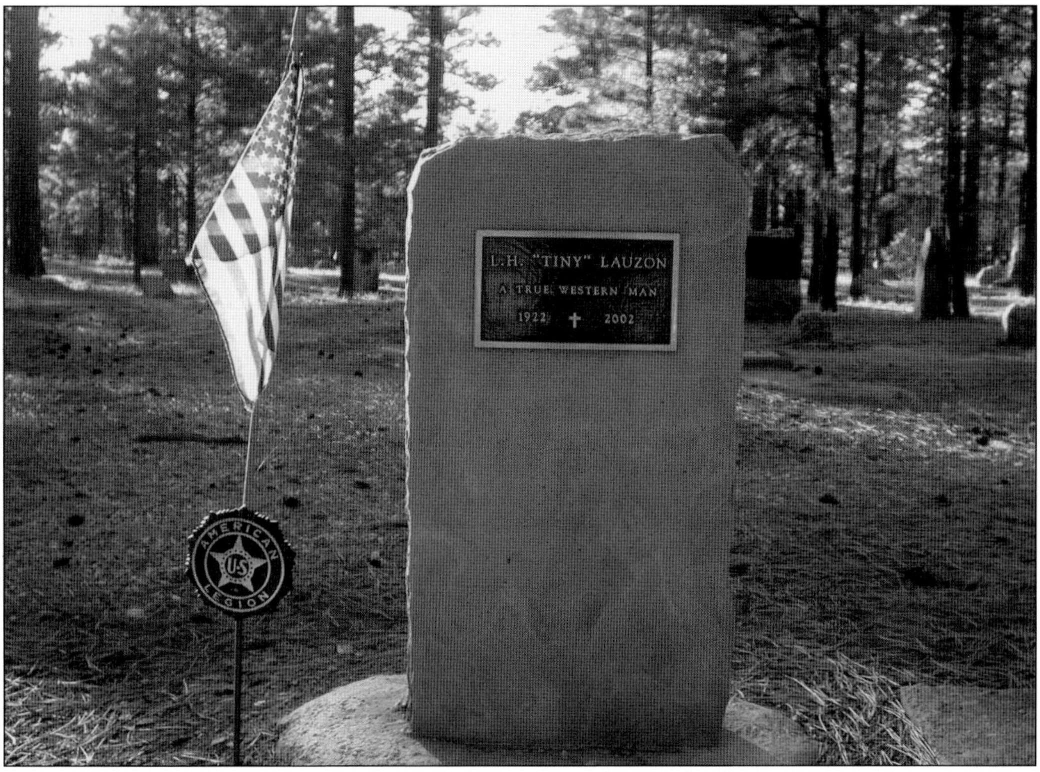

This is the grave of Loren "Tiny" Lauzon, the son of Hubert and Edith Lauzon. He was two years old when his mother died. (David Schmittinger.)

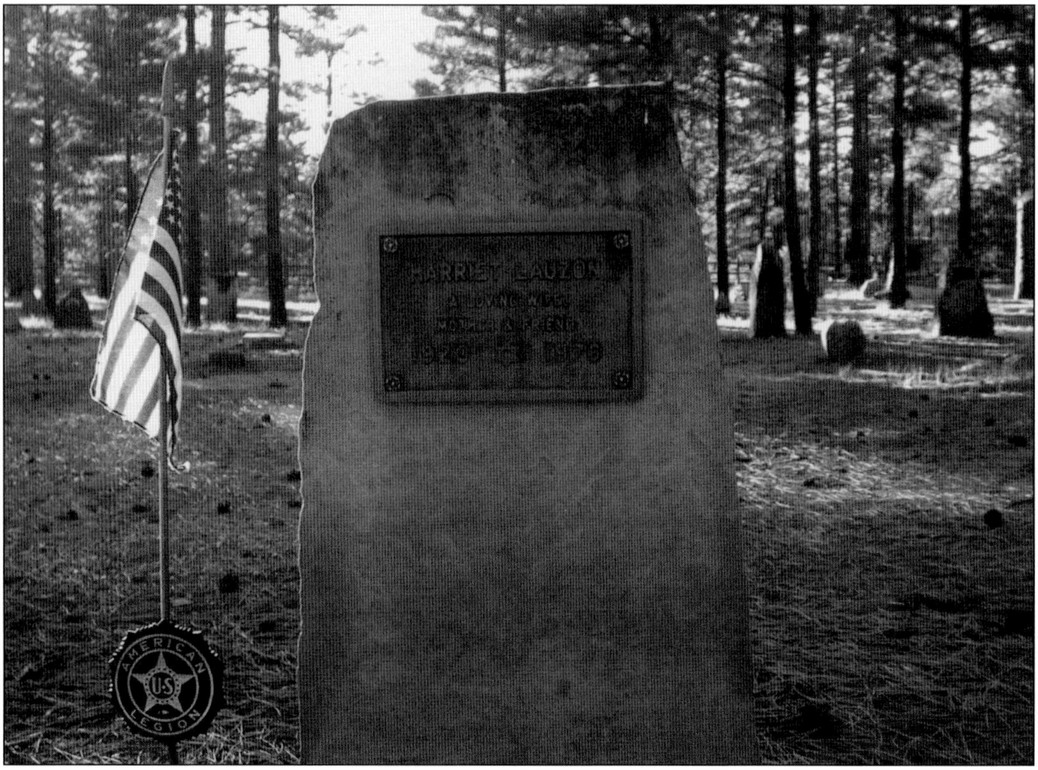

Harriet Lauzon, Loren Lauzon's wife, rests here also. She was 56 years old at the time of her death. (David Schmittinger.)

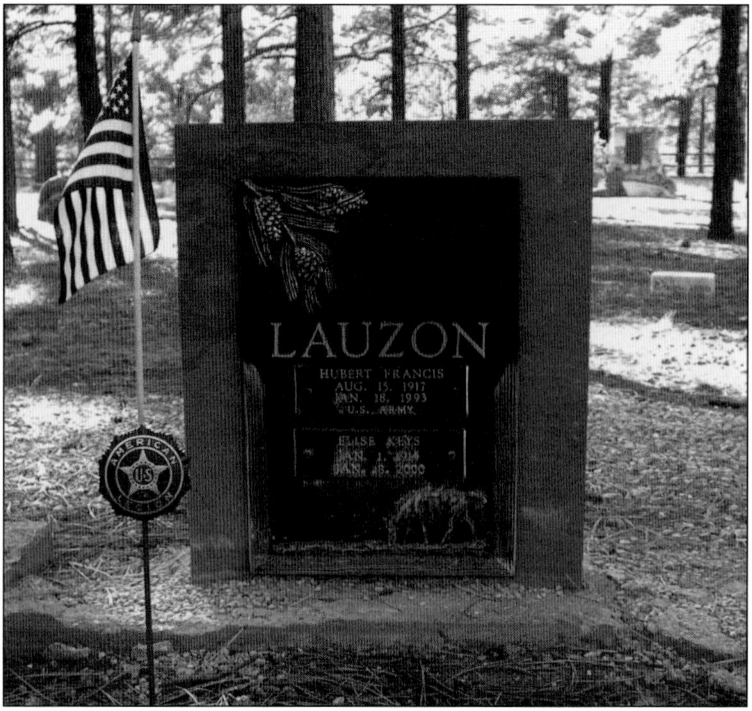

Hubert Lauzon (1917–1993), Hubert and Edith's son, and his wife, Elise (1914–2000), are buried here. (David Schmittinger.)

Seven

1956 Grand Canyon Air Crash

On the fateful day of June 30, 1956, about 11:30 a.m., two commercial jetliners, TWA Flight No. 2 with 70 people aboard (including crew) and a United Airlines DC-7, Flight 718, with 58 people on board (including crew), collided and crashed over the Grand Canyon. All 128 passengers and crew died. The point of impact was above Temple and Chuar Buttes near the confluence of the Colorado and Little Colorado Rivers on the east end of the canyon. Both planes were traveling at about 21,000 feet and around 300 miles per hour at the time of the crash.

To understand how this tragedy could have happened, one must remember the times. There was no single, universal air traffic control system—each airline company managed its own planes. Both flights had taken off from Los Angeles, California, and apparently both pilots detouring around a thunderhead had decided to give the passengers a view of the Grand Canyon. The rest, sadly, is history.

This was the worst disaster in aviation history up to that time. It spurred Congress into action and led to the creation of the Federal Aviation Administration (FAA), a single entity to handle the nation's air traffic control system. If anything positive could have come from this horrific tragedy, it was the creation of these aviation safeguards that are taken for granted today, which have undoubtedly prevented many more such accidents.

As for the victims of the Grand Canyon air crash, only 29 of the 128 were identified positively enough to be sent home to their families. The rest were interred in two mass graves. One is in Citizens Cemetery in Flagstaff, while four coffins of body parts were buried in a mass grave at the Grand Canyon Pioneer Cemetery under a monument listing the names of 31 victims.

In 2014, a memorial to the victims was erected at the Desert View overlook near the watchtower designed by Mary Colter. Temple and Chuar Buttes can be seen from this vantage point, the section of the canyon where the planes collided.

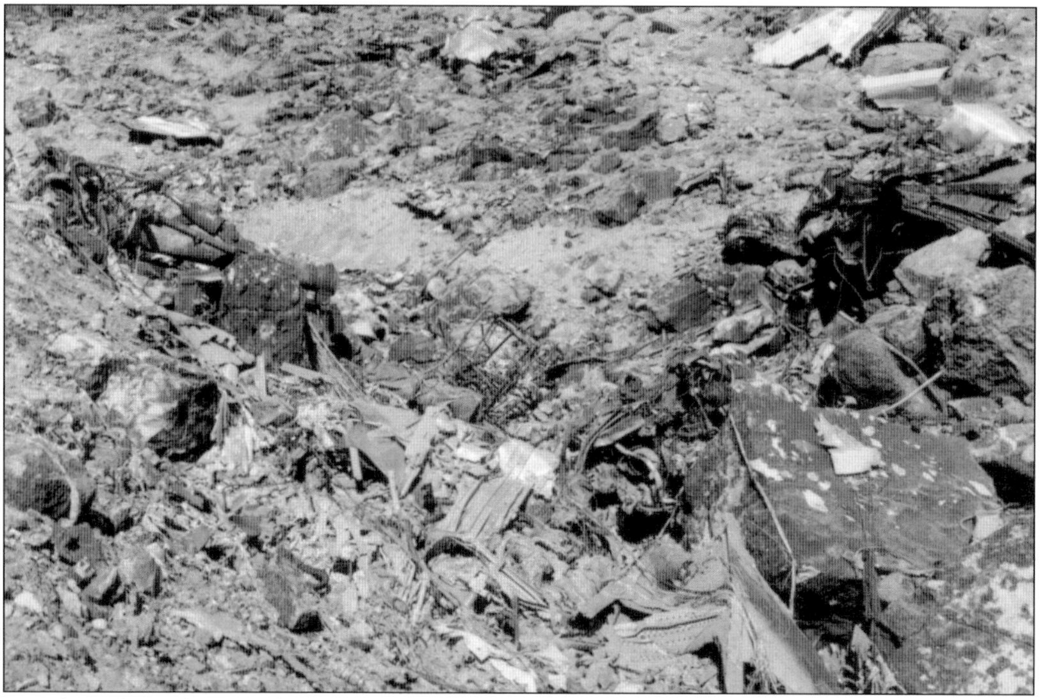

Wreckage from the two planes was spread out over a great distance, which made recovery of the bodies quite difficult. Investigators and National Park Service personnel were faced with a grisly task. These photographs show various parts of wreckage. (Both, photographs by Dan Davis; above, Grand Canyon NP Museum Collection No. 03702B; below, Grand Canyon NP Museum Collection No. 03702D.)

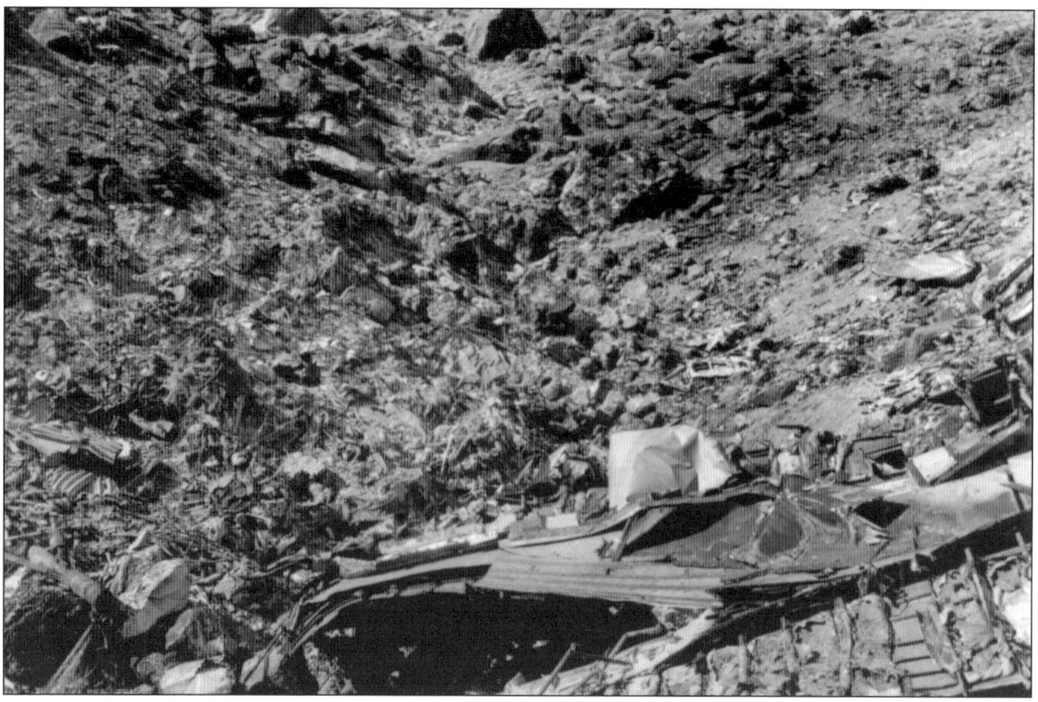

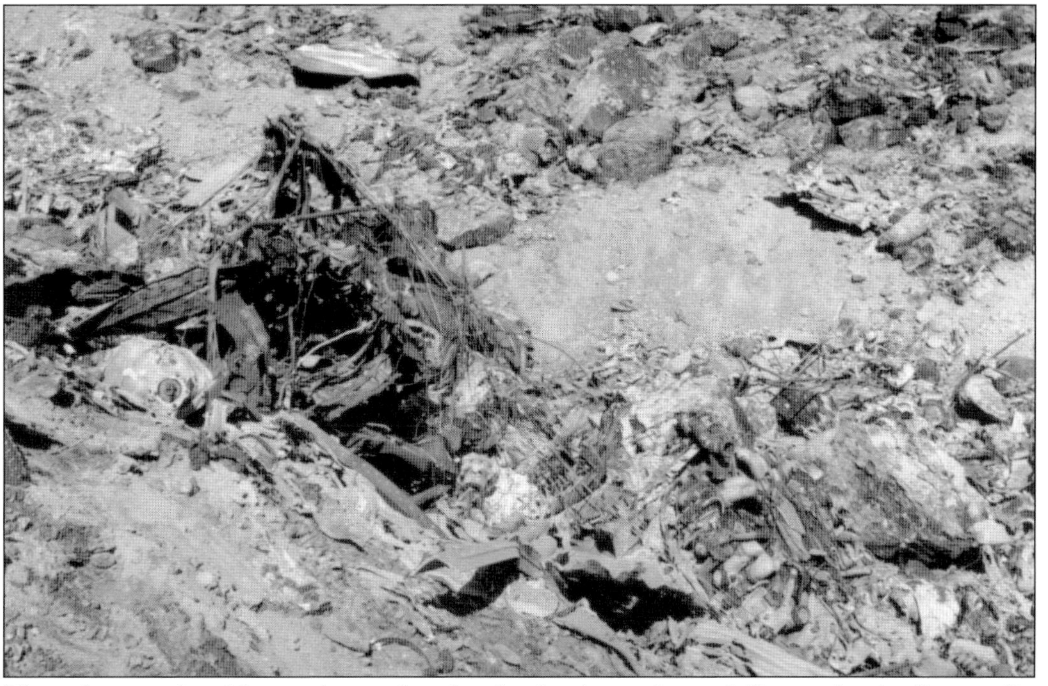

These photographs of the wreckage, taken shortly after the crash, are chilling to this day. Reportedly, small pieces of the wreckage can still be found in the canyon, but they are now protected by the Antiquities Act. Therefore, it is now a felony crime for explorers and souvenir hunters to remove them. (Both, photographs by Dan Davis; Grand Canyon NP Museum Collection No. 03702C; below, Grand Canyon NP Museum Collection No. 03702E.)

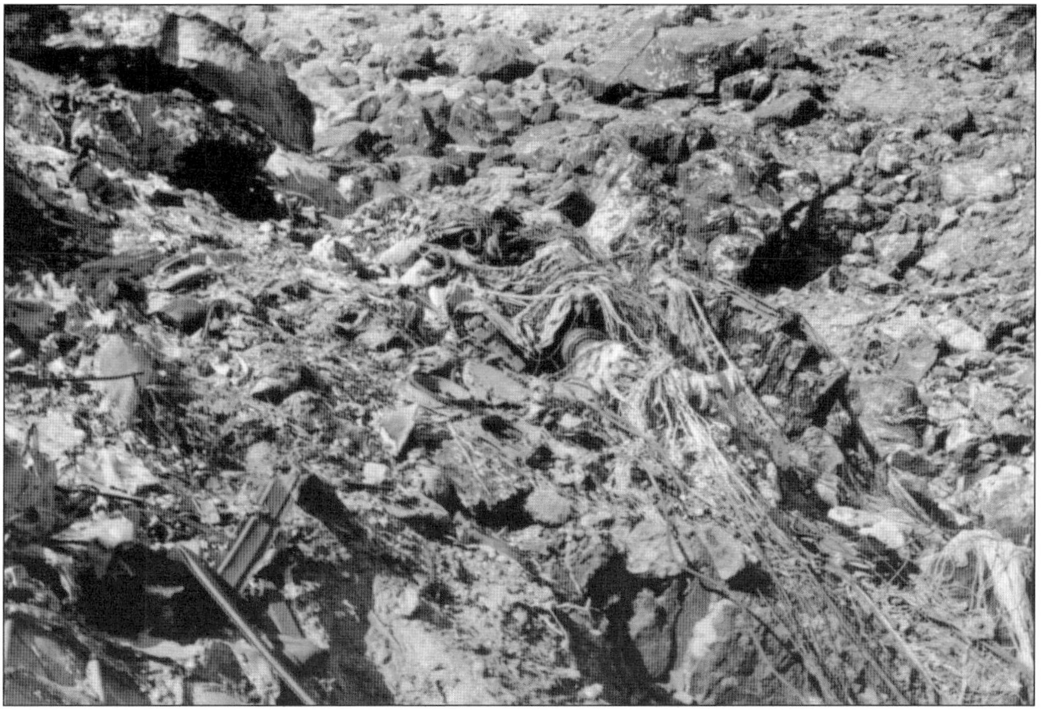

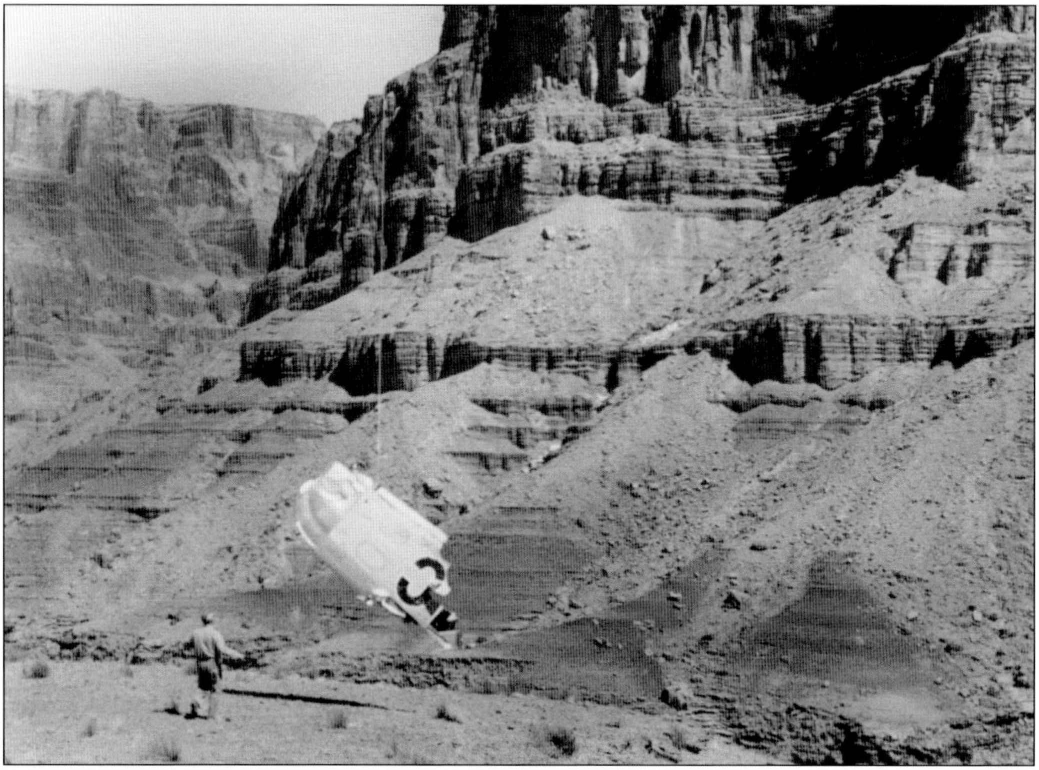

A portion of the United Airlines wing is lifted out of the canyon crash site by a helicopter not long after the terrible collision occurred. It was a Douglas DC-7 plane, No. N6324C (a portion of the 4 and C can be seen in this photograph). The large portions of the aircraft were removed as quickly as possible to discourage looting. (Photograph by Dan Davis; Grand Canyon NP Museum Collection No. 03702A.)

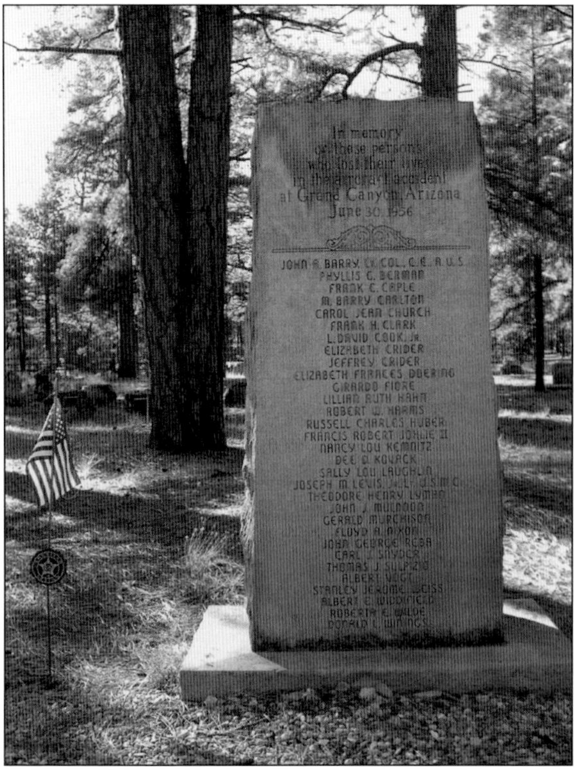

This monument was placed over the mass grave in the Grand Canyon Pioneer Cemetery, where four coffins of unidentified remains were buried. The names reflect some, but not all, of the victims who may or may not be the ones buried here, as there is another mass grave from this tragedy in Flagstaff. (David Schmittinger.)

Eight

OTHER BURIALS

The story of the Grand Canyon and its cemetery does not begin or end here. There are many more who heard the call of the canyon, came here, and worked hard to keep the national park one of the crown jewels of the world. Interred at the cemetery are park rangers, scientists, geologists, concession workers, Harvey Girls, miners, public officials, and some local characters.

This chapter pays tribute to some of these men and women who devoted their lives to this miracle of God's creation. The tales the tombstones tell give people the history of the Grand Canyon National Park. As long as the Grand Canyon Pioneer Cemetery remains an active burial ground, it will continue to serve as the final resting place for future generations of the canyon's stewards, who would probably not wish to be buried anywhere else.

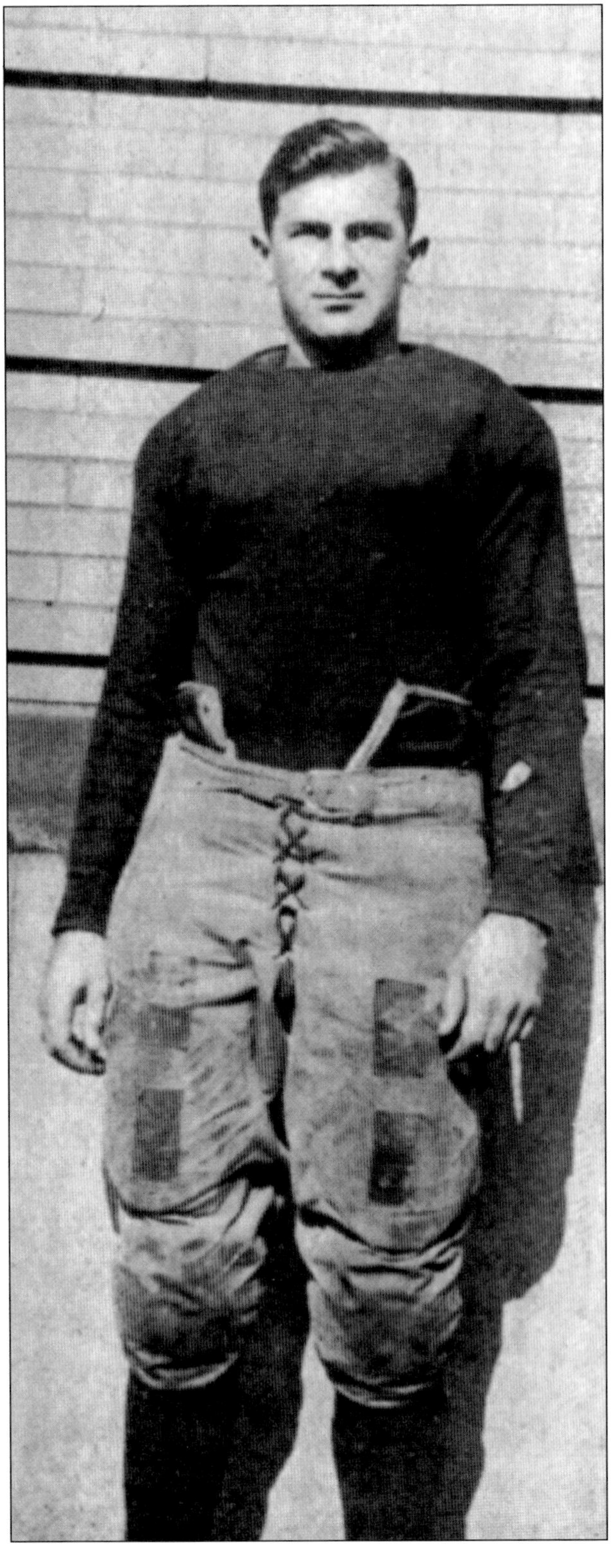

Robert Bingham attended Yale University from 1915 to 1918 and was a star football player there, leading his team to many victories, including one over Harvard. He was a student at Sheffield Scientific School at Yale at the same time and a member of the Book and Snake fraternity. (Yale University Manuscripts and Archives.)

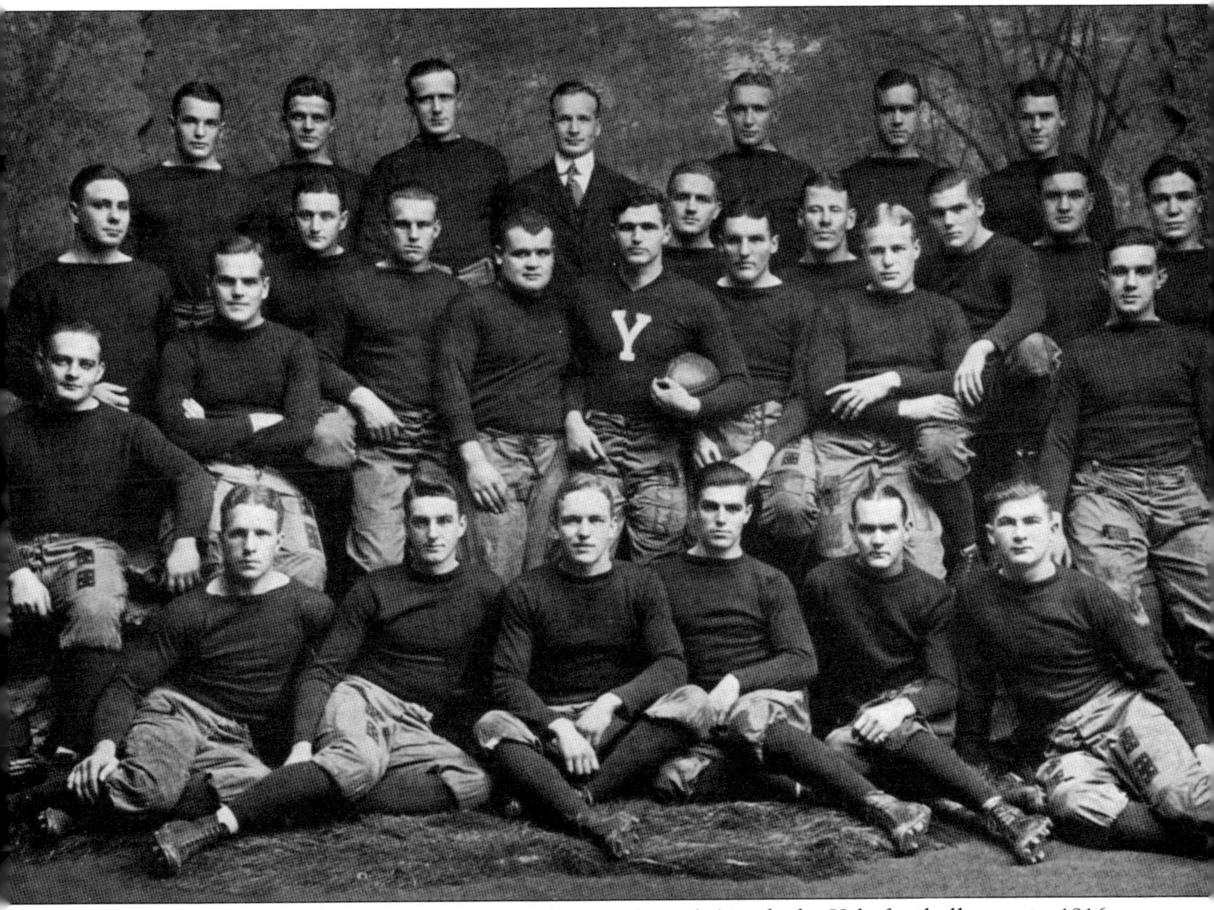

This is a photograph of Robert Bingham (first row, far right) with the Yale football team in 1916. After leaving the university, he went west for his health and became one of the first forest rangers at the Grand Canyon. Shortly after the canyon attained national park status, Bingham died in 1919 from the Spanish flu pandemic that devastated the United States following World War I, killing up to 40 million people worldwide. (Yale University Manuscripts and Archives.)

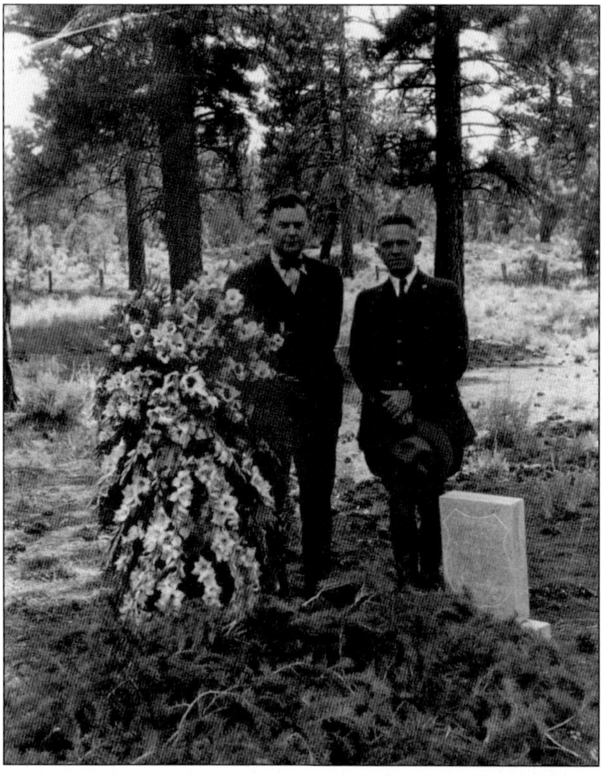

A.D. Jones (left) and park superintendent Miner R. Tillotson (right) stand by the grave of Yale football star and forest ranger Robert Bingham in this 1932 photograph. (Grand Canyon NP Museum Collection No. 00748.)

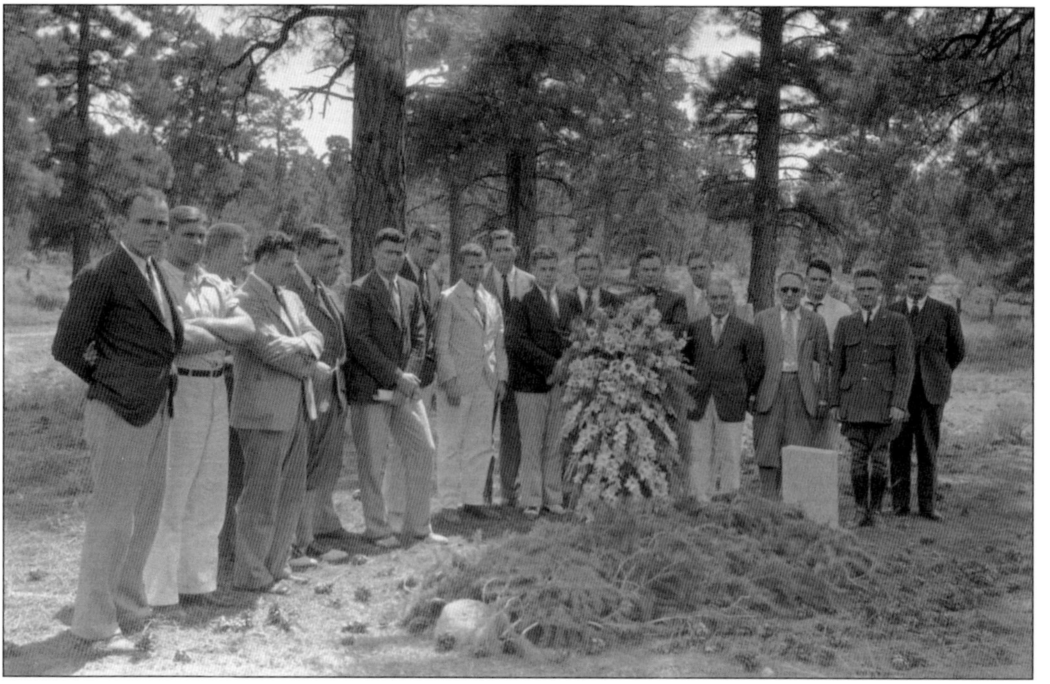

Members of the Yale, Harvard, and Princeton football teams, en route to the Olympic Games in Los Angeles, California, in 1932, made a stop at the Grand Canyon Cemetery to pay a graveside tribute to the memory of Robert Bingham. (Grand Canyon NP Museum Collection No. 00571.)

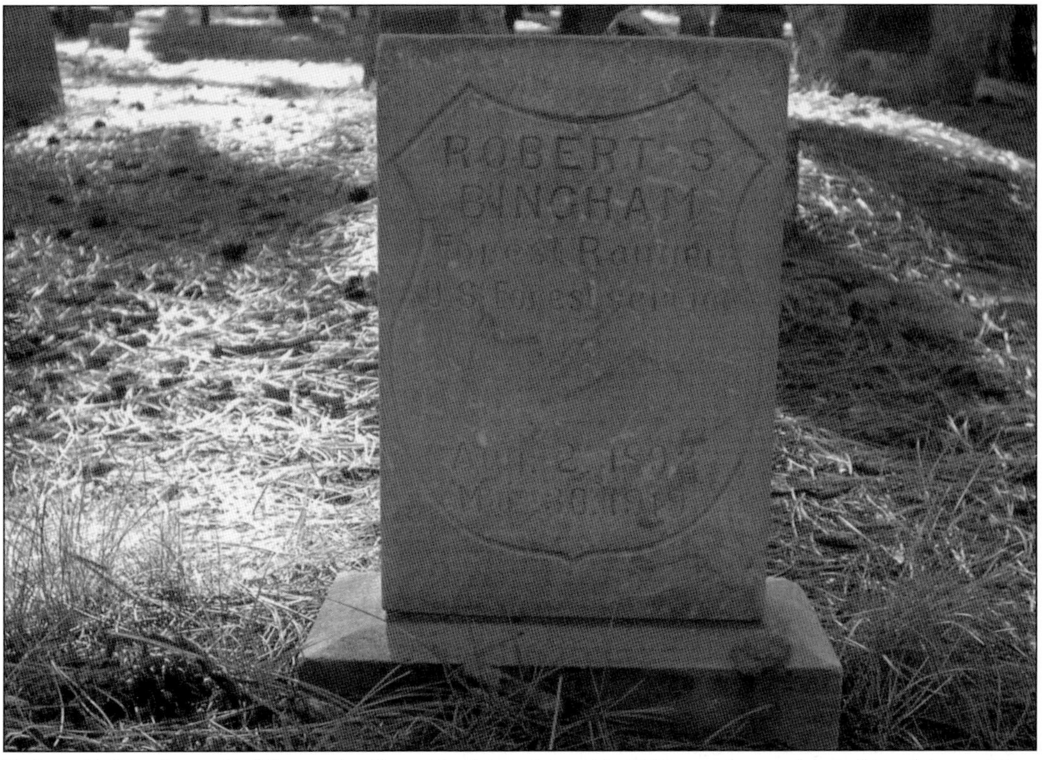

Robert S. Bingham died from the Spanish flu on May 30, 1919, not long after taking his position as a Grand Canyon park ranger. This is his tombstone as seen today. (David Schmittinger.)

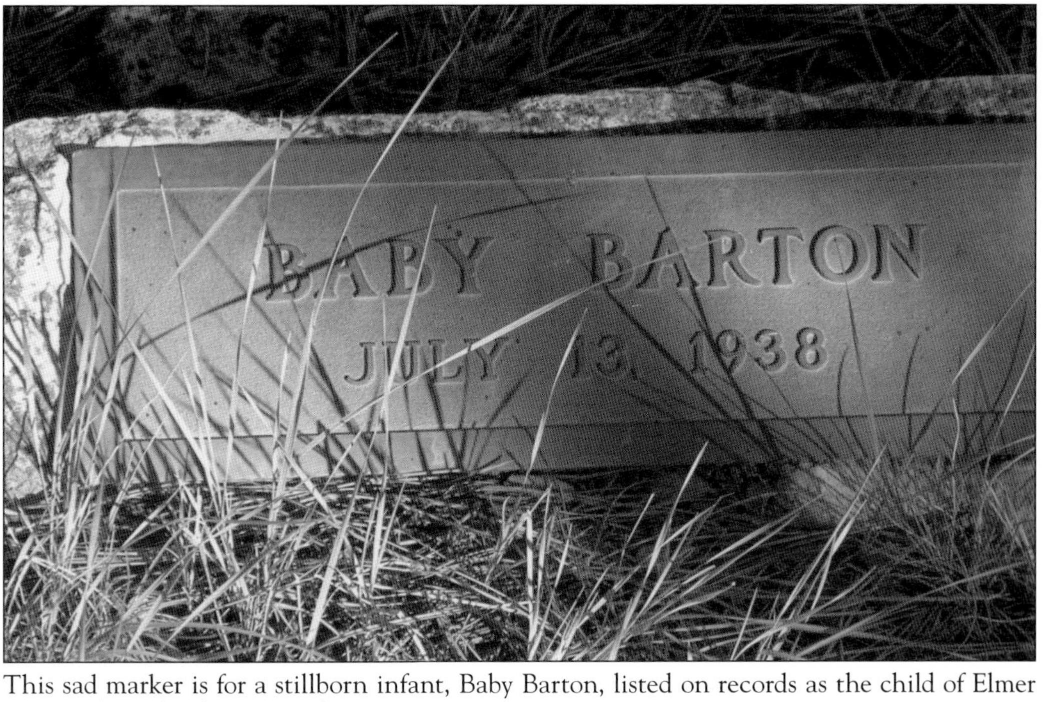

This sad marker is for a stillborn infant, Baby Barton, listed on records as the child of Elmer Barton. (David Schmittinger.)

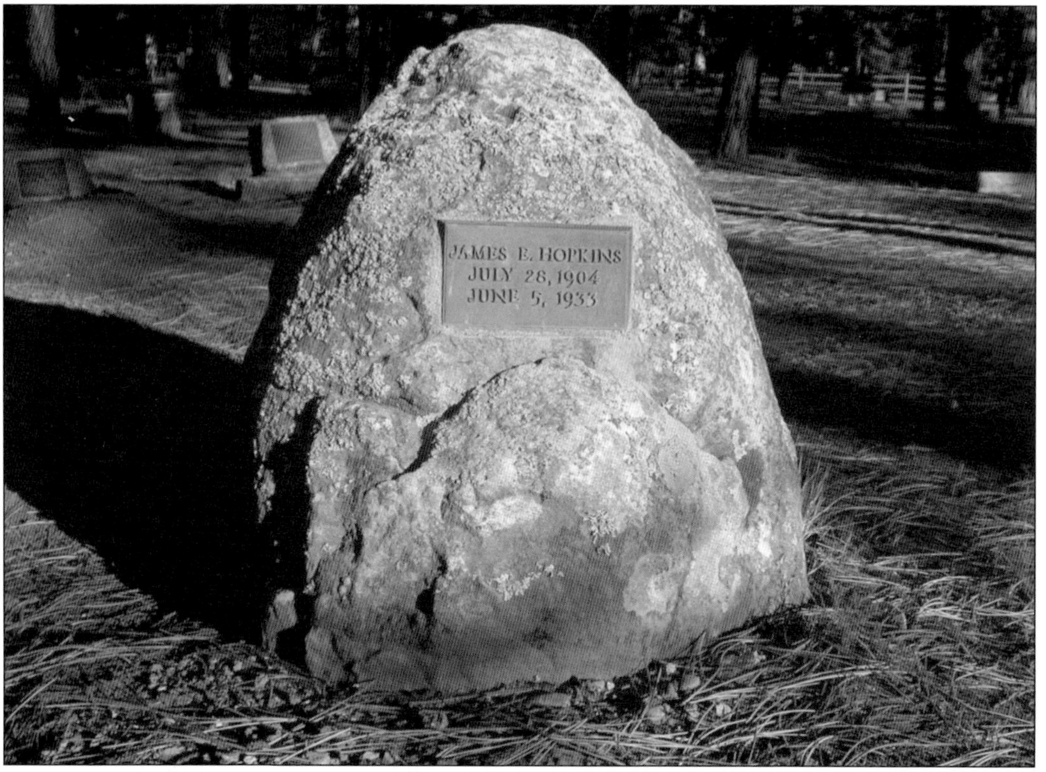

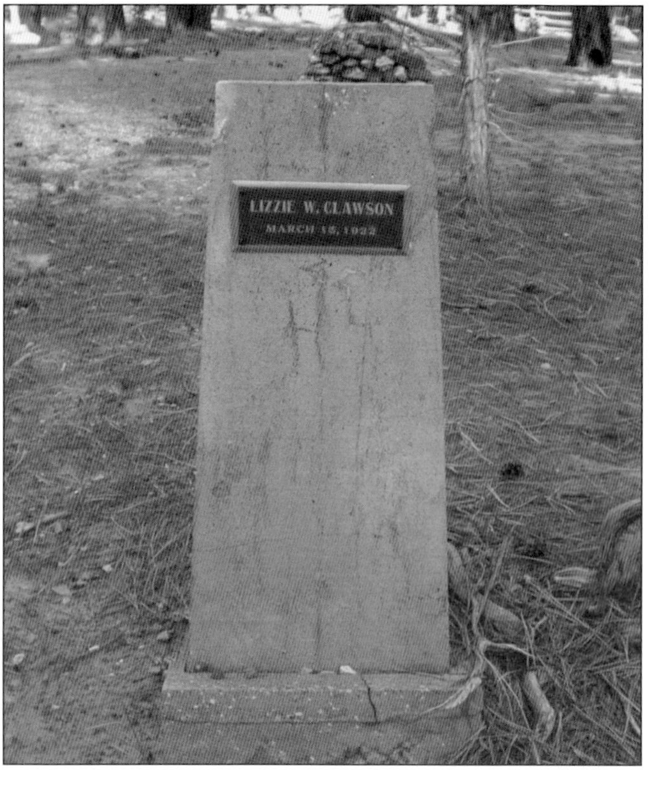

One unique aspect of the Grand Canyon Pioneer Cemetery is that many of the tombstones are made out of large rocks with plaques attached, a concept not found in many other cemeteries. This is the grave of James Hopkins (1904–1933). (David Schmittinger.)

Lizzie Clawson, who died March 15, 1922, at the age of 58, was a housewife who passed away from acute bronchial pneumonia and was one of the earliest burials here. (David Schmittinger.)

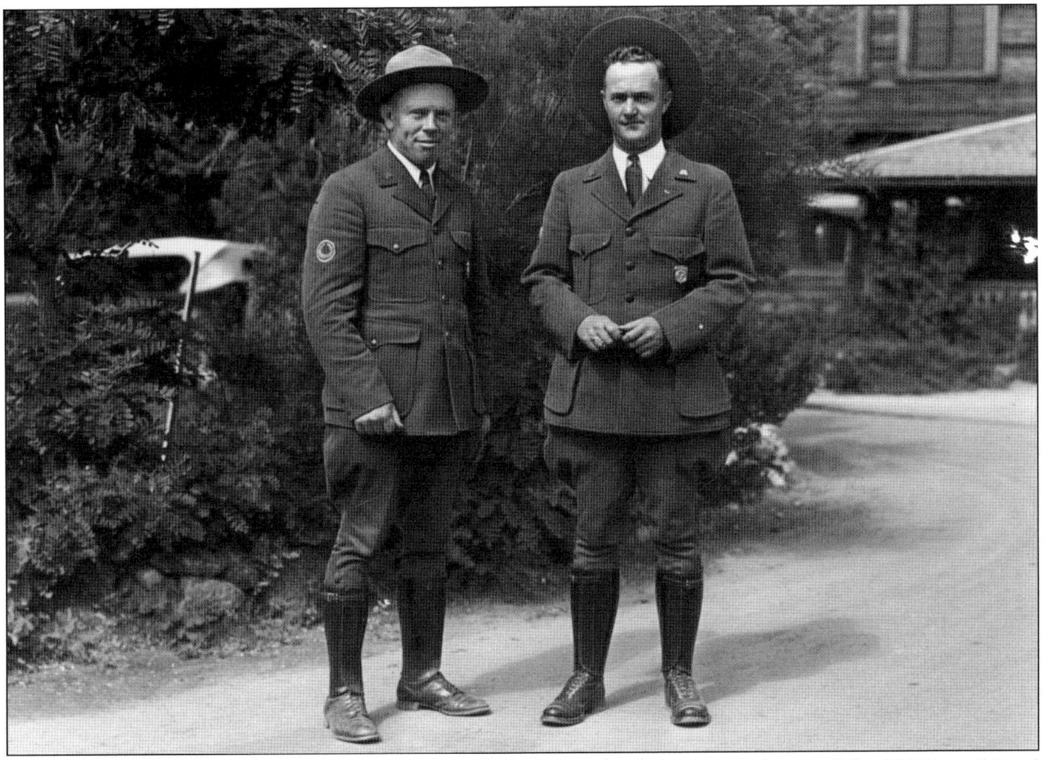

Park rangers Robert R. Williamson (left) and Carl Cox (right) pose in front of the El Tovar Hotel in June 1931. (Grand Canyon NP Museum Collection No. 00029.)

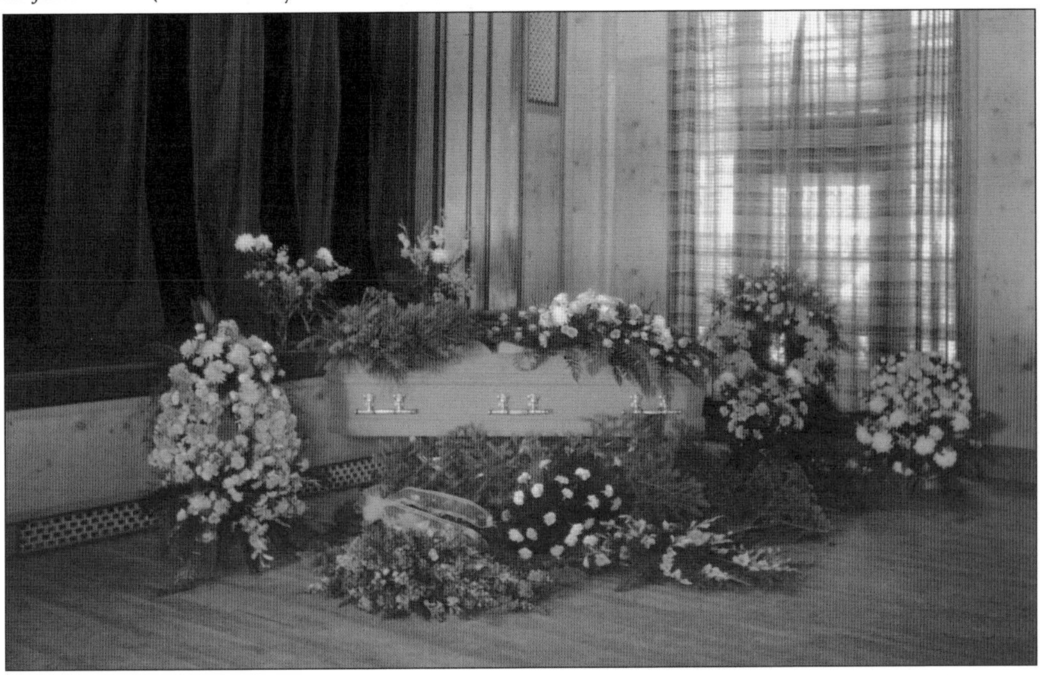

The casket of Robert R. Williamson is displayed in the Grand Canyon Community Building following his death in January 1937. (Grand Canyon NP Museum Collection No. 00576.)

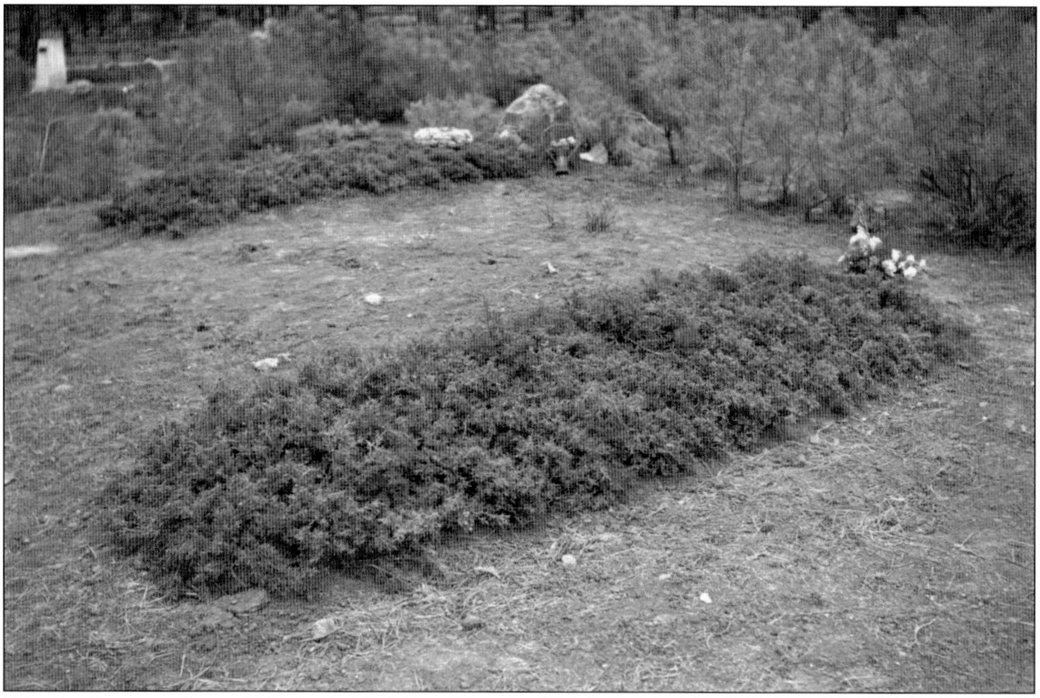

The fresh grave of ranger Robert R. Williamson is seen in this photograph taken shortly after burial. His tombstone had not yet been installed. (Grand Canyon NP Museum Collection No. 01405.)

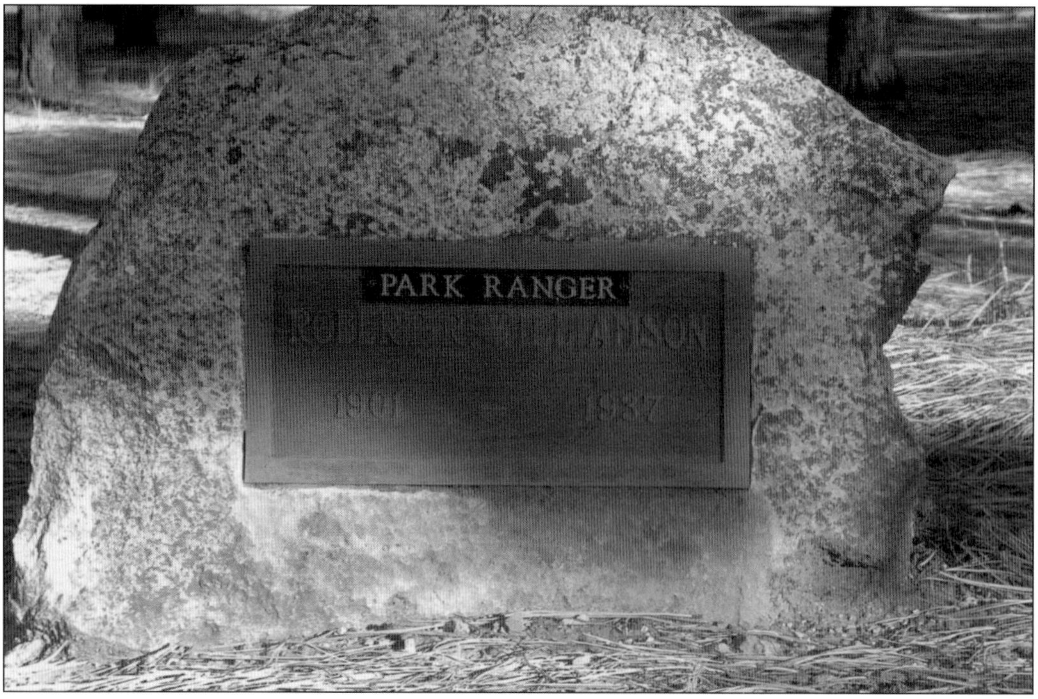

Here is the grave of park ranger Robert R. Williamson as seen today. He was 35 years old and had died of a combination of influenza and pneumonia. Such maladies were not so easily treated in 1937 as they are now. (David Schmittinger.)

Many veterans are buried here, including Cecil W. Dodd, a World War I veteran who was a wagon driver in the military from the days before automobiles and trucks. He died at the age of 34 from acute nephritis. (David Schmittinger.)

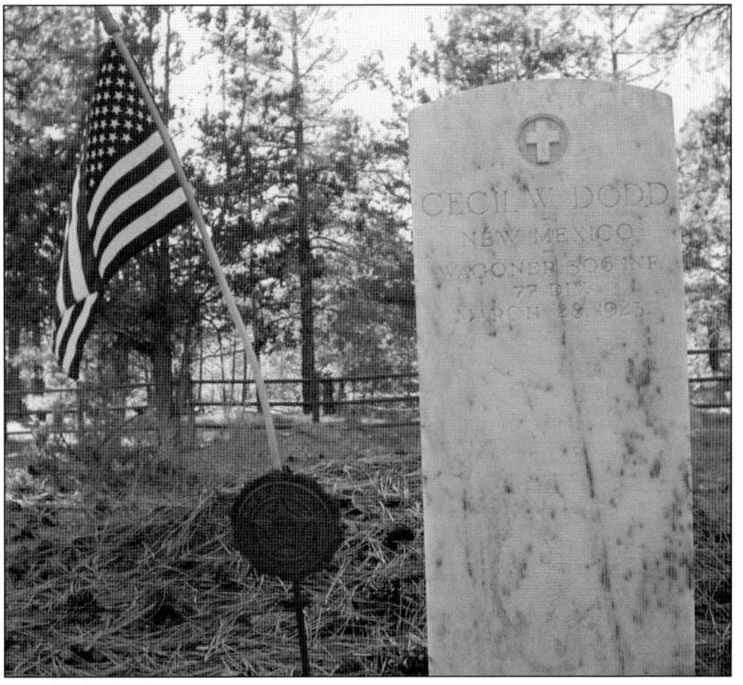

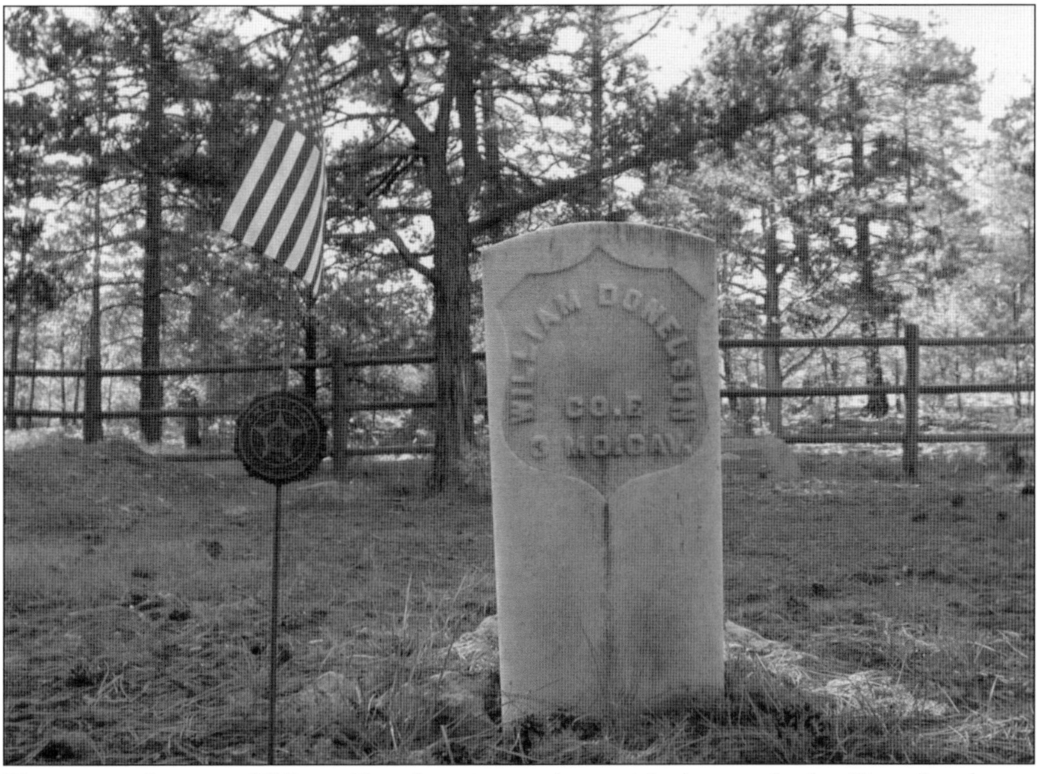

The grave of veteran William Donelson is seen here with the standard military headstone that was issued in that era. He died of apoplexy on February 9, 1933, at the age of 90. (David Schmittinger.)

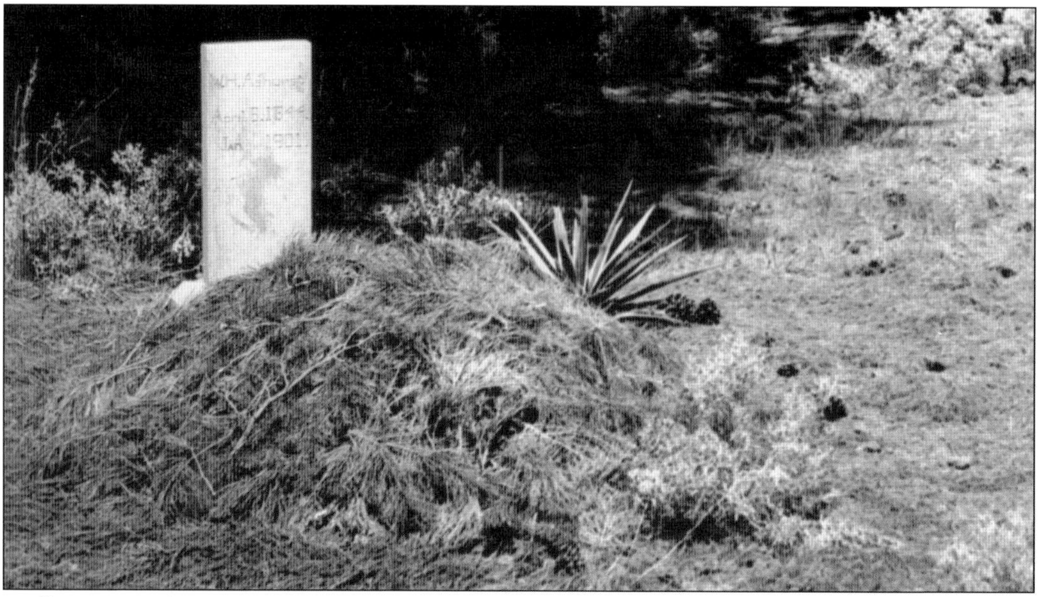

William H. Ashurst was an early prospector and mining partner of John Hance, Pete Berry, and Ralph Cameron. He was killed in a rockslide in the canyon on January 18, 1901, at the age of 57. Found by John Hance 49 days later, Ashurst was buried where he fell. In 1908, Niles J. Cameron exhumed him and reburied him at the Bright Angel trailhead. Then sometime in the mid-1930s, Ashurst was exhumed again and buried in the Grand Canyon Cemetery. This undated photograph shows an old tombstone no longer present on Ashurst's grave. (Grand Canyon NP Museum Collection No. 00566.)

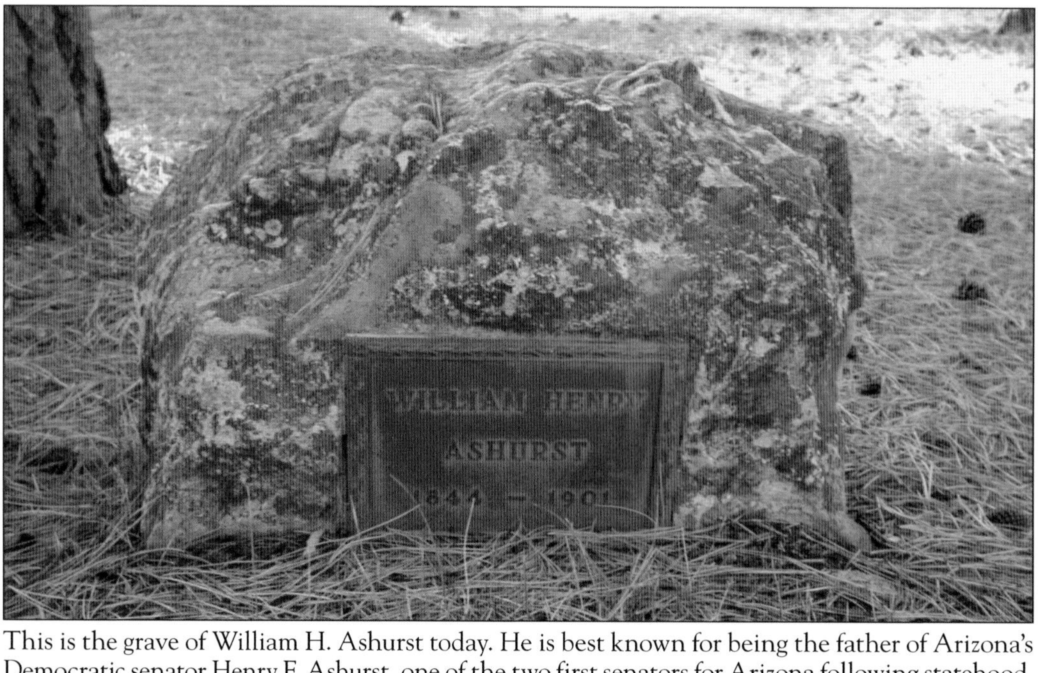

This is the grave of William H. Ashurst today. He is best known for being the father of Arizona's Democratic senator Henry F. Ashurst, one of the two first senators for Arizona following statehood. Although not the first burial in the Grand Canyon Pioneer Cemetery, William H. Ashurst has been dead the longest of anyone here. (David Schmittinger.)

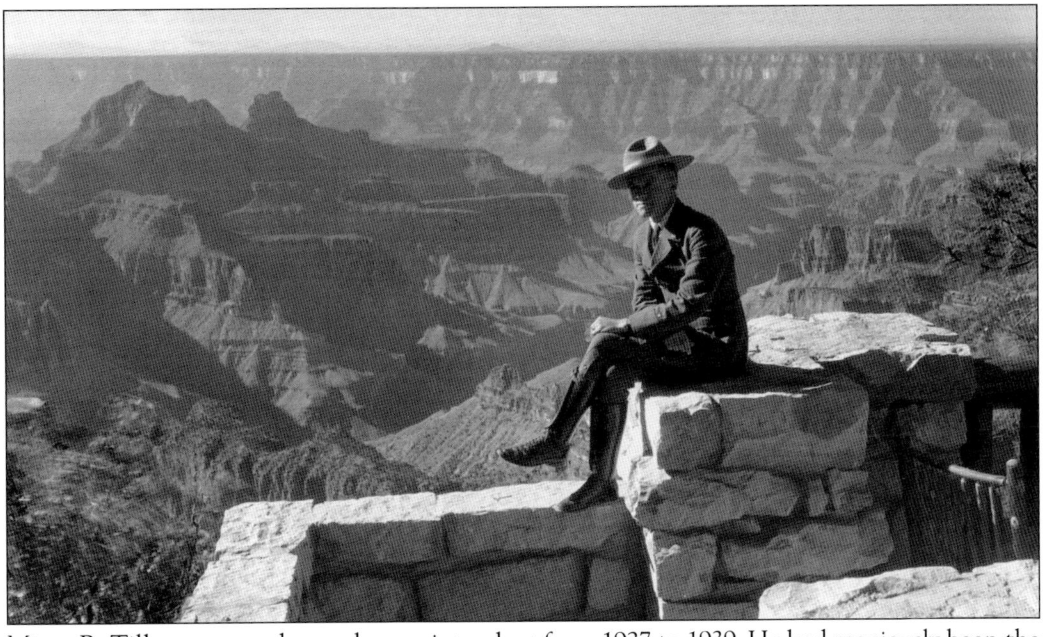

Miner R. Tillotson served as park superintendent from 1927 to 1939. He had previously been the park's chief engineer and constructed the South Kaibab Trail and the Kaibab Trail Bridge, known as the "Black Bridge," over the Colorado River, which was used for people and mule traffic. This photograph from July 25, 1930, shows him sitting outside the Grand Canyon Lodge at the North Rim. (Grand Canyon NP Museum Collection No. 00511.)

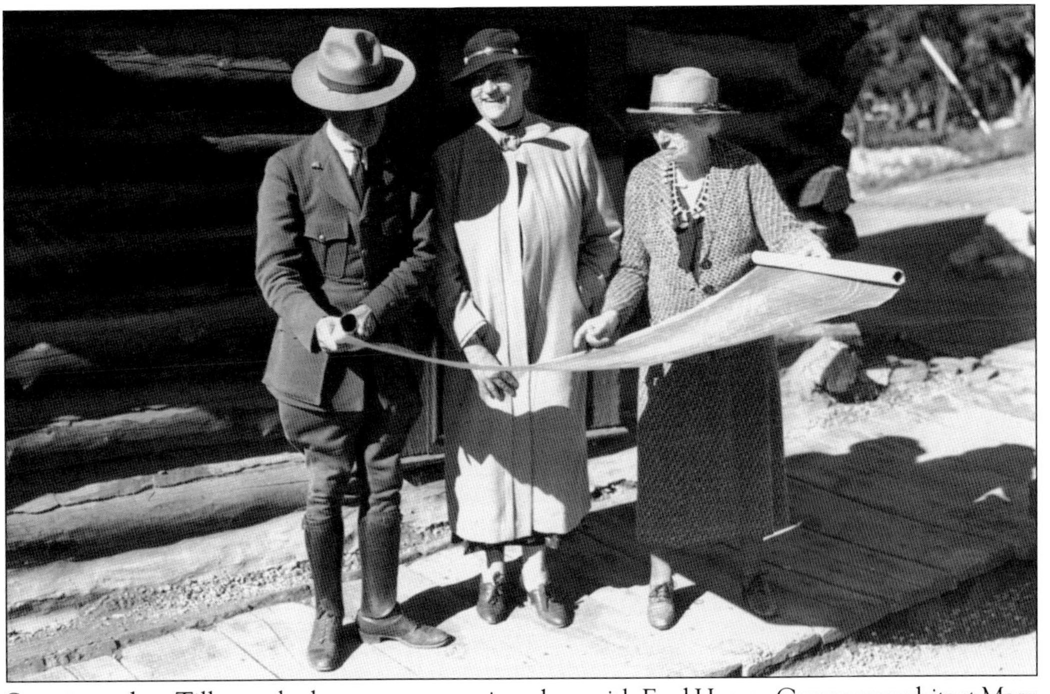

Superintendent Tillotson looks over construction plans with Fred Harvey Company architect Mary Colter (right) in this 1935 photograph. Anna Ickes, wife of Department of the Interior secretary Harold L. Ickes, stands at center. (Grand Canyon NP Museum Collection No. 16942.)

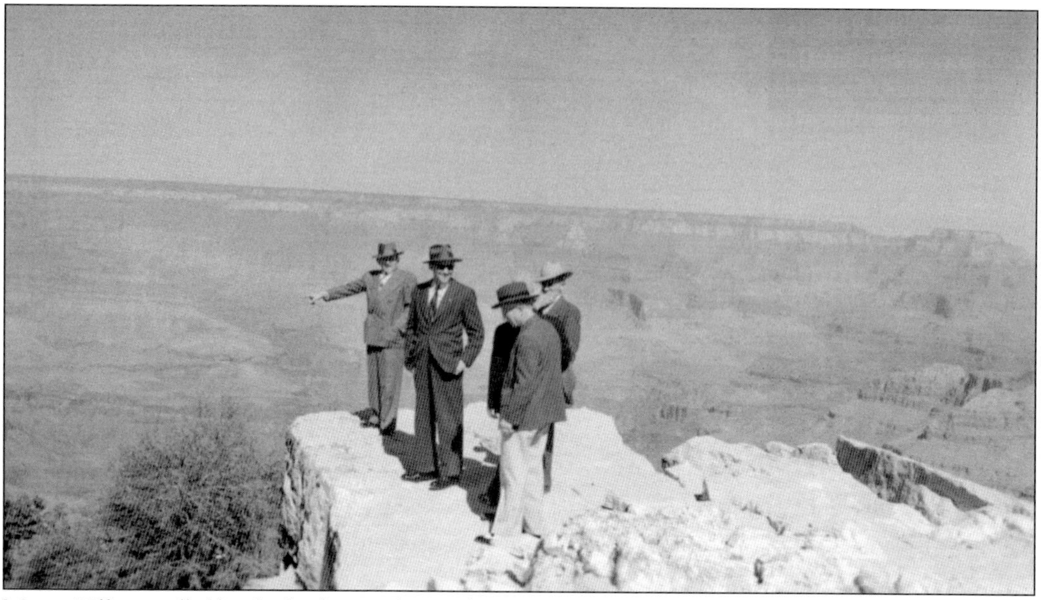

Miner Tillotson (left), who had moved up to become regional director of the National Park Service by this time, stands at Pima Point conversing with members of the US House Committee on Interior and Insular Affairs during a two-day visit to the canyon March 24–25, 1951. Also pictured are Congressmen Wayne Aspinall of Colorado, Lloyd M. Bentsen Jr. of Texas (who would become the Democratic vice presidential nominee in 1988), and Fred L. Crawford of Michigan. (Grand Canyon NP Museum Collection No. 02203.)

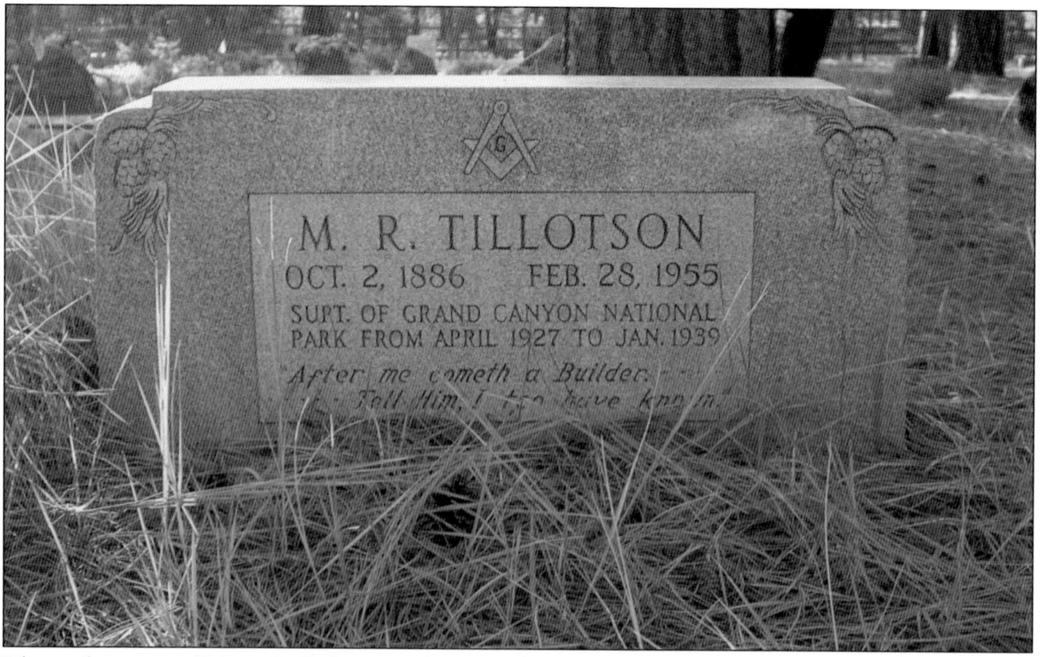

This is the grave of Miner R. Tillotson, who passed away in 1955 at the age of 69. His wife, Winifred, is buried next to him. He had served as Grand Canyon park superintendent and regional director of the National Park Service and was from Richmond, Virginia. Note the Masonic Lodge symbol on his tombstone. (David Schmittinger.)

John W. Harris was a veteran of the Spanish-American War of 1898. In his later years, he worked as a US Forest Service blacksmith at the Grand Canyon. Harris died on December 8, 1934, at the age of 58 of heart trauma resulting from influenza. (David Schmittinger.)

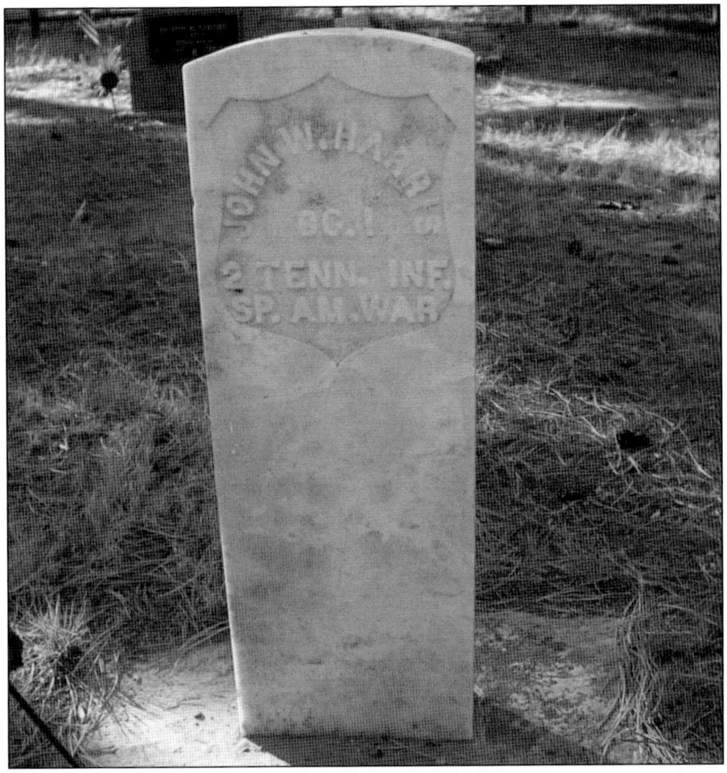

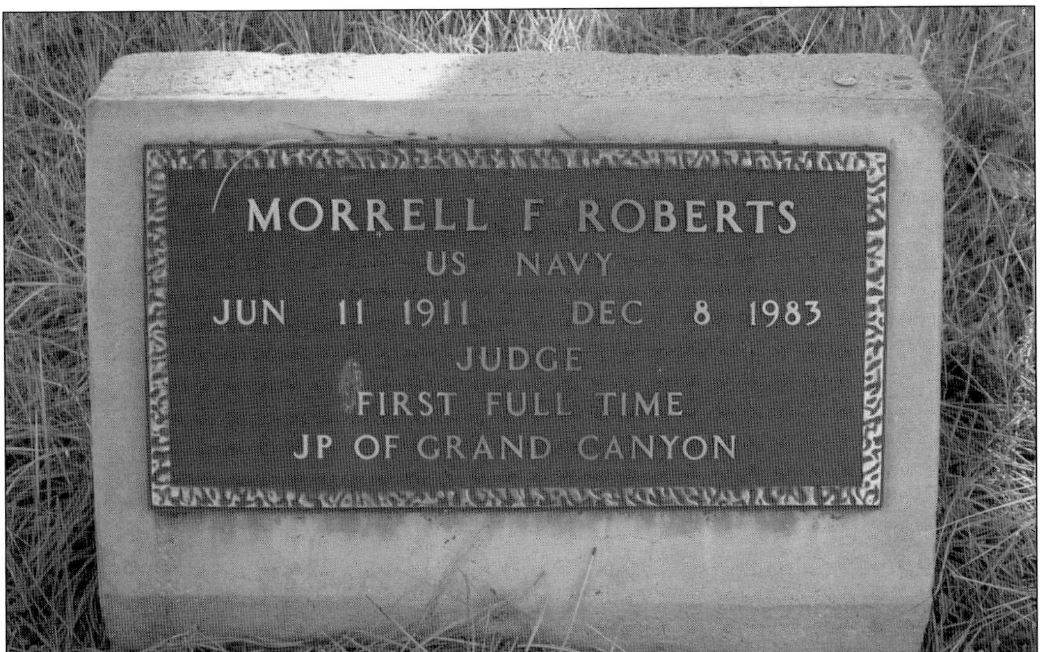

Morrell Roberts was the first justice of the peace for the Grand Canyon. With Flagstaff and Williams so far away, the Grand Canyon community decided it needed some public officials in case of problems that might arise in the area. (David Schmittinger.)

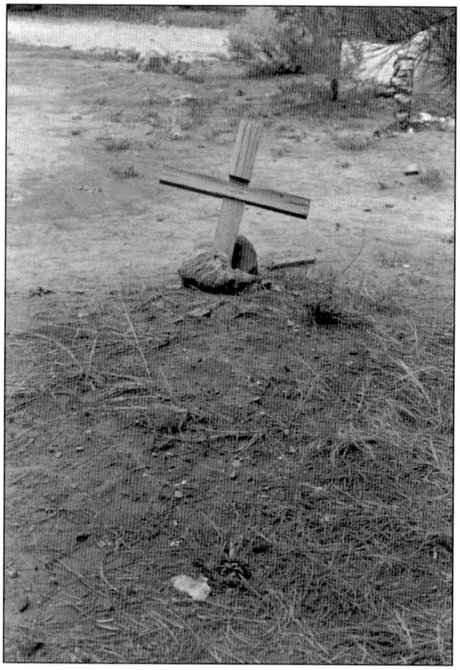

A small wooden cross marks the grave of Elsie Reed in this undated photograph. Reed was shot to death in 1924, and a coroner's inquest ruled that she had committed suicide, even though there were no powder burns on her hands. Many believed at the time that she had been murdered by her husband, Frank Reed, over rumors that she was having an illicit relationship with canyon-area rancher Martin Buggeln. The marker in this photograph no longer exists, and her grave is completely unmarked today. (Grand Canyon NP Museum Collection: Cemetery Files.)

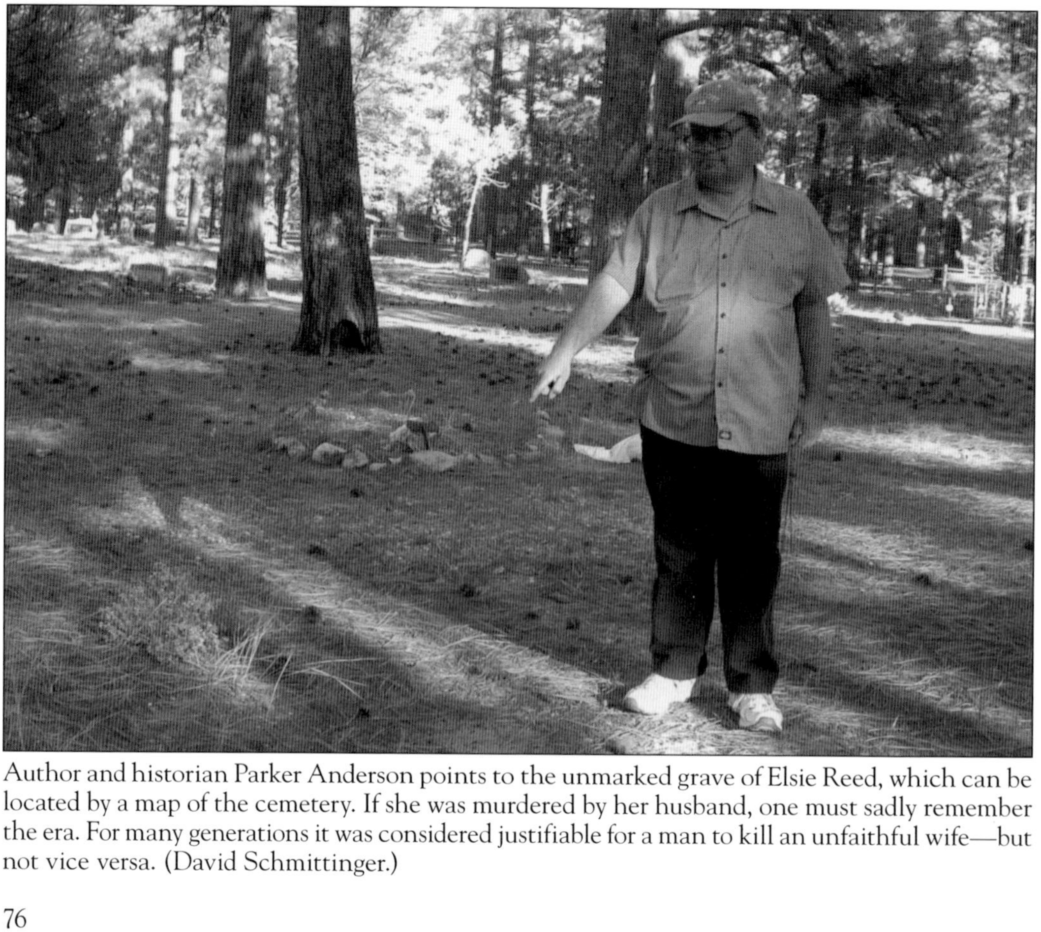

Author and historian Parker Anderson points to the unmarked grave of Elsie Reed, which can be located by a map of the cemetery. If she was murdered by her husband, one must sadly remember the era. For many generations it was considered justifiable for a man to kill an unfaithful wife—but not vice versa. (David Schmittinger.)

This is the touching gravesite of Marvin Gustafson, a US Marine Corps veteran. His lengthy epitaph reads, among other things, "His enduring legacy is his example of generosity, acceptance, kindness, modesty, loyalty, honor, courage, humor. He made a huge impact on countless souls who will forever cherish his memory; Gus loved his country, his family, and his God." (David Schmittinger.)

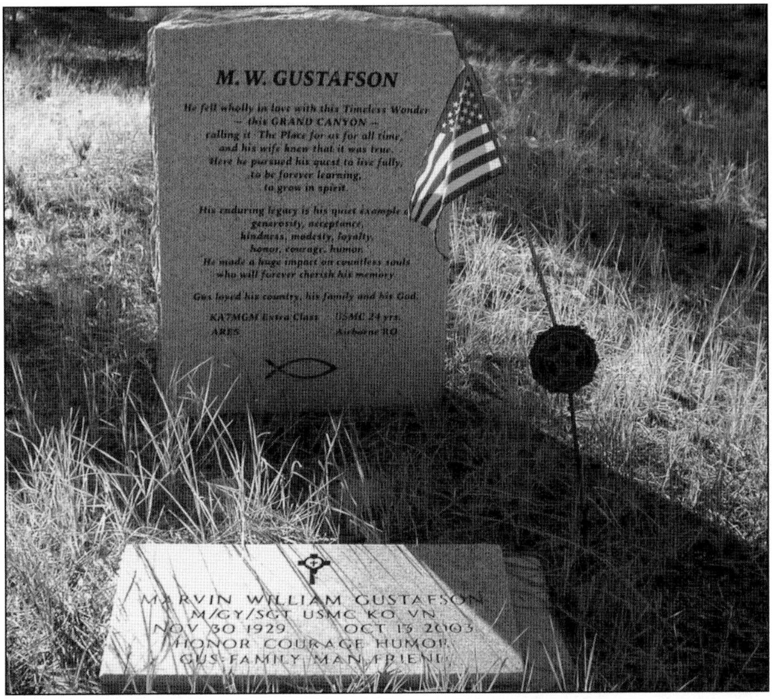

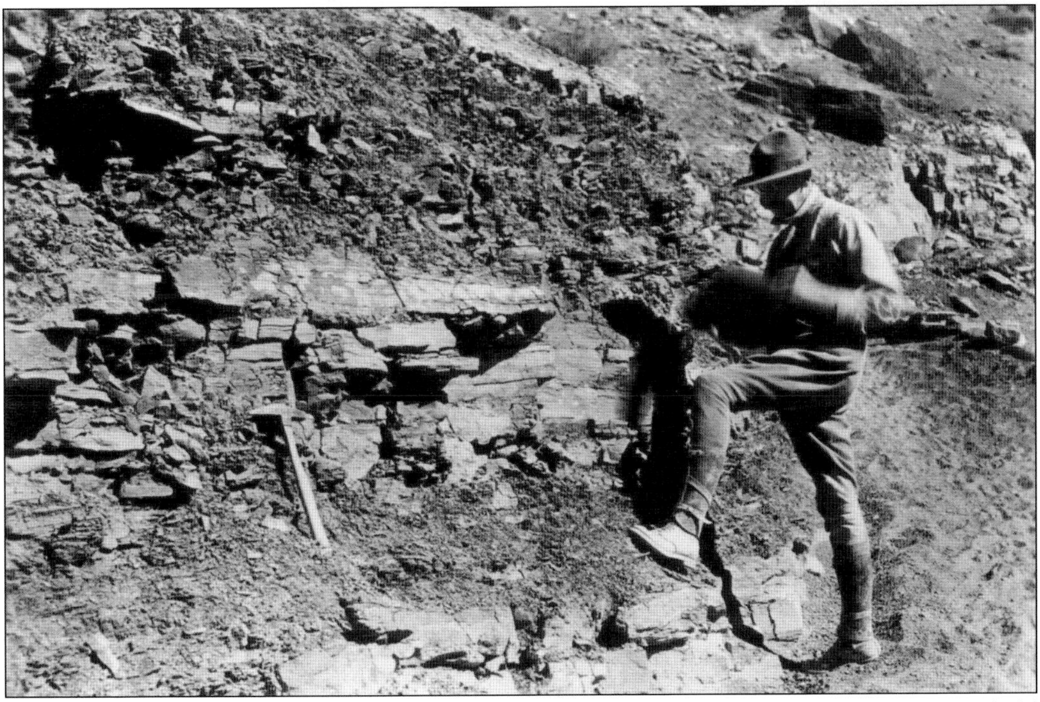

Dr. David White was the chief geologist for the US Geological Survey from 1912 to 1922, held many esteemed positions in his field, and is remembered as one of the legendary figures in geology research. He did much work on fossil study in the Grand Canyon and is seen here at work in 1929 in fossil beds that were discovered along the Yaki Trail. (Grand Canyon NP Museum Collection No. 02864.)

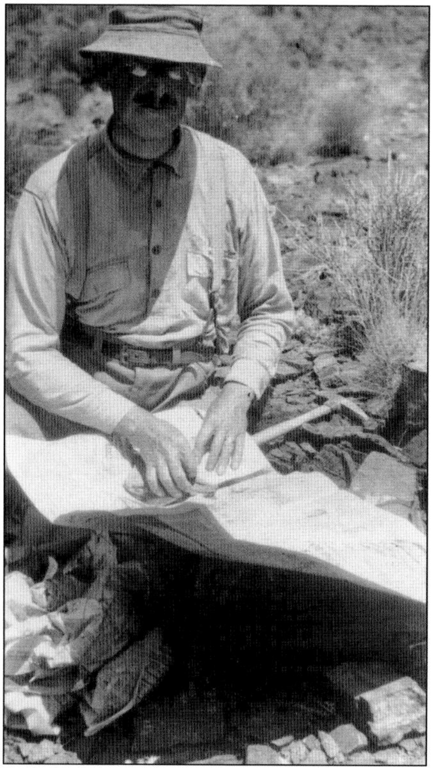

In this 1928 photograph, Dr. David White is wrapping a fossil in newspaper to remove it from the canyon for further laboratory study. (Photograph by Glen Sturdevant; Grand Canyon NP Museum Collection No. 07145.)

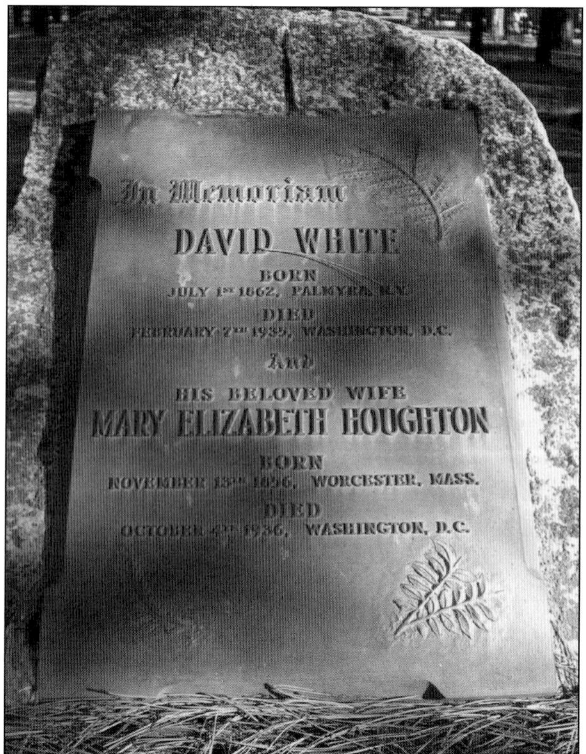

For his immense contribution to the study of fossils in the Grand Canyon, Dr. David White was buried here upon his death on February 7, 1935. He was 73 years old. His wife, Mary, who died October 4, 1936, was then interred with him. (David Schmittinger.)

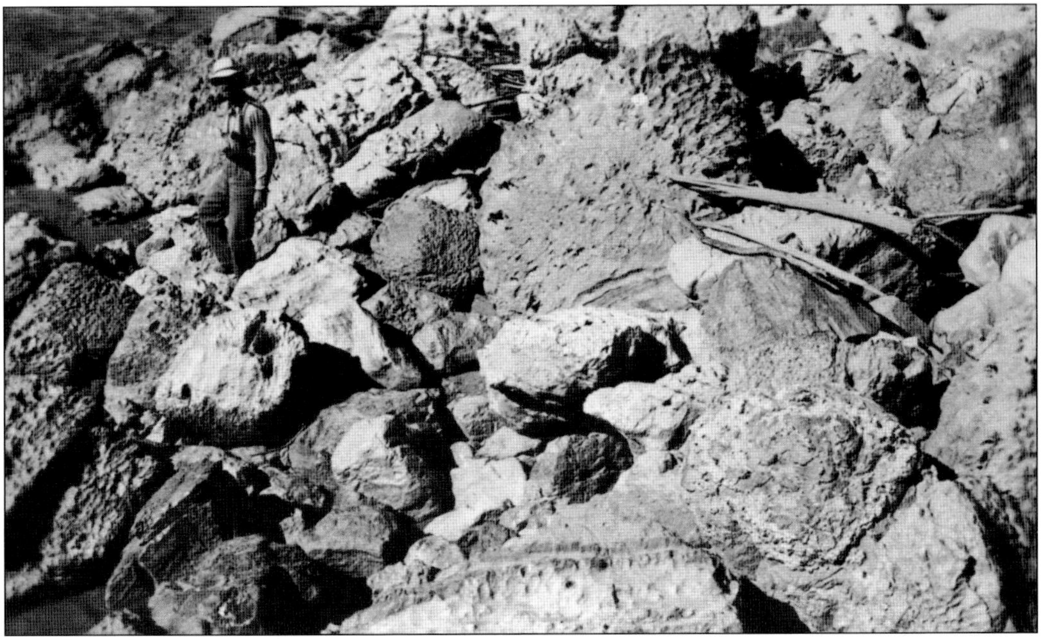

Dr. John Maxson, another famous geologist whose studies of the Grand Canyon increased the world's knowledge of this area, is seen here studying boulders along the Colorado River, at River Mile 119, on November 8, 1937. He wrote nearly 30 formal papers on Grand Canyon geology. (Grand Canyon NP Museum Collection No. 17314.)

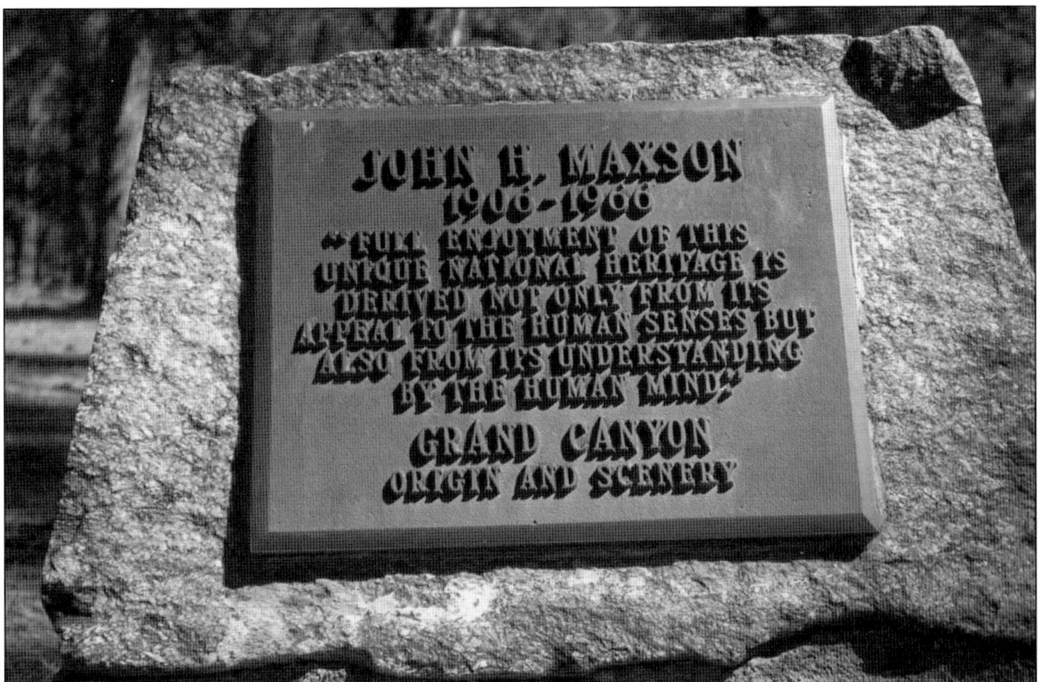

The rock used for the tombstone of Dr. John Maxson is Vishnu Schist, chosen intentionally as a nod to his accomplishments in geological research. He died in 1966 at the age of 60. (David Schmittinger.)

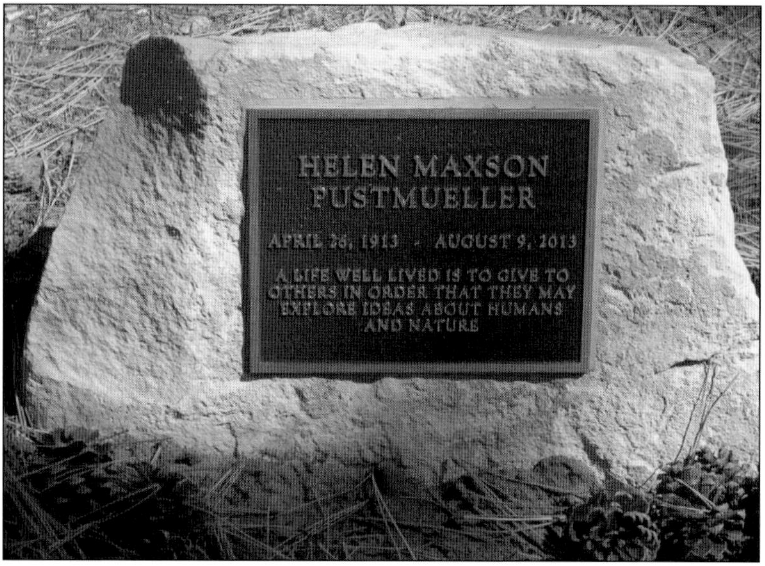

Dr. Maxson's widow, Helen Maxson Pustmueller, outlived him by 47 years and passed away on August 9, 2013, at the age of 100. She is buried next to him. (David Schmittinger.)

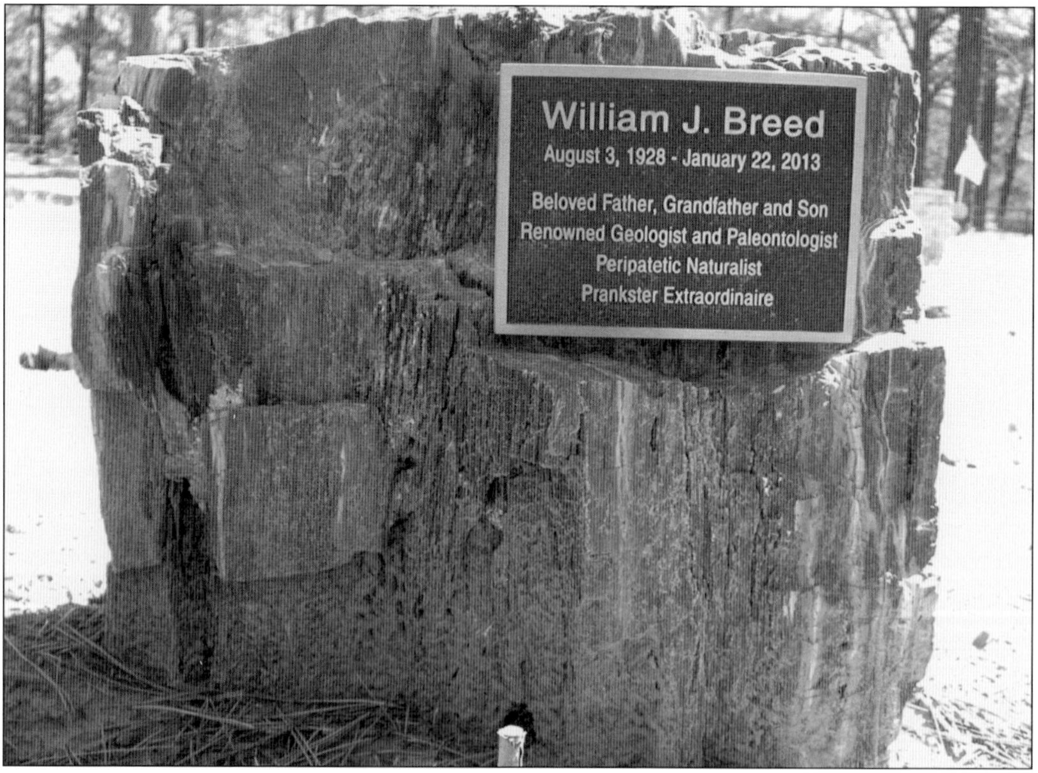

William J. Breed (1928–2013) was a geologist and paleontologist in northern Arizona and was mentored by Dr. Edwin McKee. Breed served as curator of geology from 1960 to 1978 at the Museum of Northern Arizona and head of the geology department from 1978 to 1981 for the same institution. Breed was one of the four paleontologists who famously discovered the fossil of a Lystrosaurus in Antarctica, thus providing evidence for continental drift. (Lois Schmittinger.)

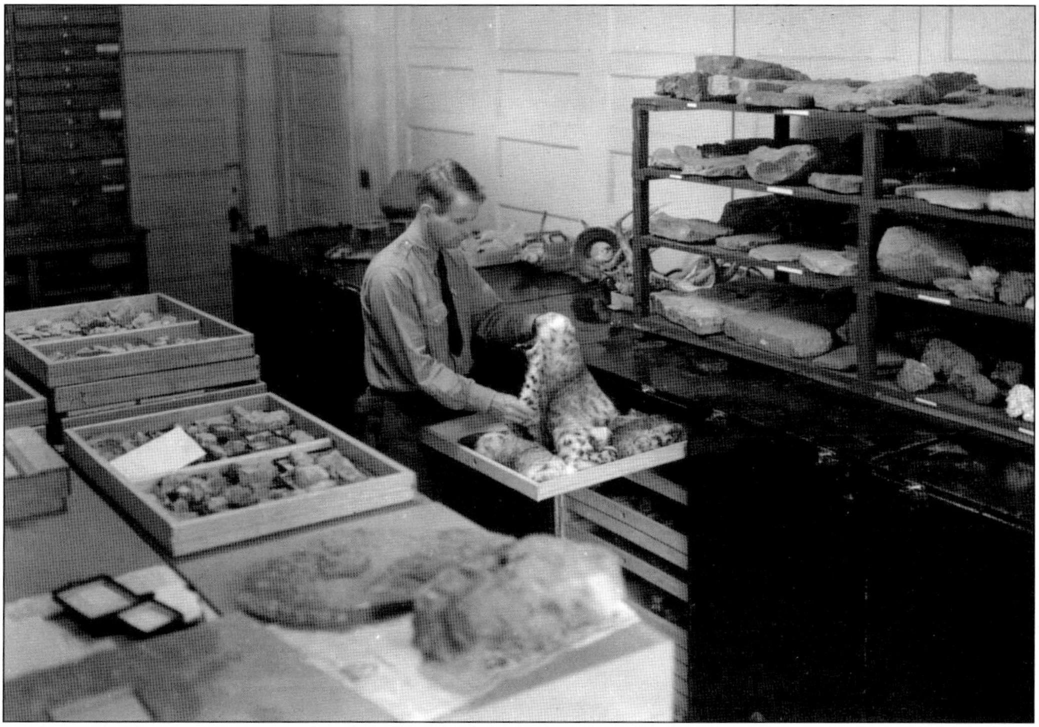

Arguably the greatest figure in Grand Canyon geology research was Dr. Edwin McKee. His books and articles are considered to be the definitive studies of the Grand Canyon rock layers and Paleozoic rocks in general. He served as park naturalist from 1929 to 1940 and is seen here studying canyon rock samples in 1935. (Grand Canyon NP Museum Collection No. 05847.)

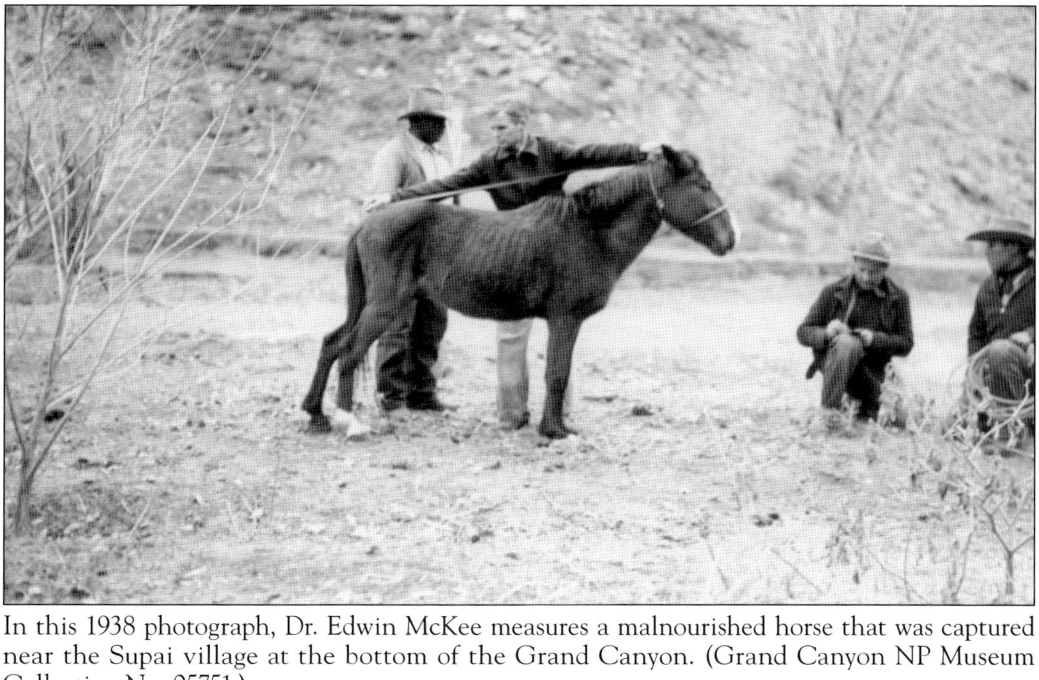

In this 1938 photograph, Dr. Edwin McKee measures a malnourished horse that was captured near the Supai village at the bottom of the Grand Canyon. (Grand Canyon NP Museum Collection No. 05751.)

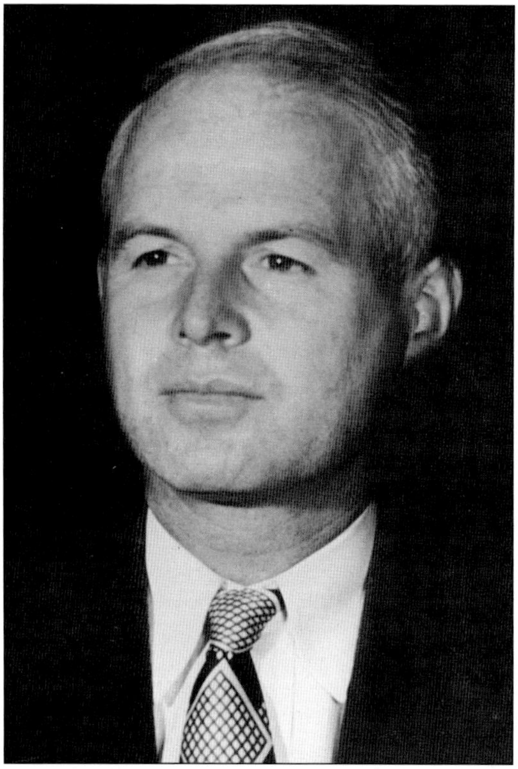

This formal portrait of Dr. Edwin McKee was taken on April 28, 1949, when he was associate professor of geology at the University of Arizona in Tucson. (Grand Canyon NP Museum Collection No. 17654.)

These are the graves of Dr. Edwin McKee (1906–1984) and his wife, Barbara (1902–1998), as seen today. (David Schmittinger.)

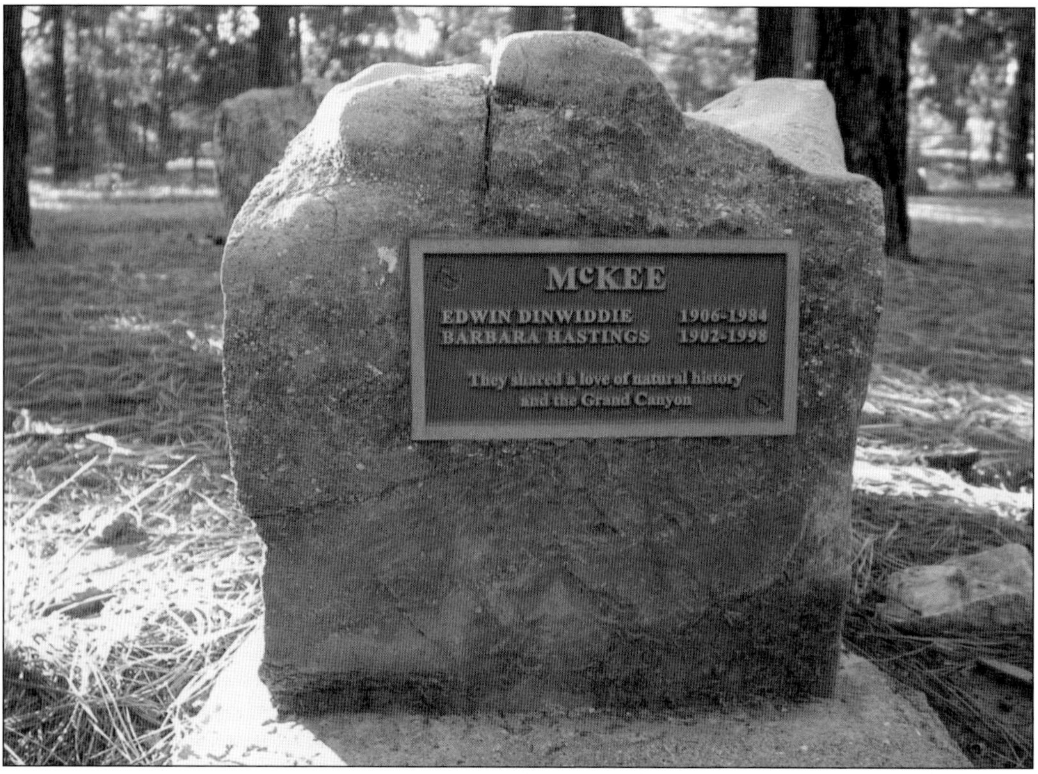

In 1925, Glen Sturdevant was hired as the first park naturalist at the Grand Canyon. He is seen here feeding a squirrel in 1926, with his son looking on. (Grand Canyon NP Museum Collection No. 13744.)

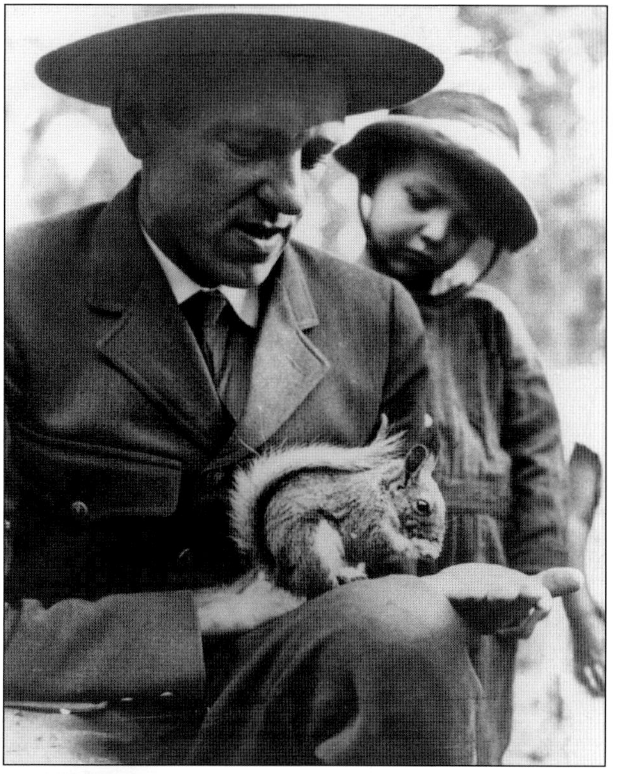

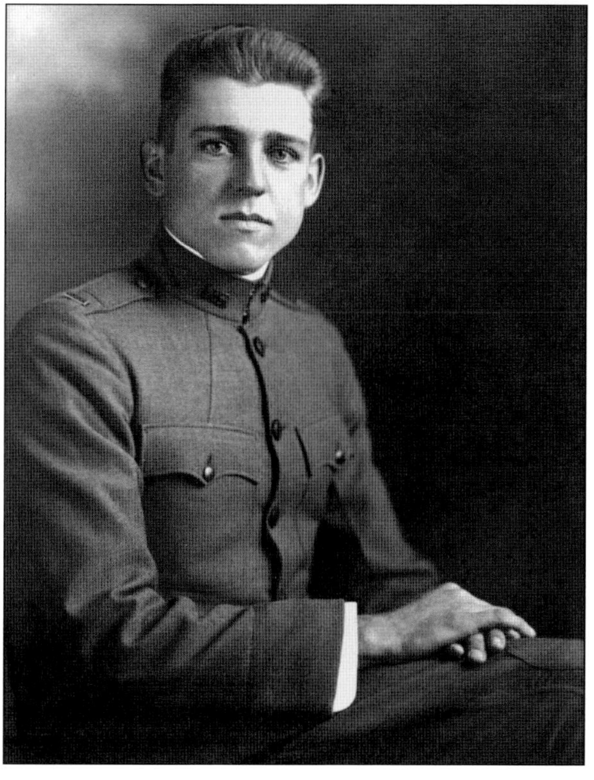

Around 1918, Glen Sturdevant poses for a formal portrait in an Army uniform before he began his work at the Grand Canyon. (Grand Canyon NP Museum Collection No. 13742.)

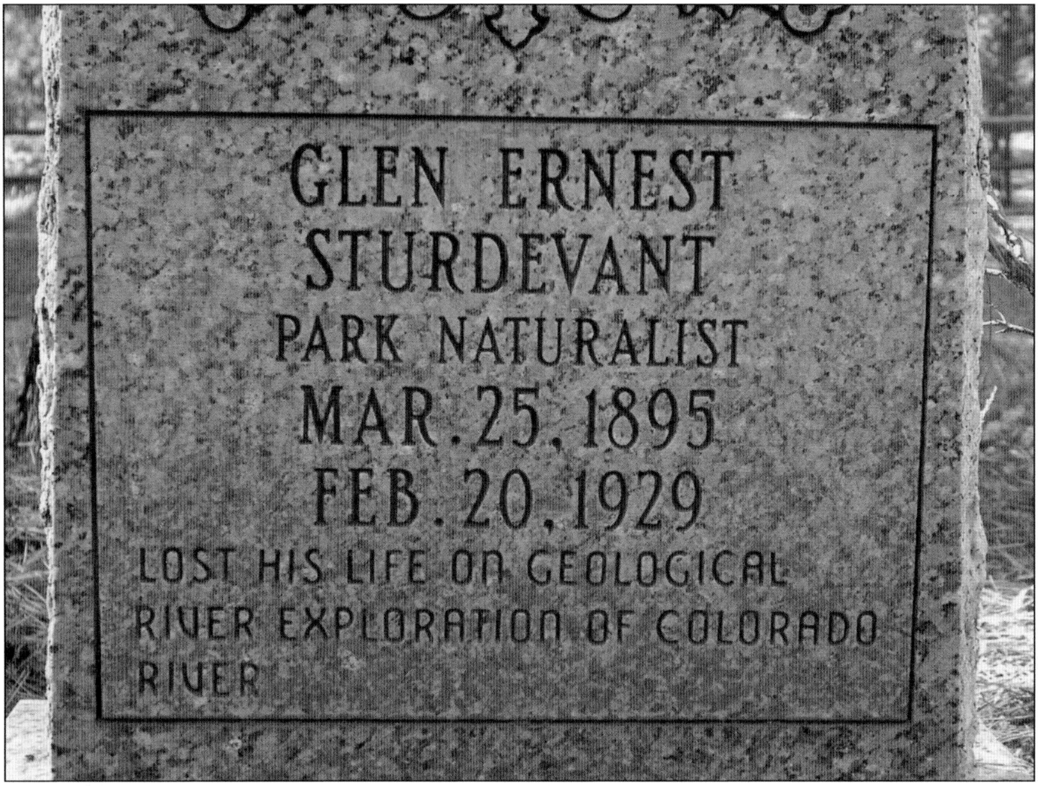

Glen Sturdevant drowned in a Colorado River boating accident while on a geological river exploration on February 20, 1929, at the age of 34, along with park ranger Fred Johnson. Ranger James Brooks survived. (David Schmittinger.)

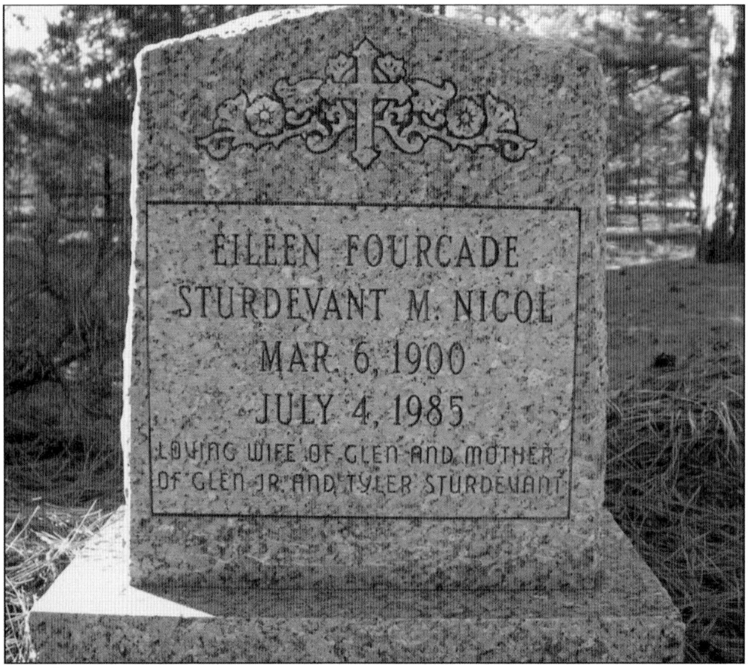

Glen Sturdevant's wife, Eileen, outlived him by 56 years. She passed away at the age of 85 and is buried next to him in the Grand Canyon Pioneer Cemetery. (David Schmittinger.)

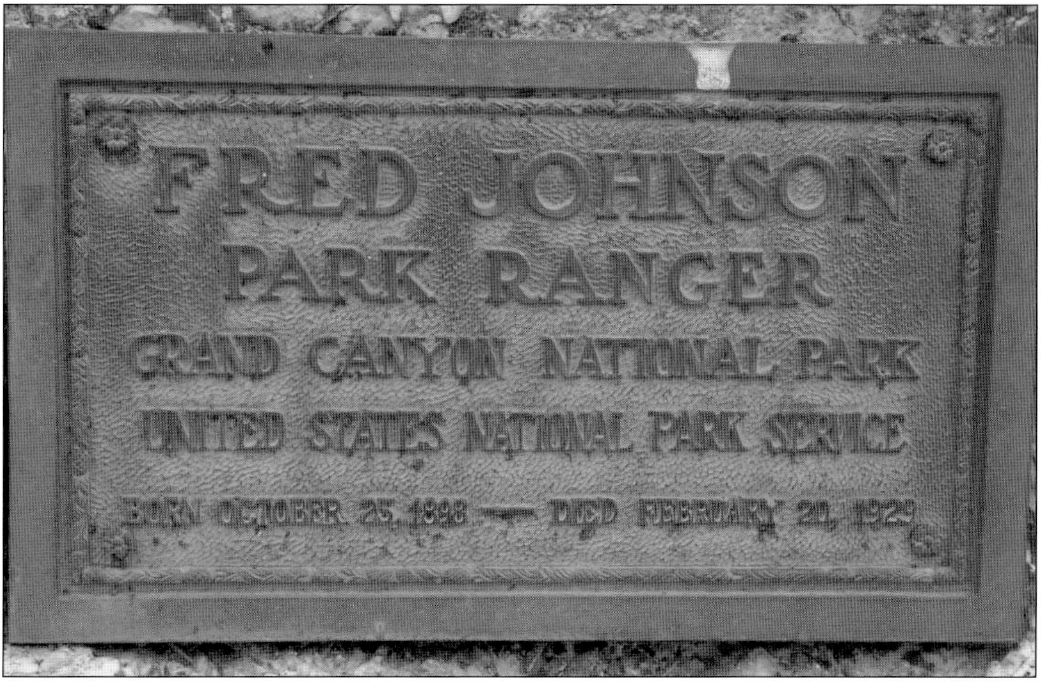

Fred Johnson drowned at the age of 31 in the same Colorado River accident that killed Glen Sturdevant. Grand Canyon historians record that his body was never found, and this is just a marker, but grave dowsers claim to have had readings at this spot. (David Schmittinger.)

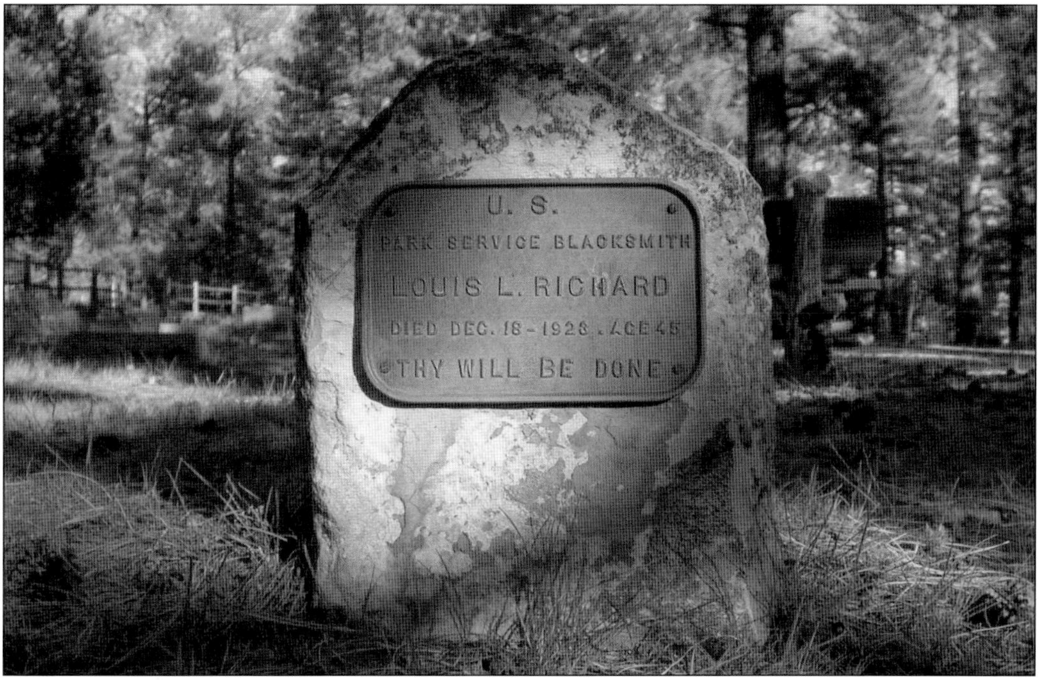

Pictured here is the grave of Louis L. Richard, an early blacksmith at the Grand Canyon who died on December 18, 1928, at age 45. Such workers were needed by the Fred Harvey Company for ironwork. (David Schmittinger.)

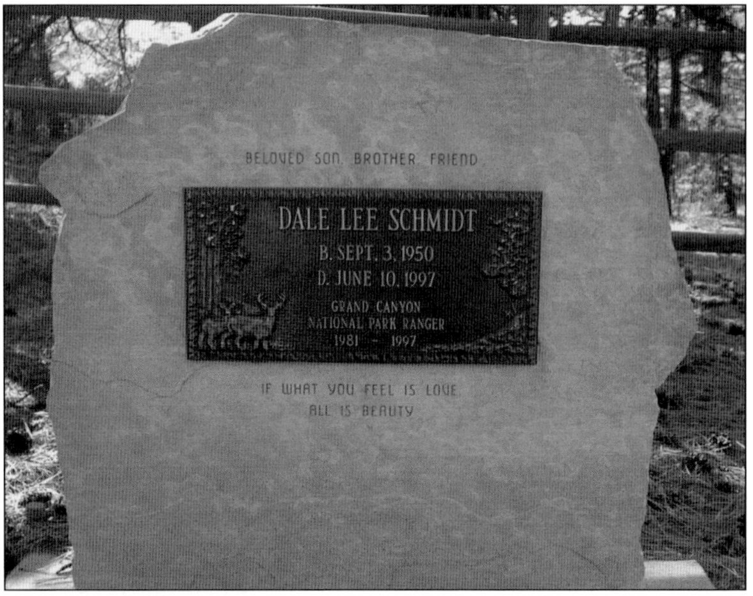

Buried here is park ranger Dale Schmidt, who served faithfully from 1981 until his death in 1997. (David Schmittinger.)

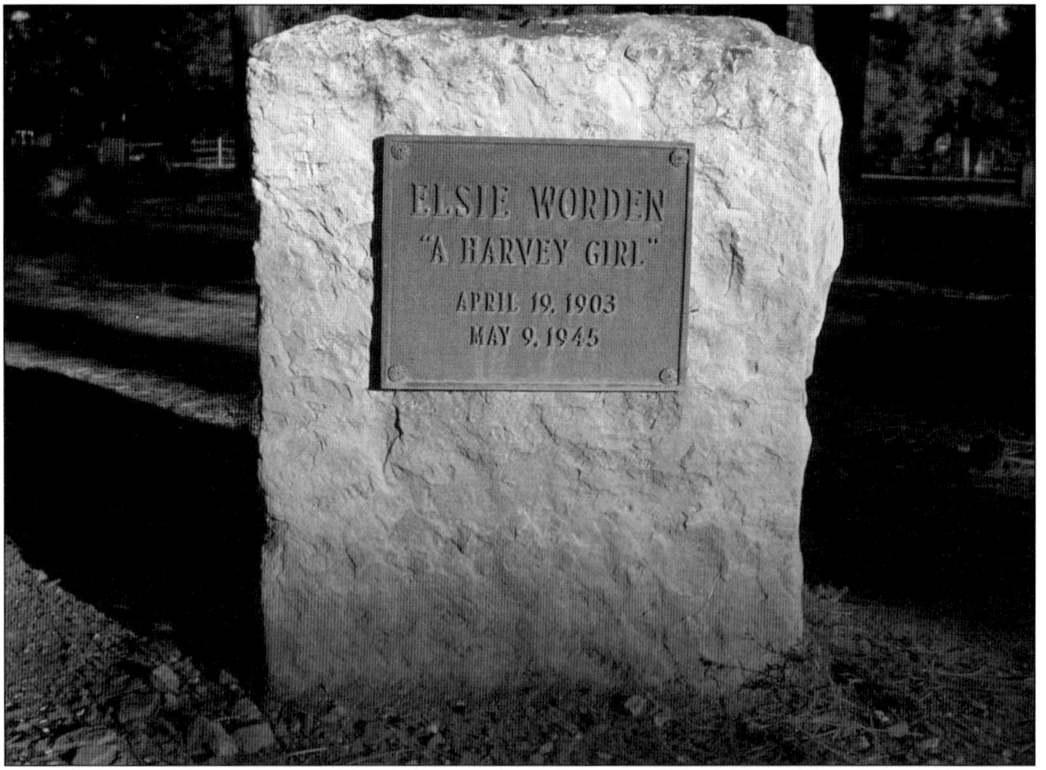

Elsie Fay Worden was the head waitress at the El Tovar Hotel at the time of her death on May 9, 1945, at the age of 42, from an intestinal obstruction. The young, beautiful waitresses who worked at the hotels and restaurants owned by the Fred Harvey Company became known as Harvey Girls and have become legendary in the development of the Southwest. Railroad workers and rich businessmen sought out the Harvey houses so they could be waited on by Harvey Girls, and often the women were fortunate enough to marry some of their clientele. (David Schmittinger.)

George W. Cravey (seen on page 36) worked as a trail guide in the early days of the Grand Canyon National Park. He was 50 years old at the time of his death on November 24, 1935, from heart complications. Note the hand-carved Masonic symbol at the top of his tombstone. (David Schmittinger.)

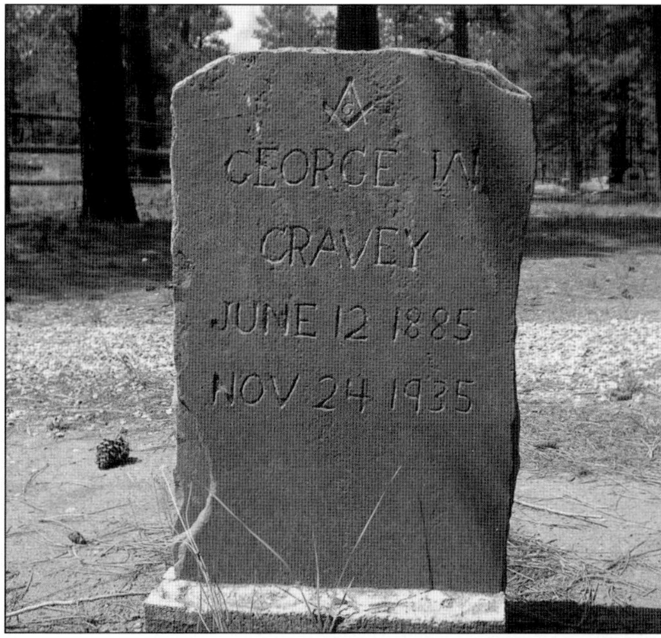

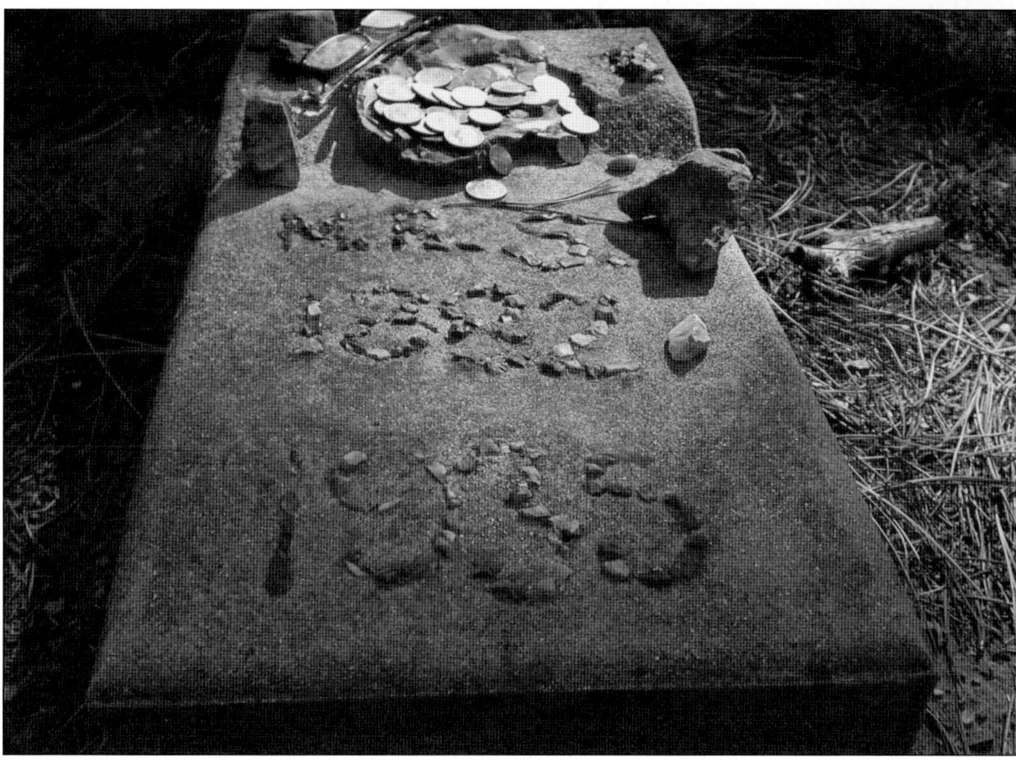

There has been much speculation about this grave marked simply M.R.S. Some genealogists believe it is the grave of Martin Rodriquez Sandoval, a truck driver for the railroad who died on July 19, 1935. Corroborating evidence could be taken from the fact that other members of a Sandoval family are buried in the cemetery. Because of the mystery surrounding the grave, visitors often leave coins on the tombstone. (Lois Schmittinger.)

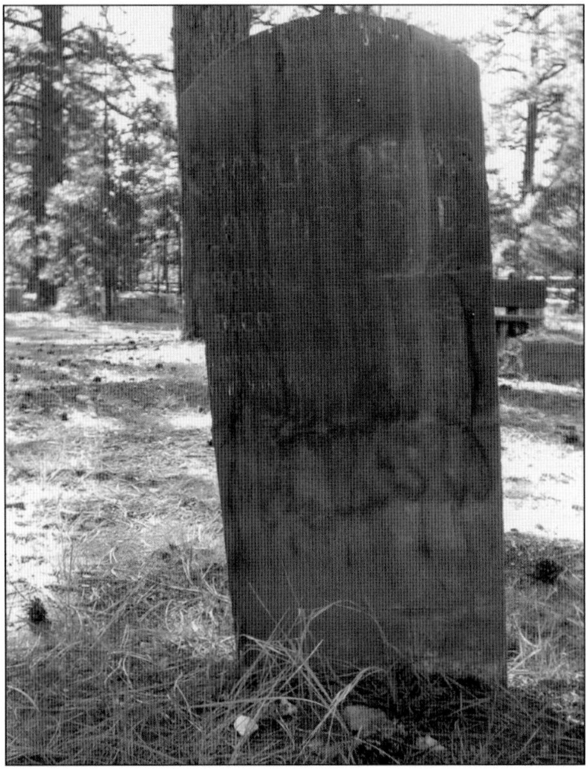

The badly aged and weathered wooden marker for early canyon resident Charles Oscar Sinclair Lovenskiold, who was born in Zamboanga, Philippines, is pictured here. The 19 year old was an auto mechanic who died in 1925 of peritonitis in the Havasupai Indian Reservation village of Supai. (David Schmittinger.)

Pictured here is a homemade tombstone for early canyon resident Mark A. Tral (1905–1927), who was 22. His family clearly put a lot of love and effort into this marker. (Lois Schmittinger.)

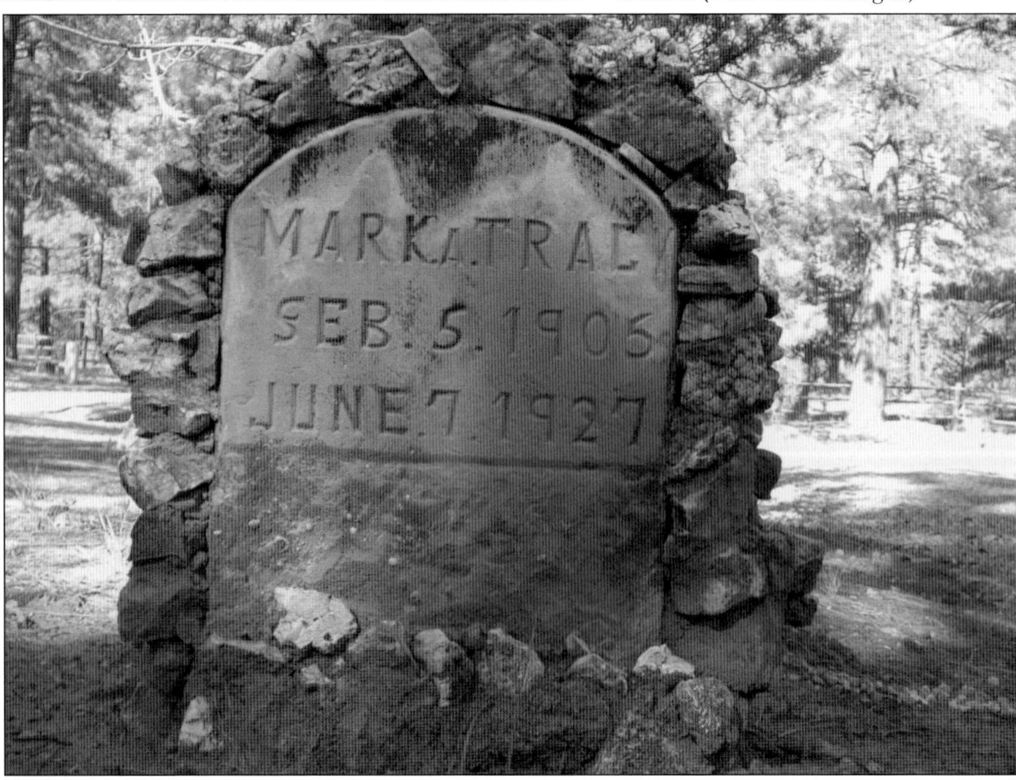

John George Verkamp, who was born in Cincinnati, Ohio, became the first curio dealer at the Grand Canyon. He sold trinkets and souvenirs to the early tourists. (Grand Canyon NP Museum Collection No. 15134.)

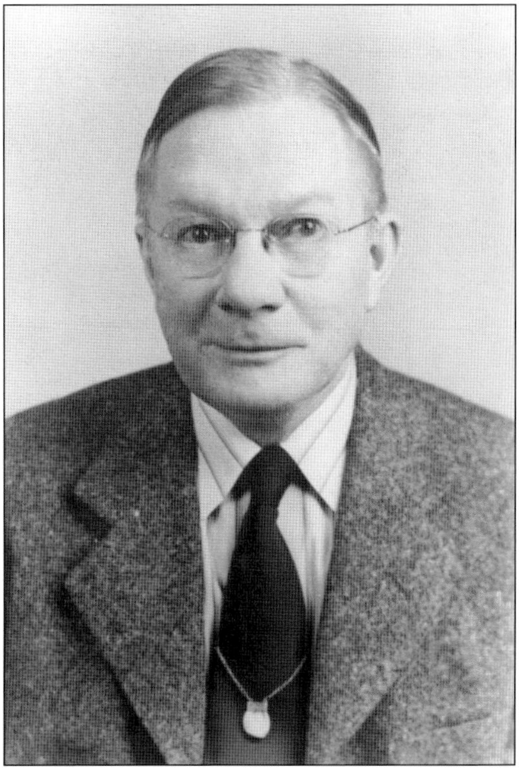

This is the Verkamp souvenir store in 1951. It continued to operate for many years following John Verkamp's death in 1944, as his children and grandchildren inherited the family business. (Grand Canyon NP Museum Collection No. 03631b.)

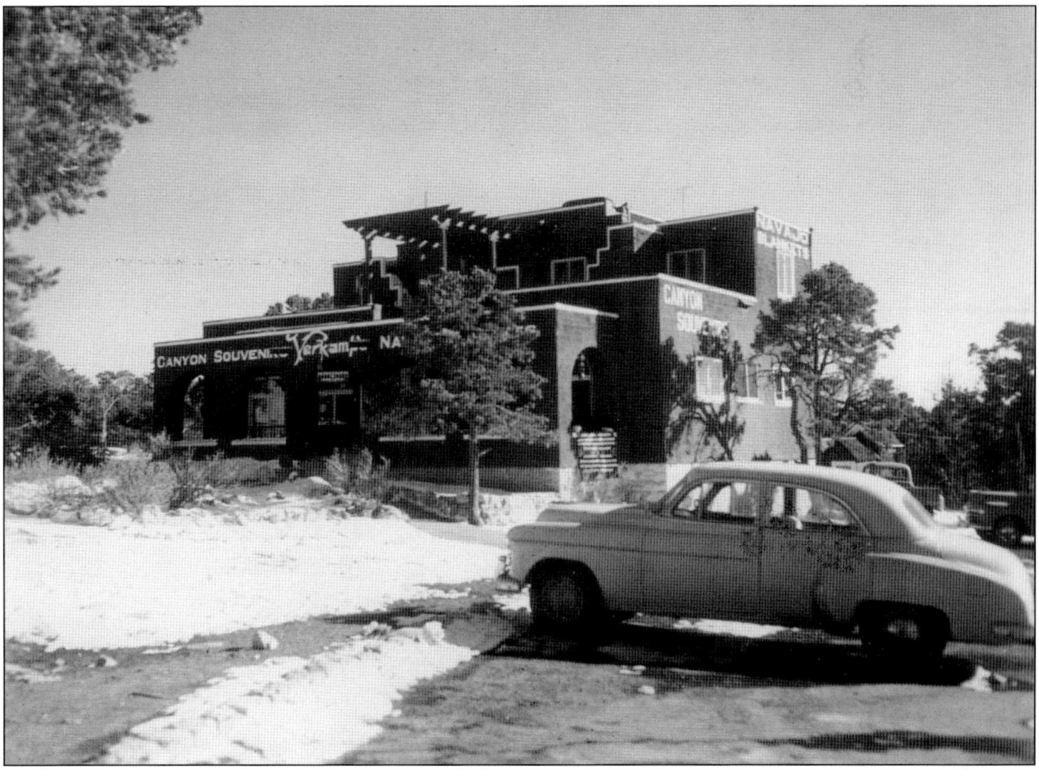

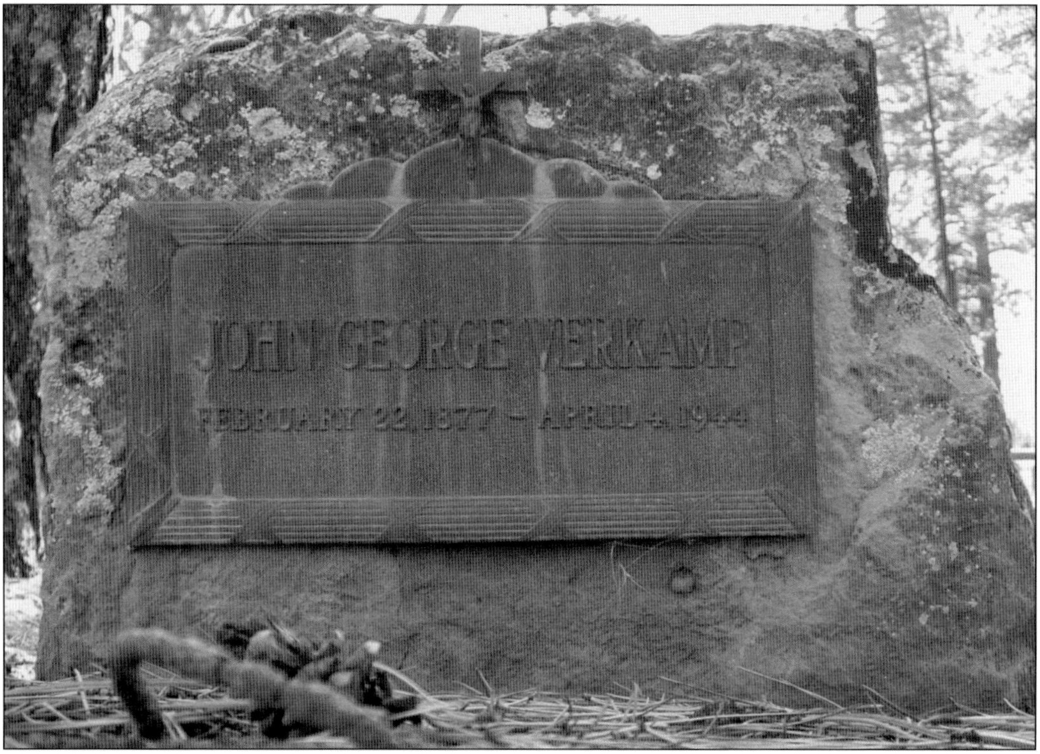

John George Verkamp died in 1944 at age 67 of heart failure, leaving his store to be carried on by his descendants. Many other Verkamp family members are buried in the Grand Canyon Pioneer Cemetery as well. (Lois Schmittinger.)

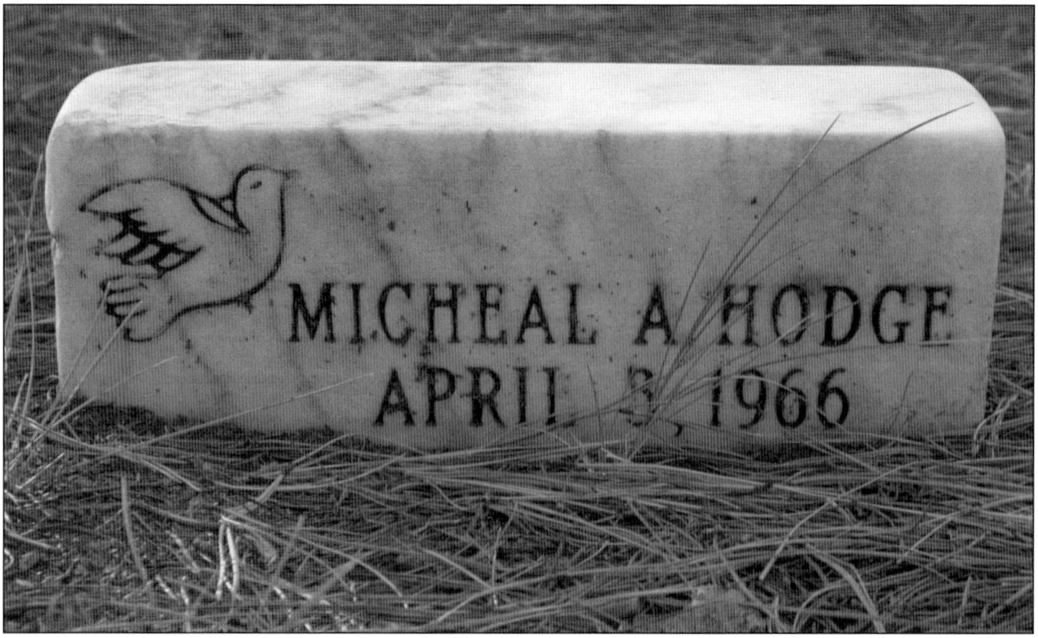

Infant Michael Hodge was born and died in 1966. He was the son of Vonda Lee Litrenta Hodge. (David Schmittinger.)

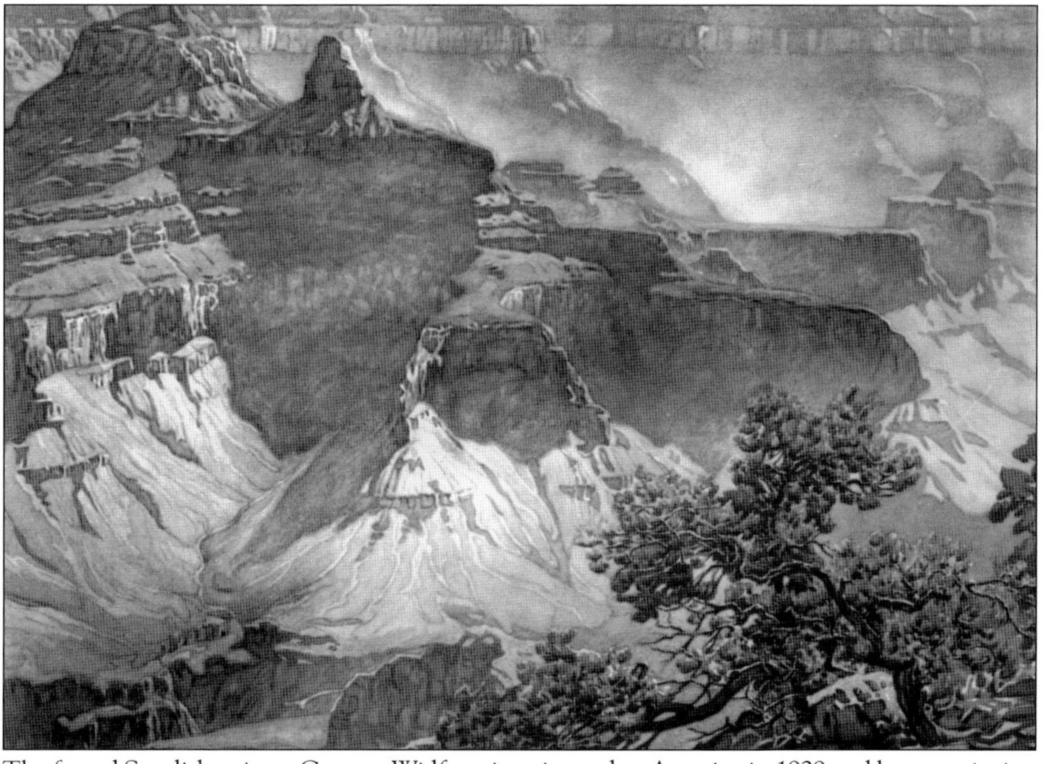

The famed Swedish painter Gunnar Widforss immigrated to America in 1929 and began painting landscapes of America's national parks. The Grand Canyon, where he settled, was his favorite. This painting by Widforss is of the Zoroaster Temple rock formation in the Grand Canyon. This photograph of the painting was taken on June 23, 1964. (Photograph by Merrill D. Beal; Grand Canyon NP Museum Collection No. 04903.)

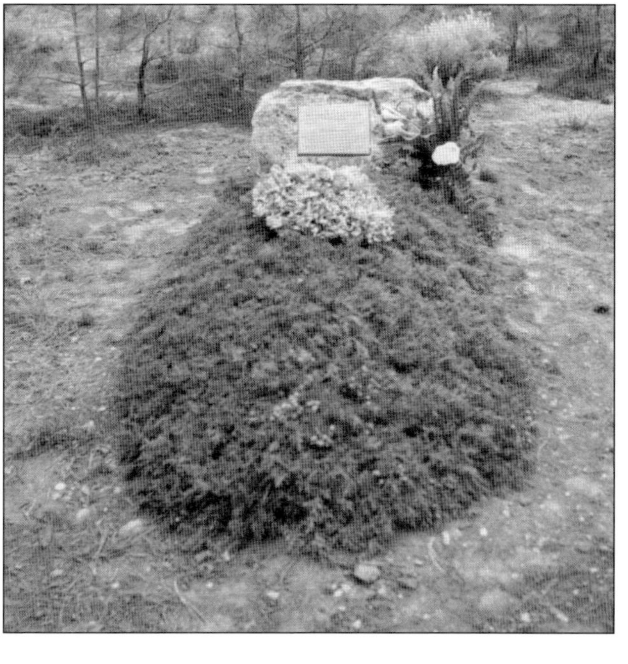

This is the grave of Gunnar Widforss in 1937, three years after his death. Told by his doctor to leave the canyon because the high altitude was bad for his health, Widforss died of a heart attack while preparing to move. (Grand Canyon NP Museum Collection No. 01410.)

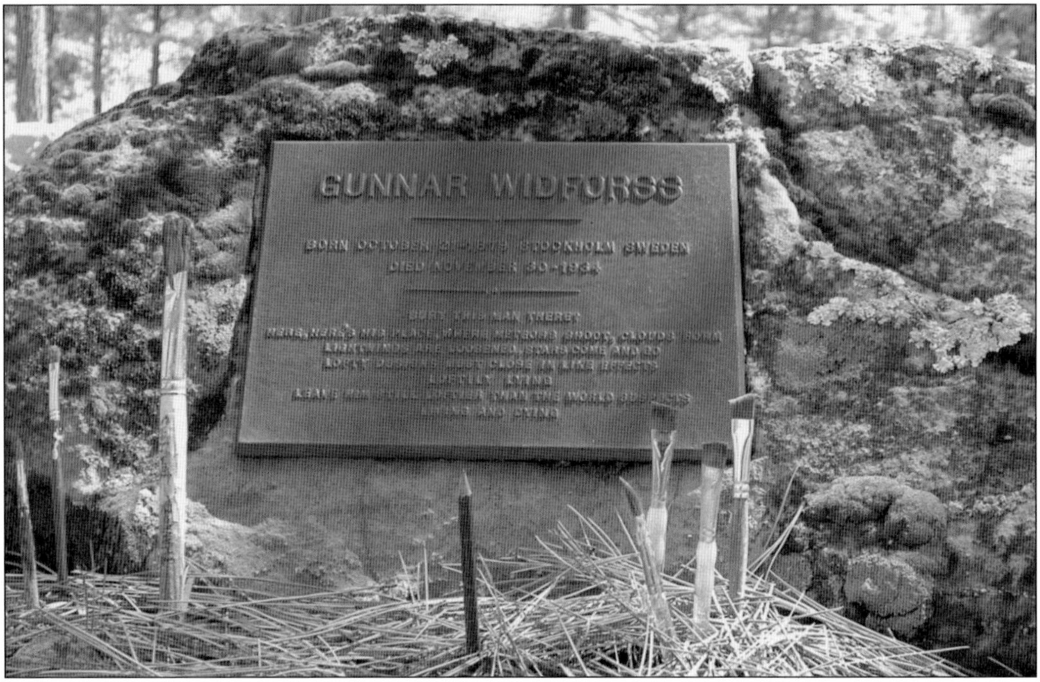

This is the grave of Gunnar Widforss as it appears today. Admirers sometimes leave paintbrushes on his grave. Reproductions of his Grand Canyon art were sold on postcards by the Fred Harvey Company for many years. (David Schmittinger.)

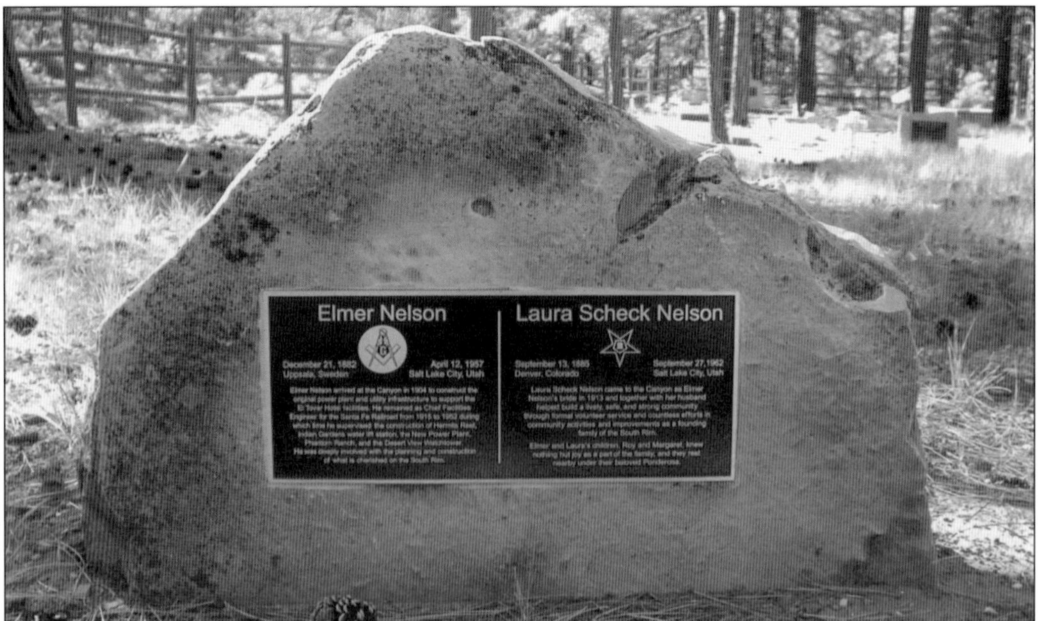

Pictured here is the final resting spot of Elmer and Laura Nelson. Elmer came to the Grand Canyon as an electrical engineer for the El Tovar Hotel and stayed on to supervise construction aspects of many of the Grand Canyon's most significant facilities, including Phantom Ranch and Mary Colter's watchtower. Note the Masonic symbols on their tombstones. (David Schmittinger.)

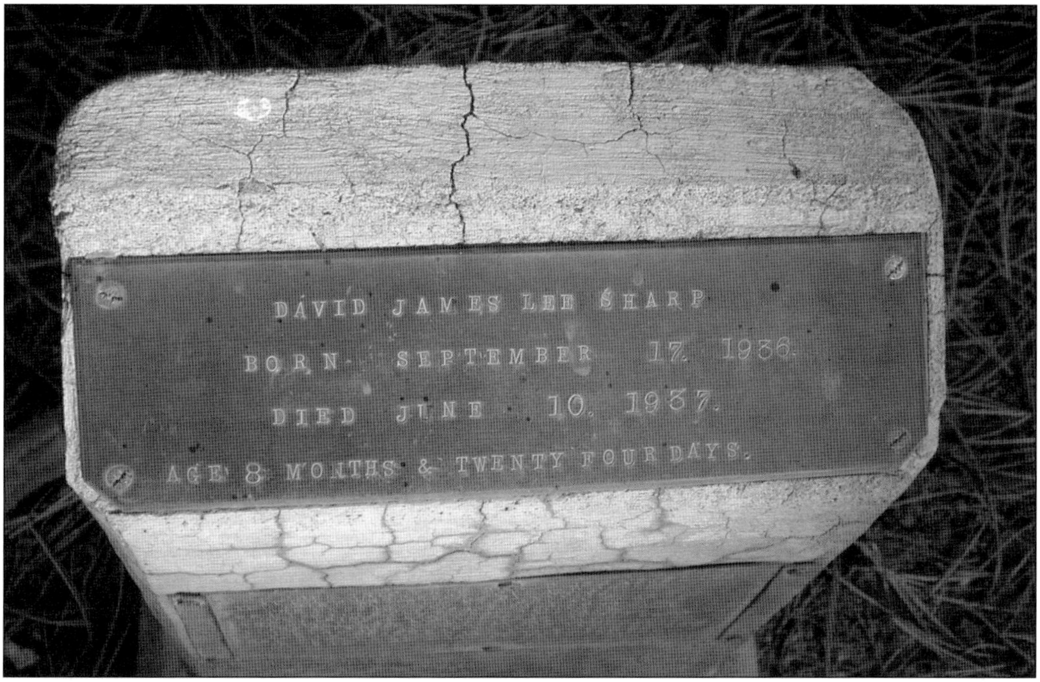

This is the sad and touching marker for David Sharp, an eight-month-old baby who died on June 10, 1937, of acute dysentery. He was the son of Grover Cleveland Sharp, a government road worker. The epitaph's author is unidentified. (David Schmittinger.)

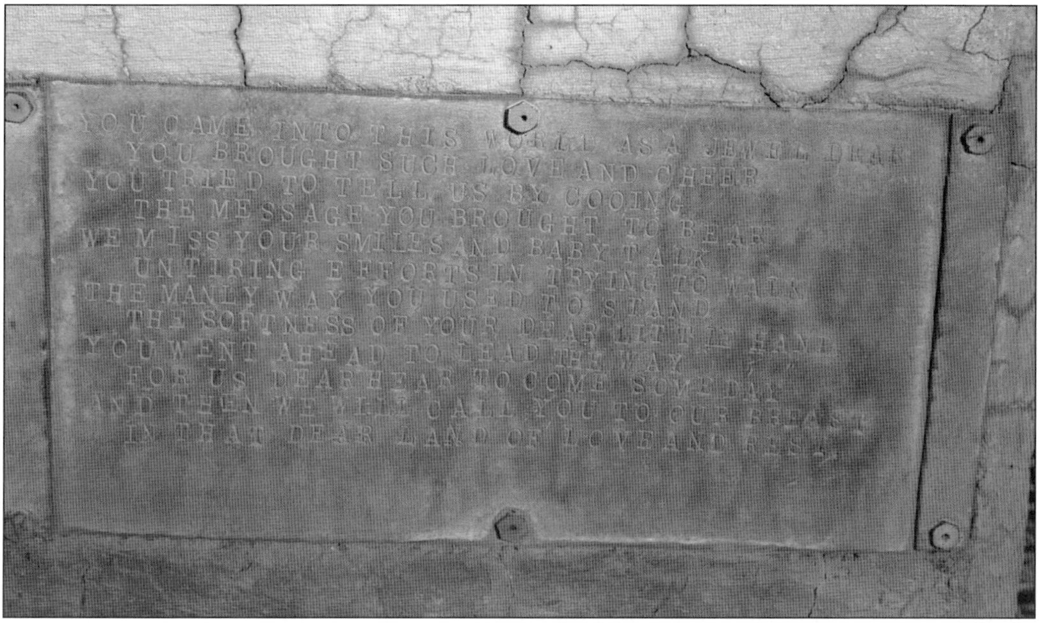

The epitaph on David Sharp's grave reads, "You came into this world as a jewel dear / you brought such love and cheer / you tried to tell us by cooing / the message you brought to bear / we miss your smiles and baby talk / untiring efforts in trying to walk / the manly way you used to stand / the softness of your dear little hand / you went ahead to lead the way / for us dear hear to come someday / and then we will call you to our breast / in that dear land of love and rest."

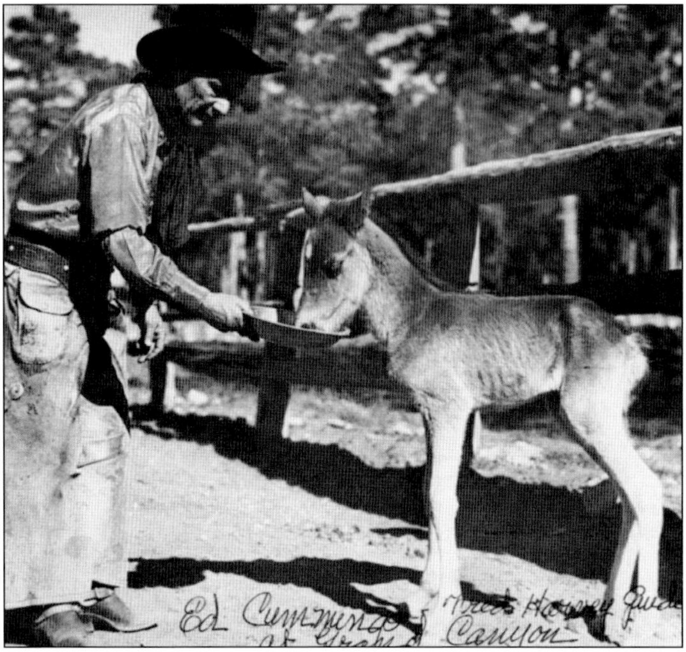

Edwin Cummings worked at the Grand Canyon for 30 years as a trail guide, ranger, amateur geologist, and furniture maker. He built much of the furniture originally used at the watchtower, Phantom Ranch, and Hermit's Rest and helped architect Mary Colter locate colorful rocks to imbed in her structures. This undated photograph shows him feeding a young burro, probably in the 1920s. (Sharlot Hall Museum; po1947p.)

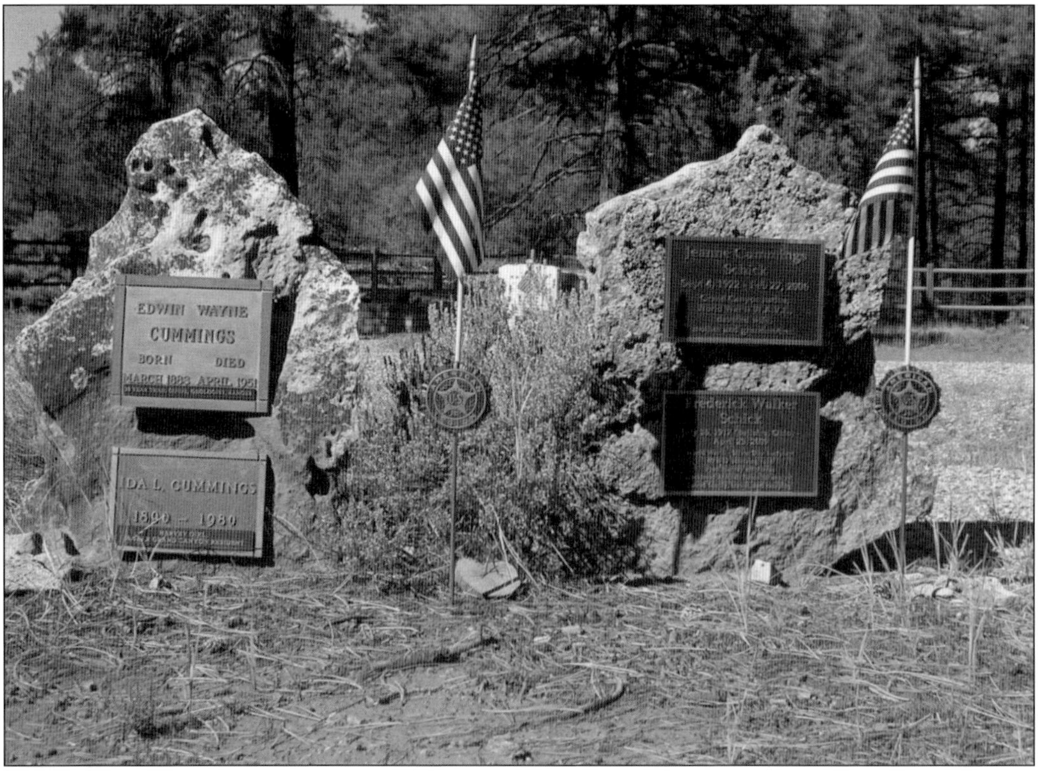

The grave of Edwin Cummings, who died in 1951 of acute myocardial failure, is seen here. His wife, Ida, who was a Harvey Girl, outlived her husband by 29 years and was interred here with him upon her death in 1980. Their daughter and son-in-law, Jeanne and Fredrick Schick (both of whom lived into their 90s), are buried next to them. (David Schmittinger.)

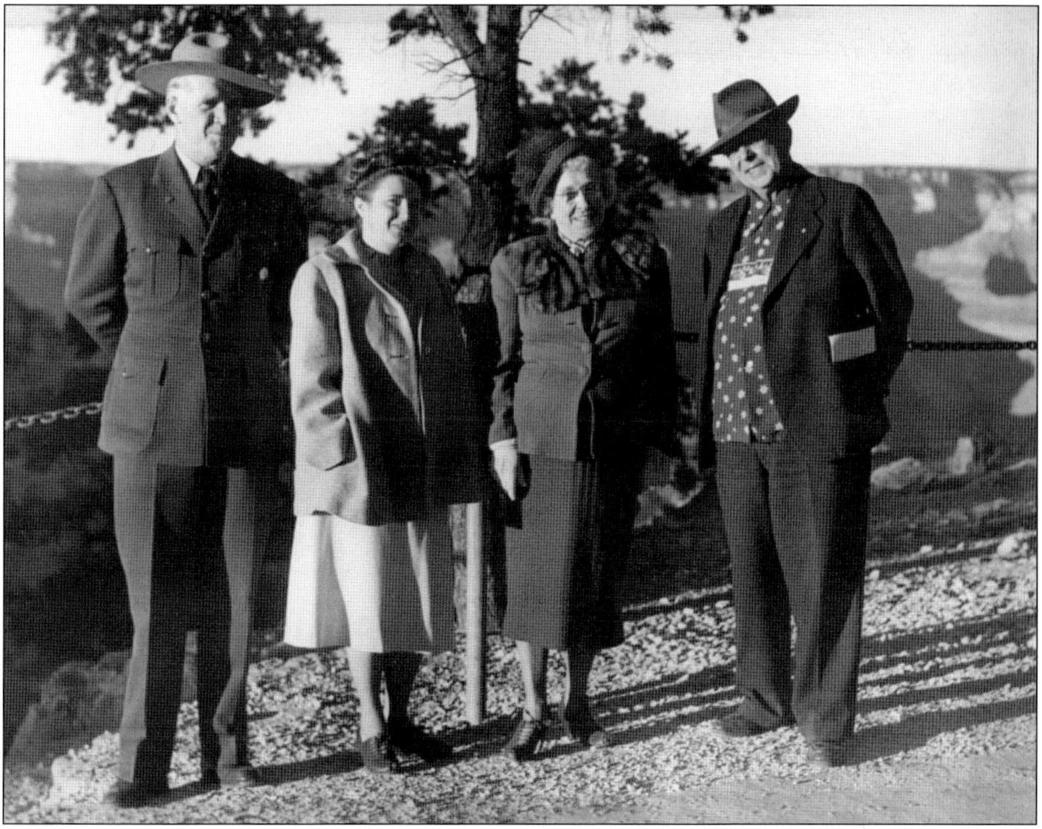

Lemuel "Lon" Garrison (also seen on page 56) was a major figure in the history of the National Park Service. Among his many positions in his long career, he was director of the Albright Training Academy at the Grand Canyon and superintendent of Yellowstone National Park beginning in 1956. He is seen here at left with his wife, Inger, a well-known sculptress and potter, standing beside him. Others in the photograph are US congressman Louis Crampton (from Michigan) and his wife. (Grand Canyon NP Museum Collection No. 02140.)

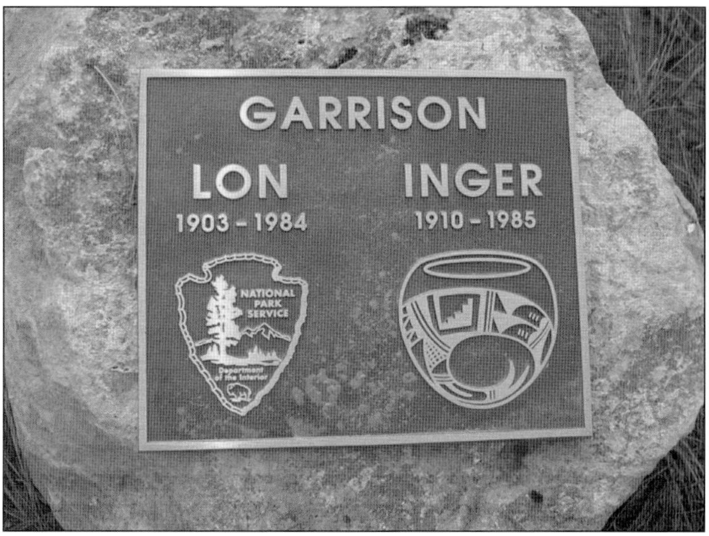

These are the graves of Lon and Inger Garrison. Lon was the first superintendent responsible for limiting the number of campers in Yellowstone at any given time by ending the construction of new campsites there. (David Schmittinger.)

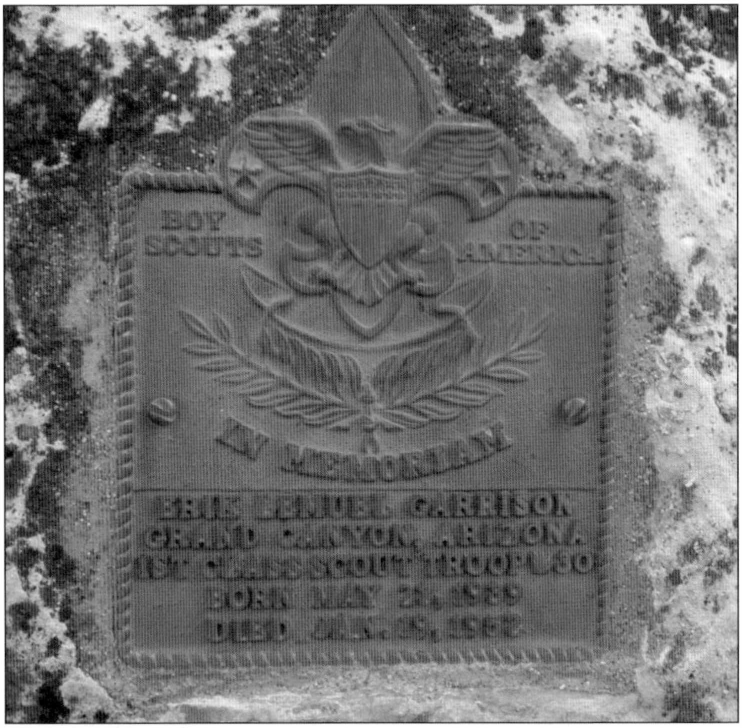

Erik Garrison (1939–1952), the son of Lon and Inger Garrison, was a Boy Scout who died at the age of 12 when he became tangled in a tow rope at the Bill Williams Ski Run. (David Schmittinger.)

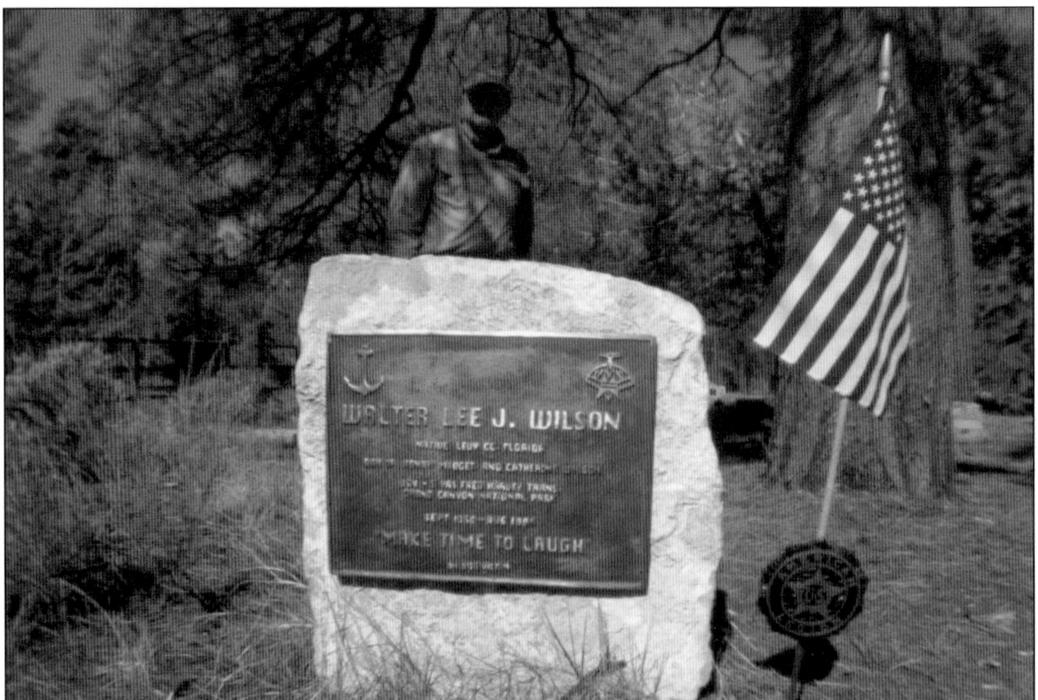

Here is the grave of Walter Lee J. Wilson, a Navy veteran who later served as an employee of the Fred Harvey Company for five years. He died of AIDS. Canyon explorer David Schmittinger is seen in the background. (Parker Anderson.)

Custer "Shorty" Yarberry worked as a mule packer at the bottom of the Grand Canyon beginning in the 1920s. After retiring, he spent his remaining days drifting around the South Rim, regaling tourists with colorful stories of dubious authenticity, much as John Hance had done many years earlier. He reportedly claimed to have planted the large cottonwood trees at Indian Gardens, but positive proof is lacking. (Grand Canyon NP Museum Collection, grca5134.)

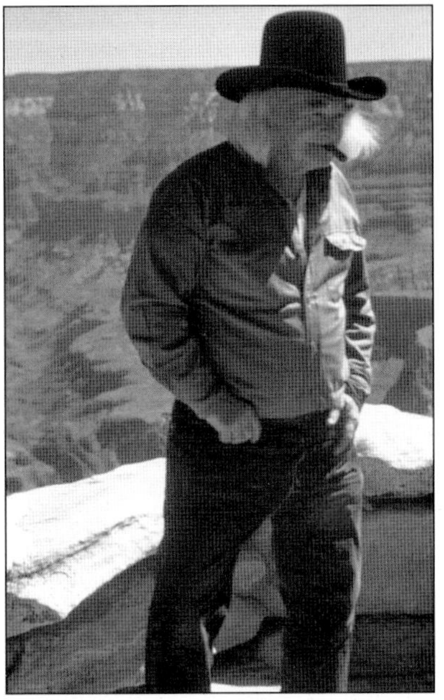

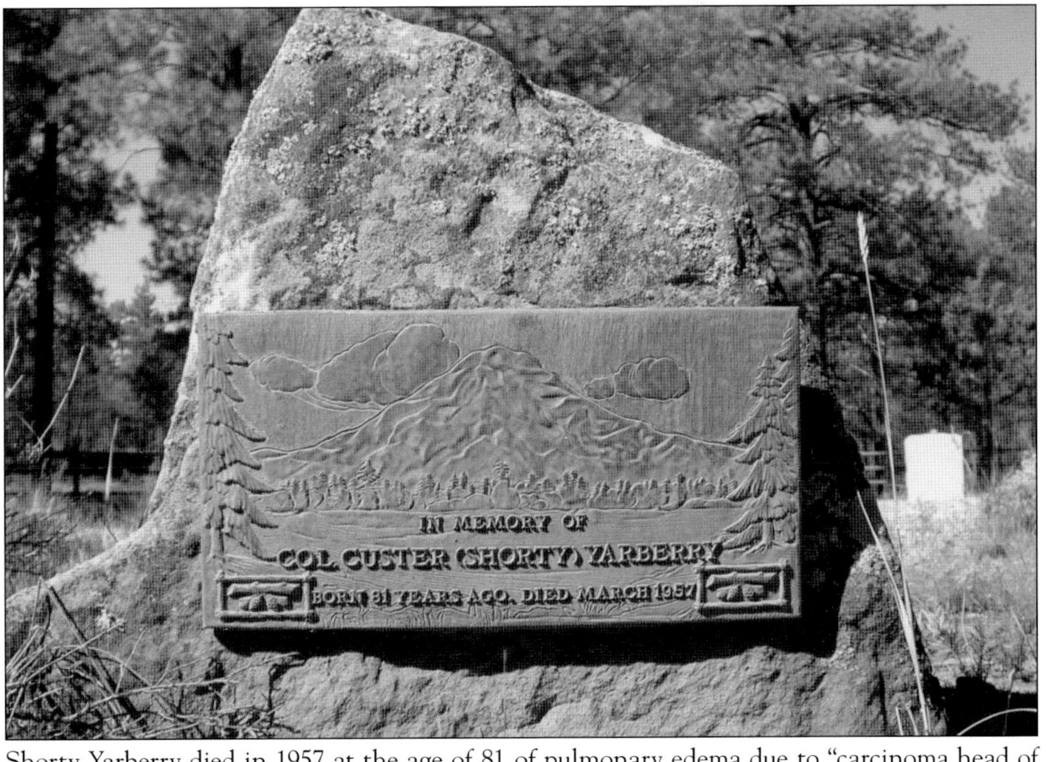

Shorty Yarberry died in 1957 at the age of 81 of pulmonary edema due to "carcinoma head of pancreas metastatic," according to his death certificate. His tall tales may have even extended to his own name. The origin of his title of "Colonel" is not known, and when his death certificate became public record in 2007, it revealed his real name was Clarence, not Custer. It seems that colorful individuals such as Yarberry have existed at Grand Canyon National Park during every era of its existence. (Lois Schmittinger.)

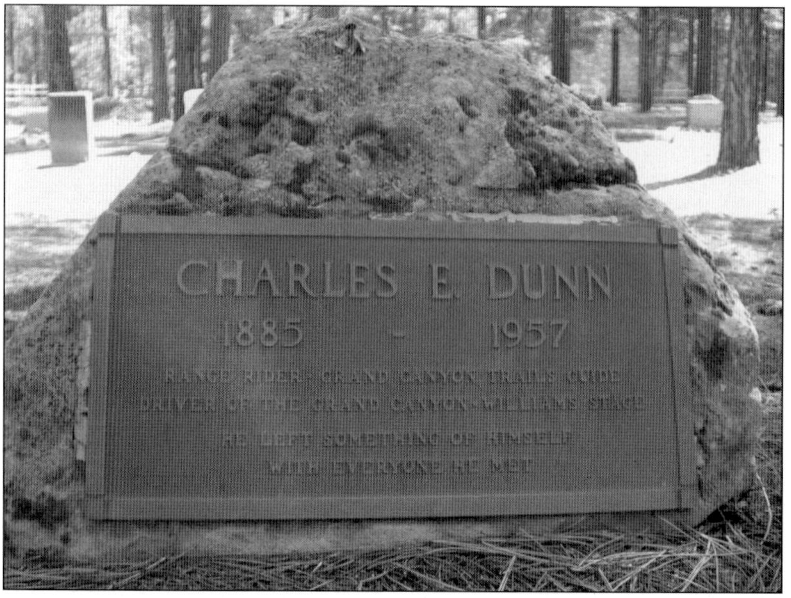

Charles Dunn was a teamster for the Grand Canyon-Williams stage, and he also became a trail guide for the canyon. He passed away on August 15, 1957, at age 71, of a heart attack. (Lois Schmittinger.)

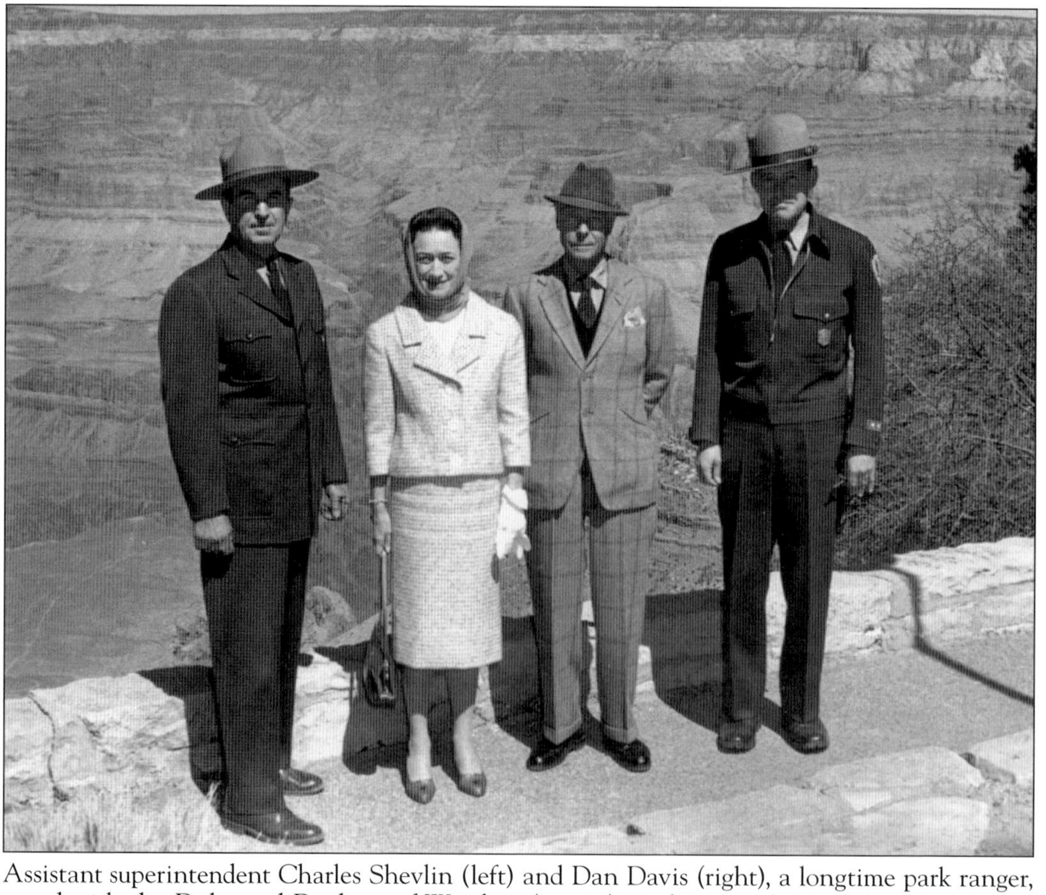

Assistant superintendent Charles Shevlin (left) and Dan Davis (right), a longtime park ranger, stand with the Duke and Duchess of Windsor (center) in this March 17, 1959, photograph. (Photograph by Steve Leding; Grand Canyon NP Museum Collection No. 03444.)

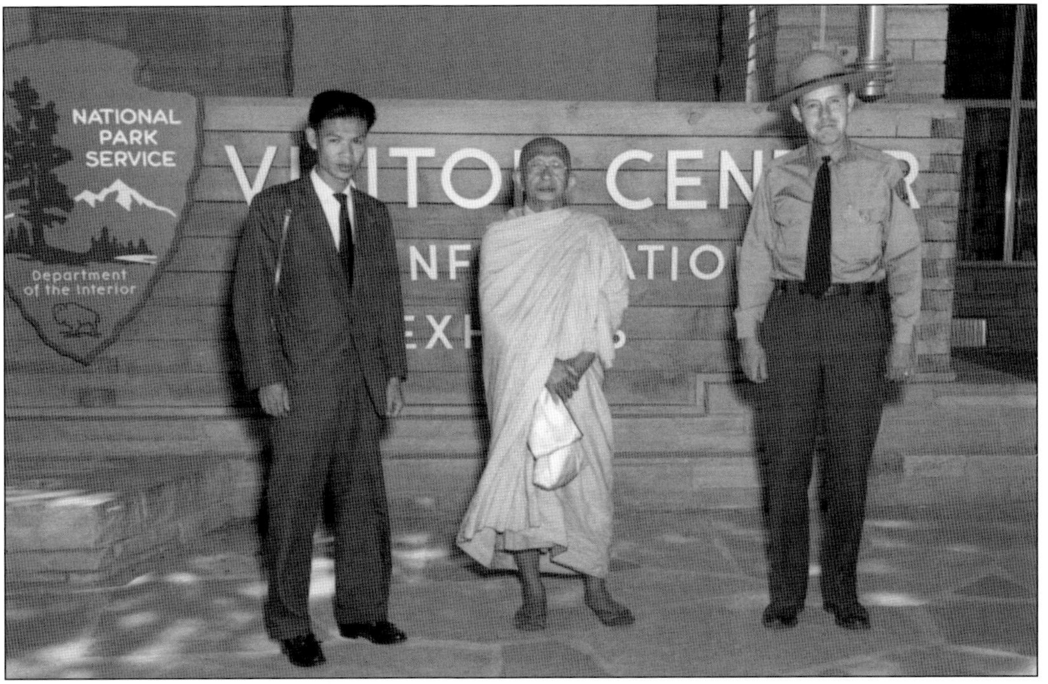

Park ranger Dan Davis (right) poses for a photograph with an important Grand Canyon visitor, His Eminence the Venerable IV Tuoth, Chief of Bonzes (the Buddhist monks) for the province of Battambang, Cambodia. Standing at far left is the Buddhist monk's interpreter, Soly Keomony, in this 1959 photograph. (Photograph by Steve Leding; Grand Canyon NP Museum Collection No. 03366.)

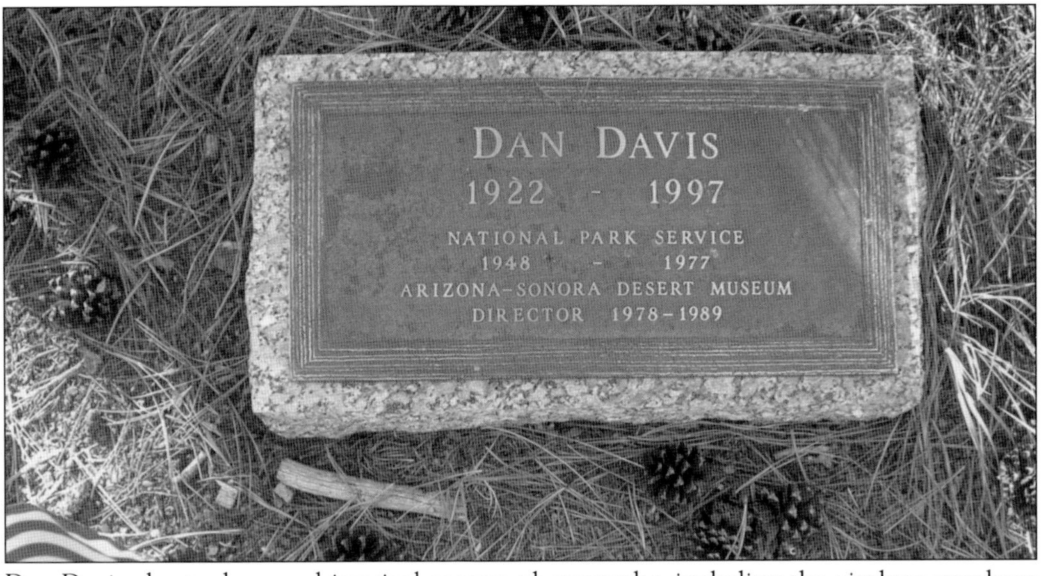

Dan Davis also took many historical canyon photographs, including the airplane wreckage photographs found in chapter 7. He left the Grand Canyon in 1978 to become director of the Arizona-Sonora Desert Museum in Tucson, where he served until 1989. Like so many others, he returned to the canyon in death and is buried in the Grand Canyon Pioneer Cemetery. (Lois Schmittinger.)

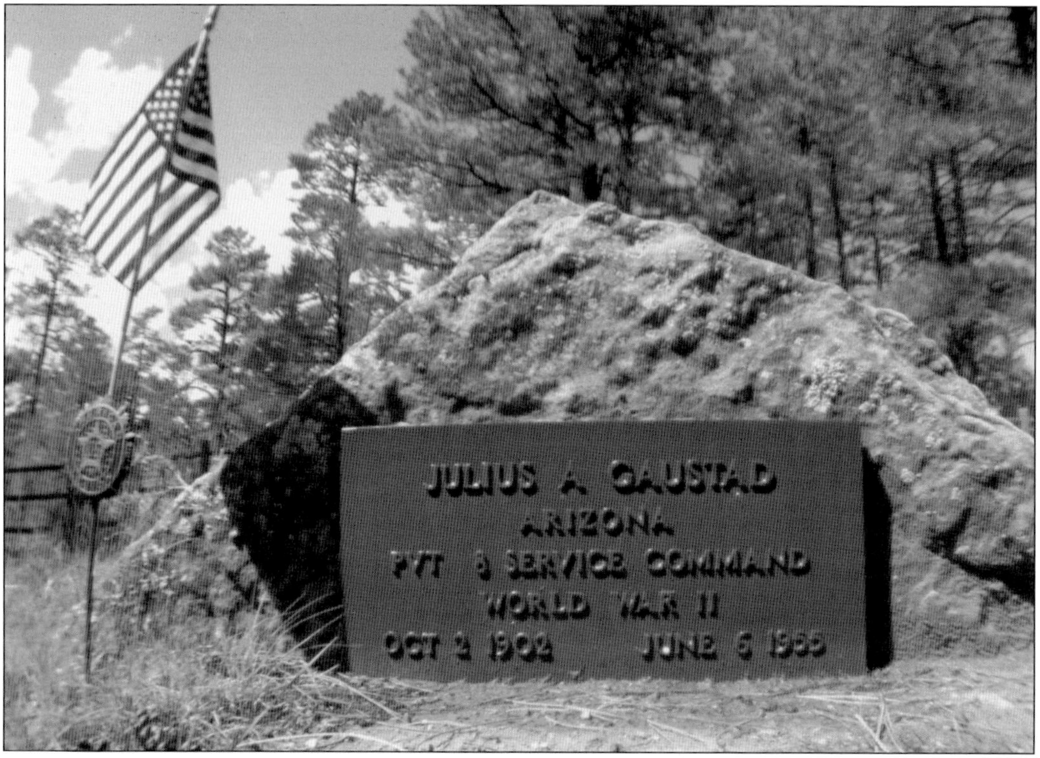

Many veterans are buried in the cemetery, including World War II veteran Julius Gaustad, a native of Arizona who literally dropped dead at 4:00 a.m. at his doctor's office in 1955. He had worked with the CCC and as an electrician during the installation of the first cross-canyon telephone lines. (David Schmittinger.)

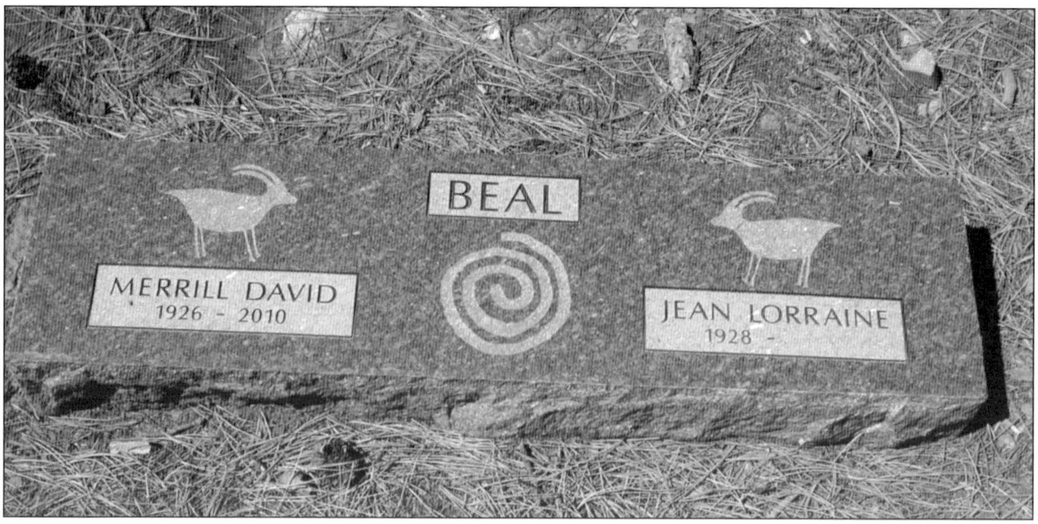

Merrill D. "Dave" Beal served as Grand Canyon park naturalist in the 1960s and worked his way up to become superintendent of the Great Smoky Mountains National Park from 1978 to 1983. He died in Eugene, Oregon, in 2010, and like so many others, returned to the canyon in death. He was the son of famed Idaho historian Merrill D. Beal, who wrote the book *I Will Fight No More Forever.* (David Schmittinger.)

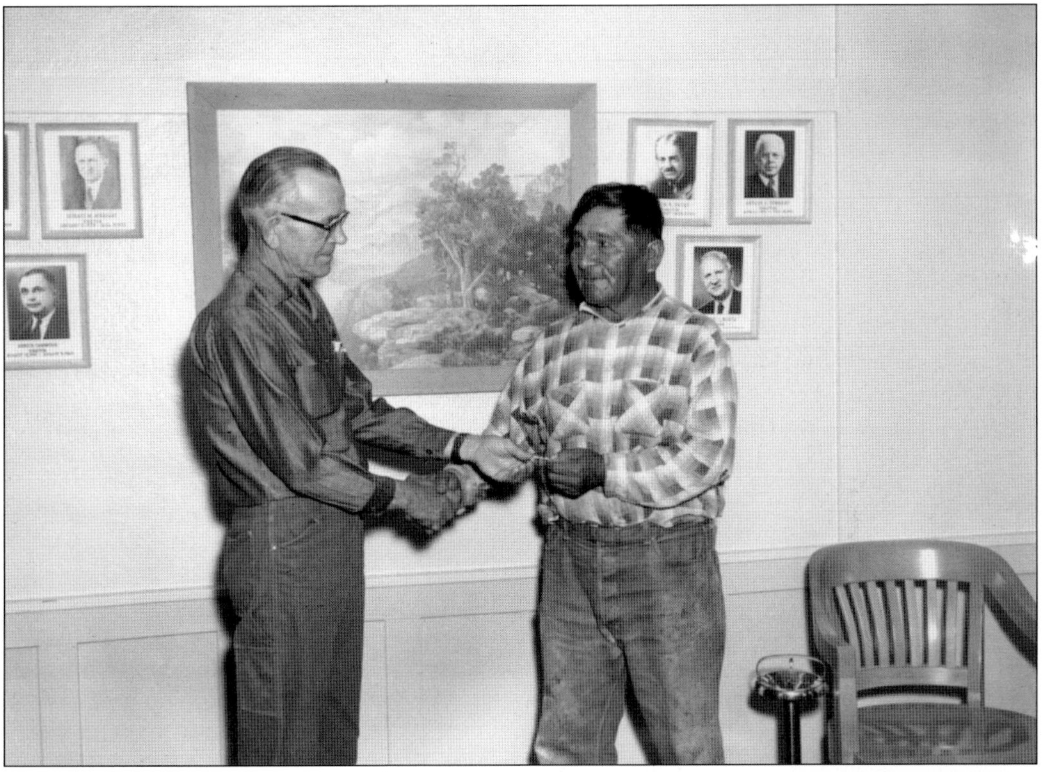

Elmer Watahomigie was a National Park Service employee for many years and a member of a prominent Havasupai family. He was very well liked and is seen here, on the right, receiving his 30-year pin from park official Otis Hicks. That is probably a Widforss painting behind them. (Grand Canyon NP Museum Collection No. 04263.)

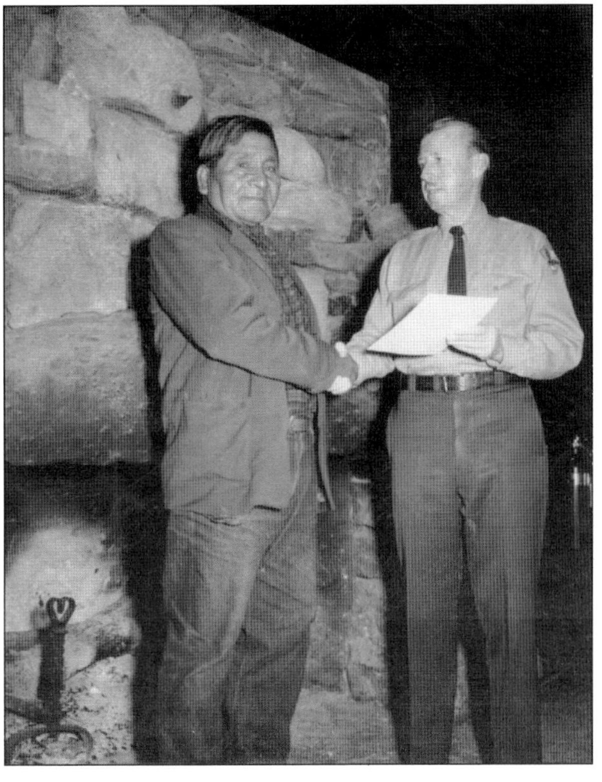

This is the retirement party for Elmer Watahomigie on February 5, 1964. Park superintendent John S. McLaughlin (right) is speaking. (Grand Canyon NP Museum Collection No. 04578.)

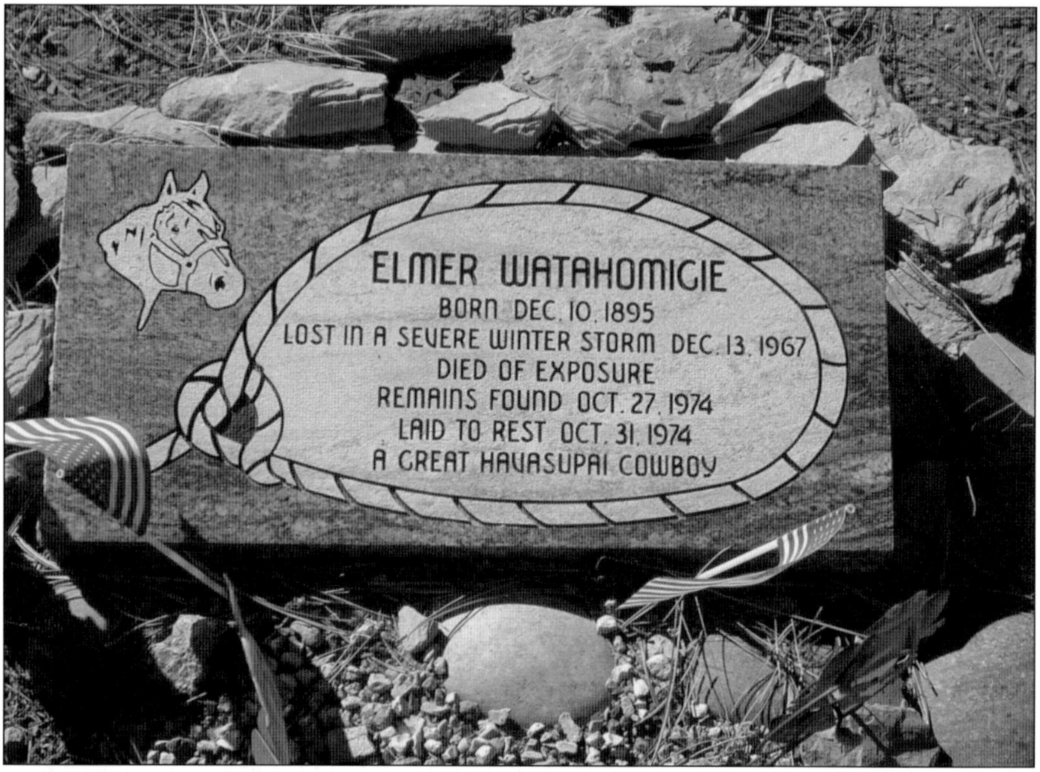

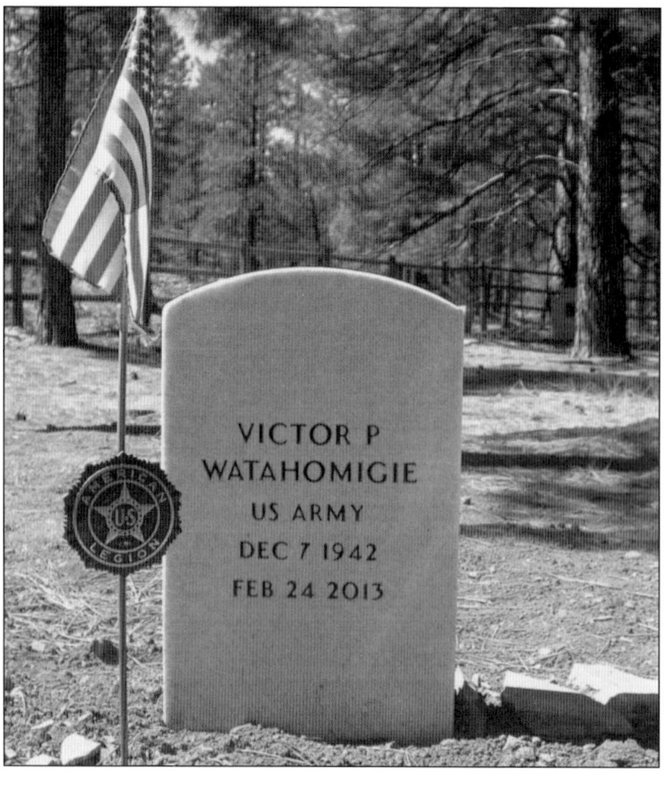

Elmer Watahomigie was caught in a severe blizzard while driving home on the night of December 13, 1967. When his truck broke down, he attempted to walk the rest of the way. Eventually taking shelter under a ledge in Cataract Canyon, he froze to death. His body was not found until seven years later by deer hunters. (David Schmittinger.)

Victor Watahomigie, Elmer's son, was also a park ranger at Indian Gardens, and he later worked at the Grand Canyon water treatment plant. Upon Victor's death on February 24, 2013, he was laid to rest beside his father. (David Schmittinger.)

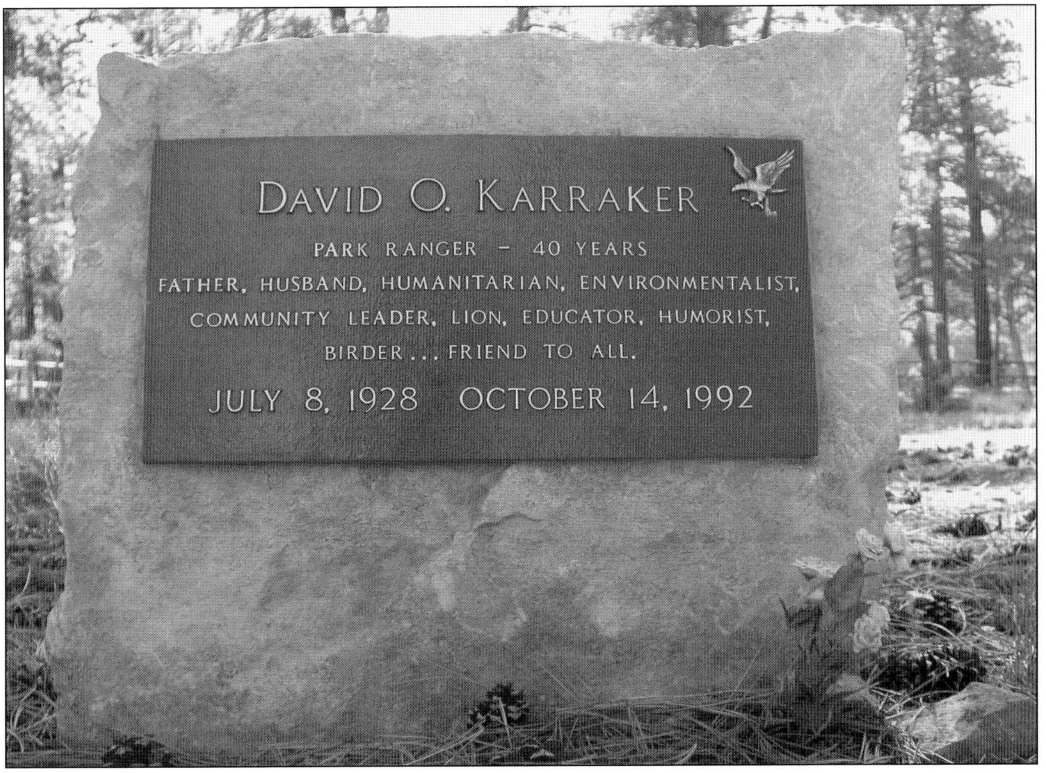

David Karraker (1928–1992) served as a Grand Canyon park ranger for 40 years. Many rangers have made the canyon their lifelong career. (David Schmittinger.)

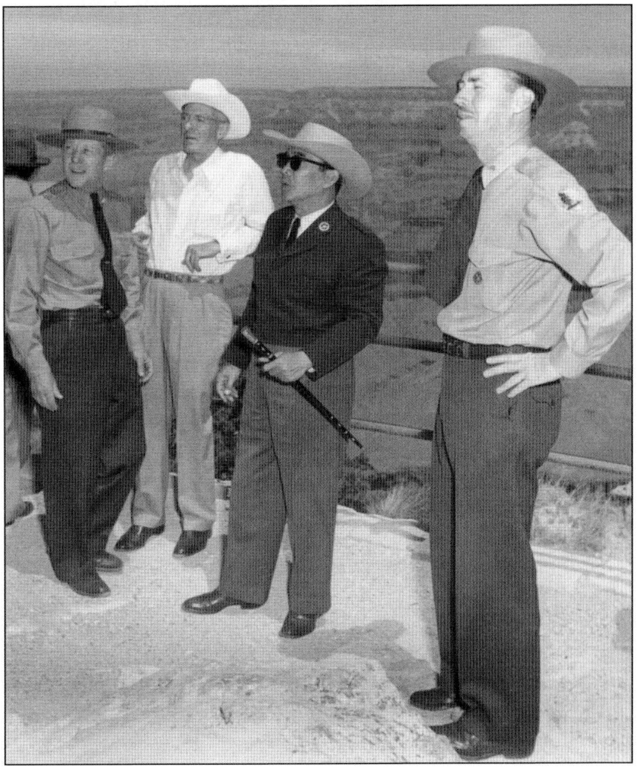

Pictured here from left to right on May 30, 1956, are park naturalist Louis Schellbach, US ambassador to Indonesia Hugh Cumming Jr., President Sukarno of Indonesia, and park superintendent John S. McLaughlin. Park superintendents are usually called upon to accompany important guests on their tours of the park. (Photograph by Steve Leding; Grand Canyon NP Museum Collection No. 03135.)

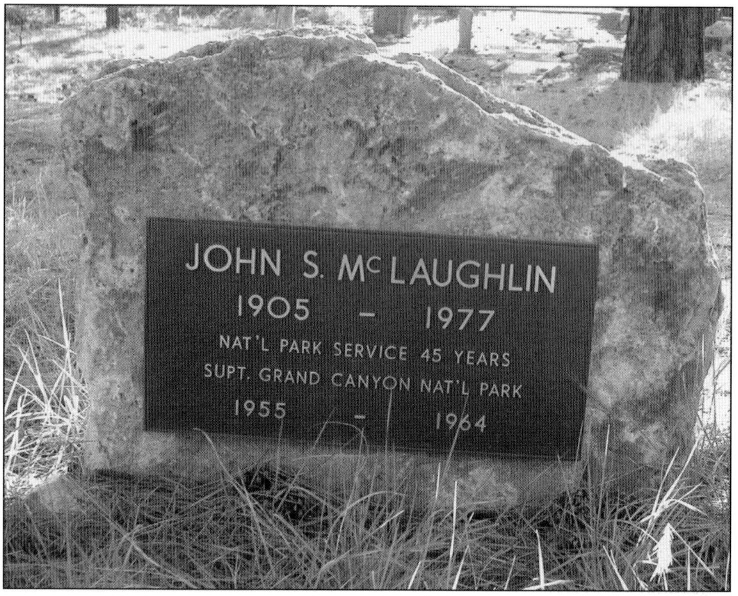

John S. McLaughlin, a lifelong National Park Service employee, was superintendent of Grand Canyon National Park from 1955 to 1964. (David Schmittinger.)

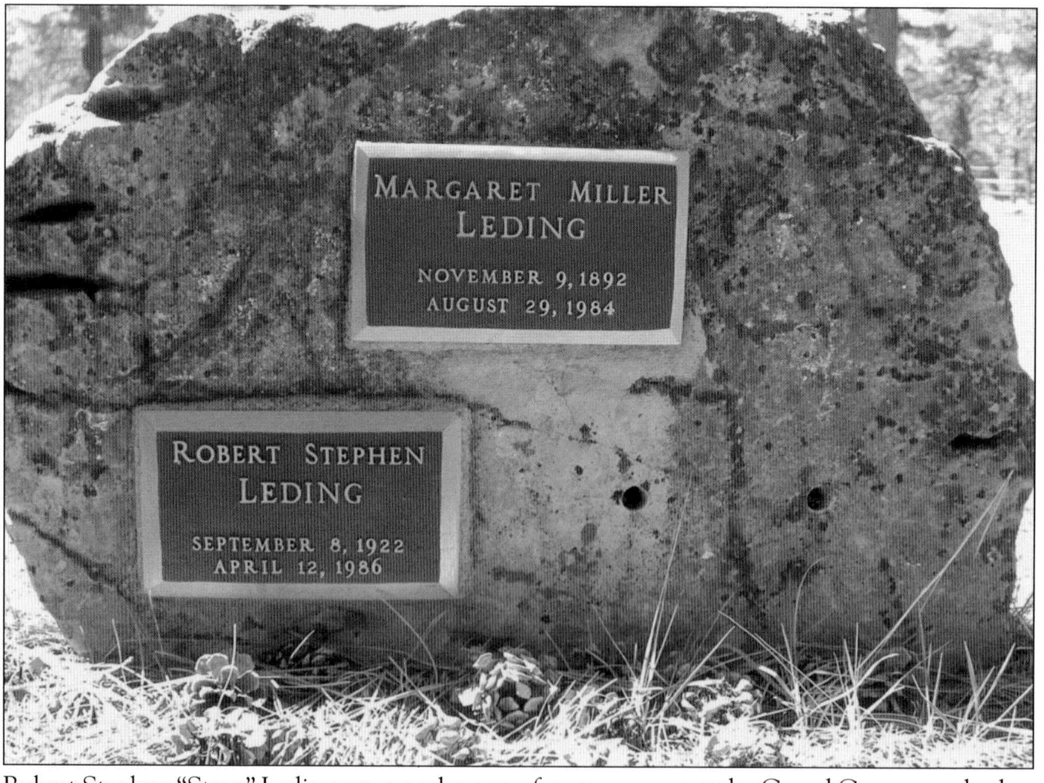

Robert Stephen "Steve" Leding was a park ranger for many years at the Grand Canyon and other national monuments. As a photographer, he shot many historical images of Grand Canyon events during his years there. The name Margaret on this marker is presumably his mother, while his father, Albert, is buried nearby. Steve Leding died in 1986. His widow, Vivian, passed away in 2011 and is reportedly interred here as well, but at the time of this writing does not have a marker. (David Schmittinger.)

Robert Stephen Leding Jr., the son of Steve and Vivian Leding, was killed in a car accident in 1967. (David Schmittinger.)

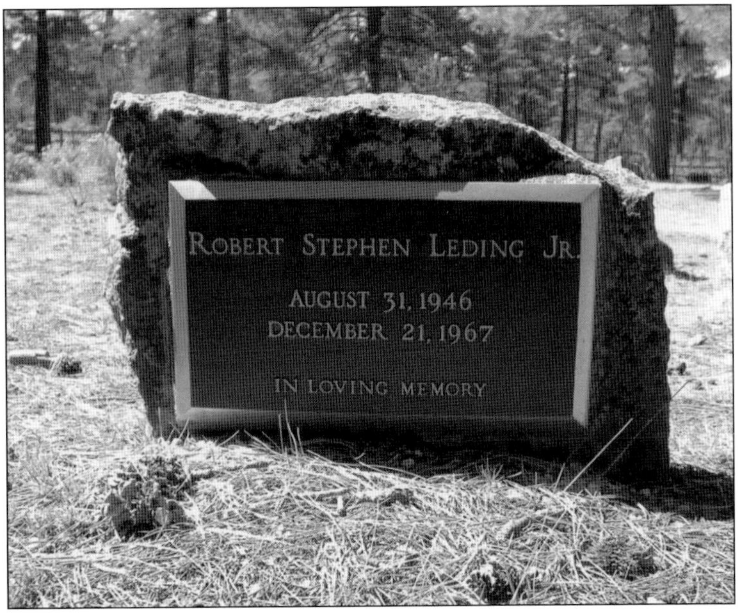

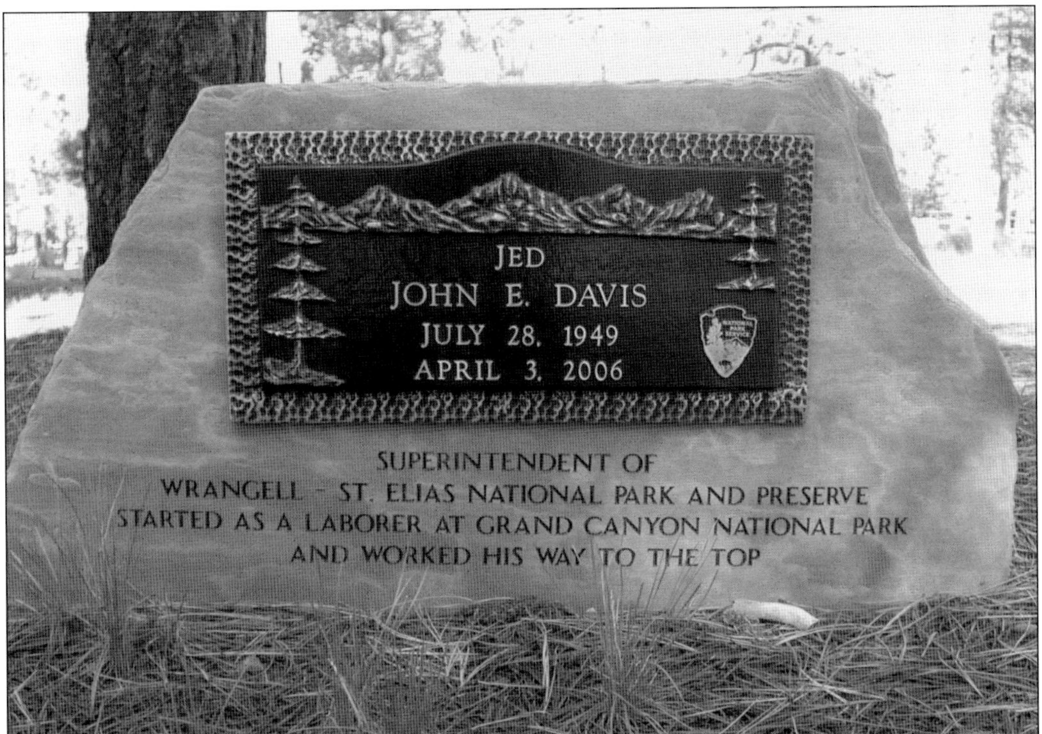

John "Jed" Davis began his National Park Service career as a carpenter and plumber at the Grand Canyon and slowly worked his way up in the NPS. Moving to Alaska in 2000, he became deputy superintendent of Glacier Bay National Park and in 2004 was named superintendent of Wrangell-St. Elias National Park and Preserve, a position he held at the time of his death on April 3, 2006, in Anchorage, Alaska. As with so many others, he returned to the Grand Canyon to be buried. (David Schmittinger.)

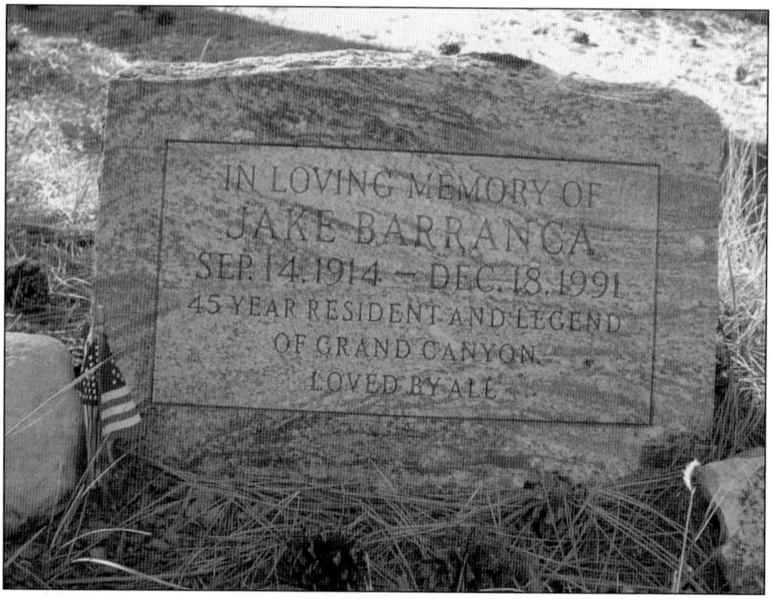

Jake Barranca (1914–1991) was one of the longest-term residents of the Grand Canyon in more modern times. He was here for 45 years until his death. (David Schmittinger.)

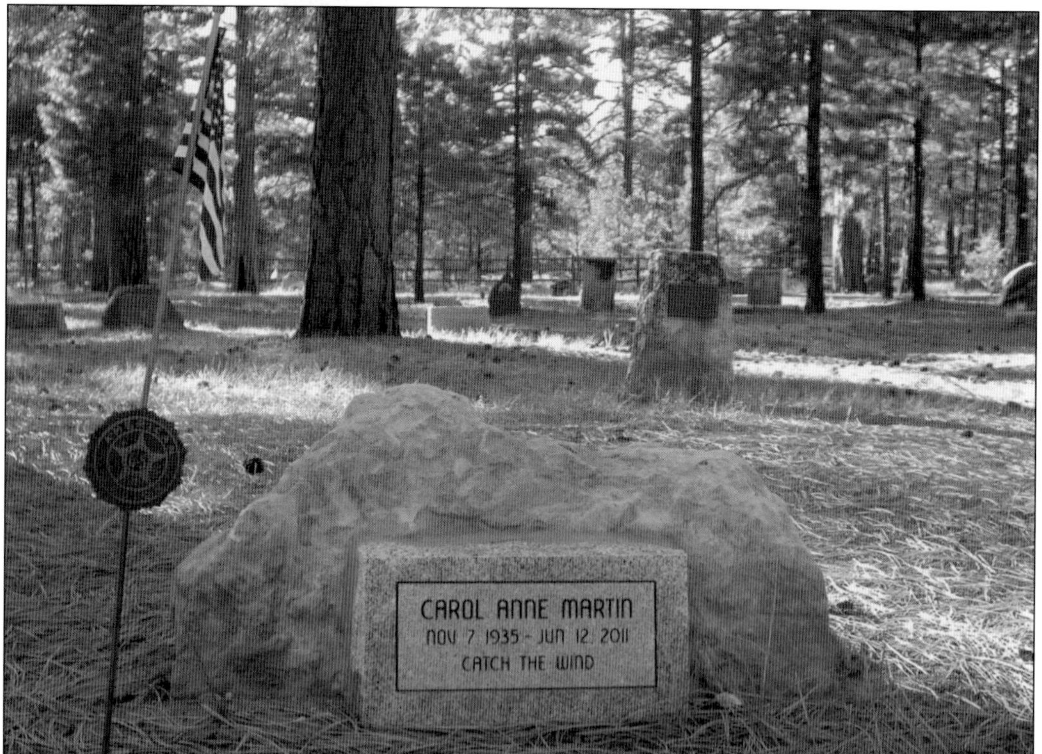

Carol "Carla" Martin was another long-term National Park Service employee who worked her way up, becoming one of the first female superintendents in the NPS (at Tuzigoot National Monument from 1971 to 1974). She also served as chief of the Western Archaeological Center in Tucson (1974–1995). Her grave, next to her husband, Phil, who died in 1965 in a boating accident, is very modest compared to others in the Grand Canyon Pioneer Cemetery, with a stone that does not list her many accomplishments. (David Schmittinger.)

Kenneth Patrick started working at the Grand Canyon as a trail guide and a heavy equipment operator. He is seen here in this 1956 photograph hiking down the Old Tanner Trail to join a search party looking for the body of Boyd Moore, who drowned in the Colorado River. (Grand Canyon NP Museum Collection No. 03033.)

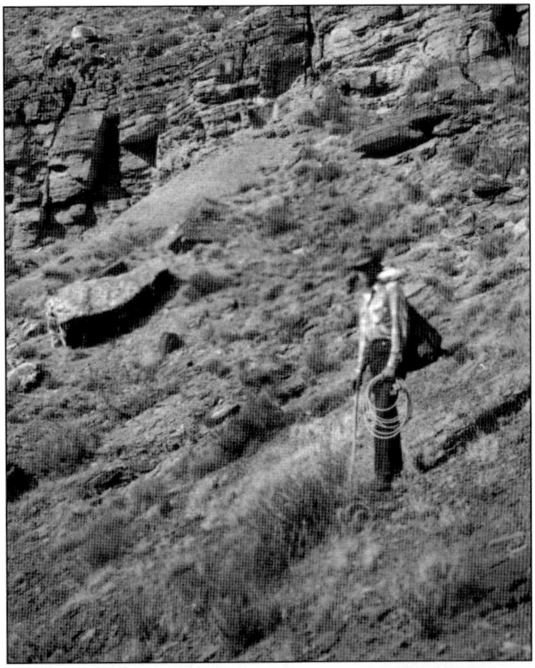

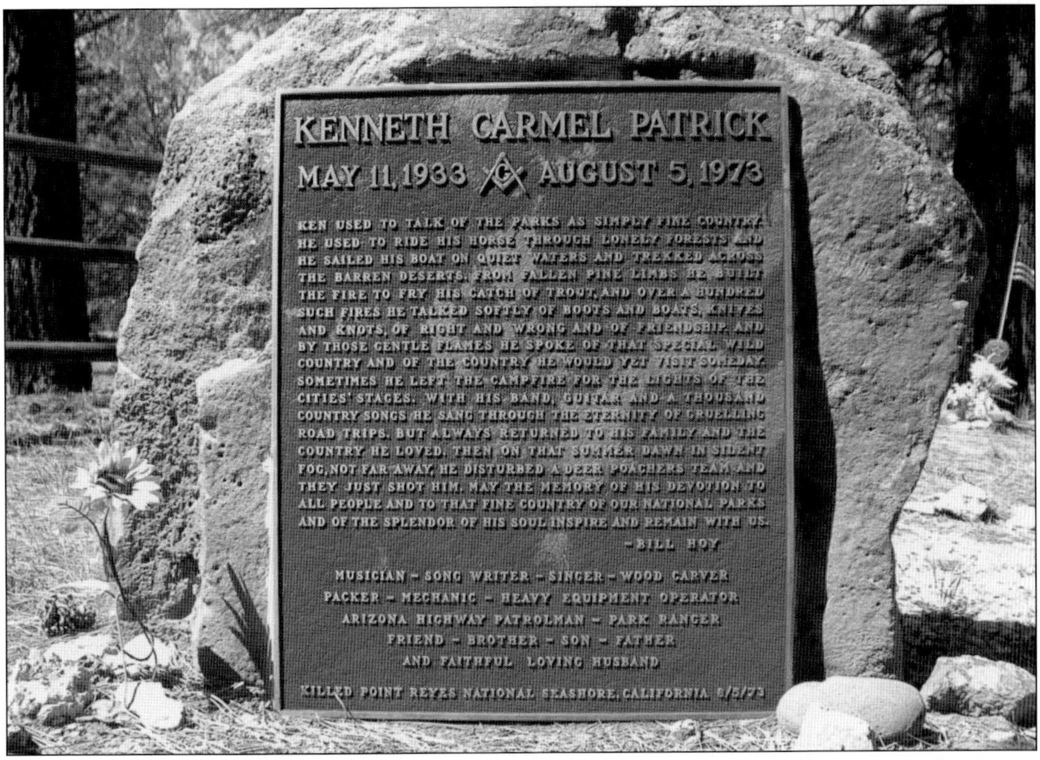

The grave of Kenneth Patrick is unusually detailed. He later became a park ranger at the Organ Pipe Cactus National Monument and then at Point Reyes National Seashore, where he was murdered by deer poachers in 1973, the first National Park Service ranger to be murdered in the line of duty. (David Schmittinger.)

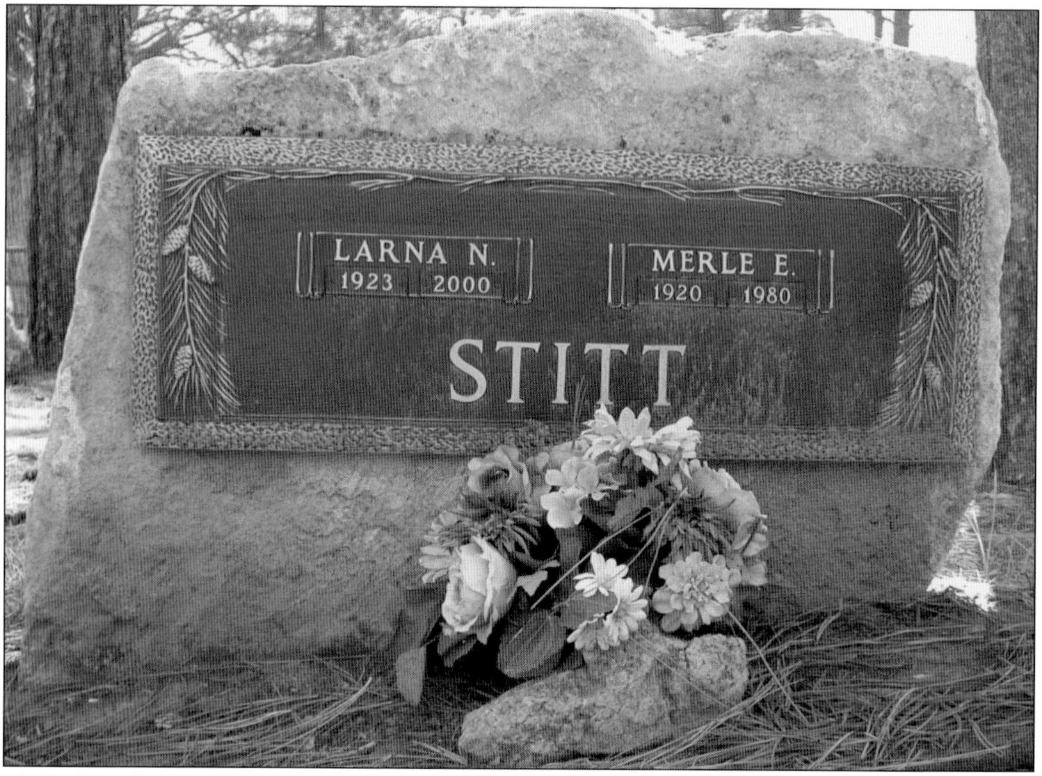

Merle Stitt (seen on page 125) served as superintendent of Grand Canyon National Park from 1972 until January 1980. He passed away only four months after retiring. Both he and his wife, Larna, who died in 2000, rest here. (Lois Schmittinger.)

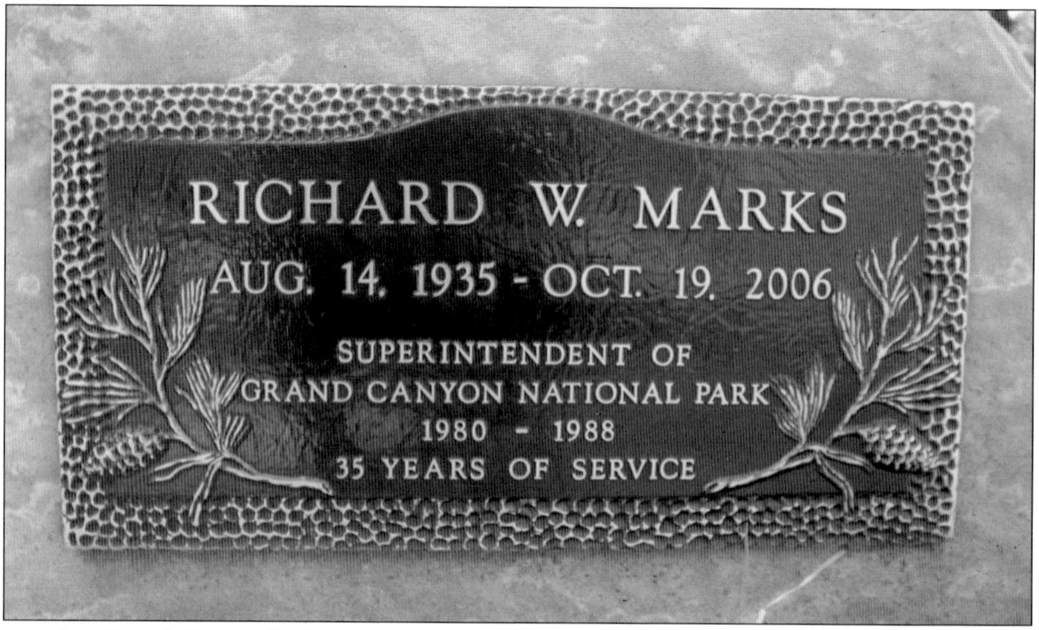

Another Grand Canyon Park superintendent who is buried here is Richard Marks (1935–2006), who succeeded Merle Stitt in 1980. (David Schmittinger.)

Millard Wilcox (1907–1993), among other accomplishments, worked on the Trans-Canyon Water Line from Roaring Springs (which supplies all of the water for North and South Rim visitors) to Indian Gardens, both as a surveyor and chief inspector. (David Schmittinger.)

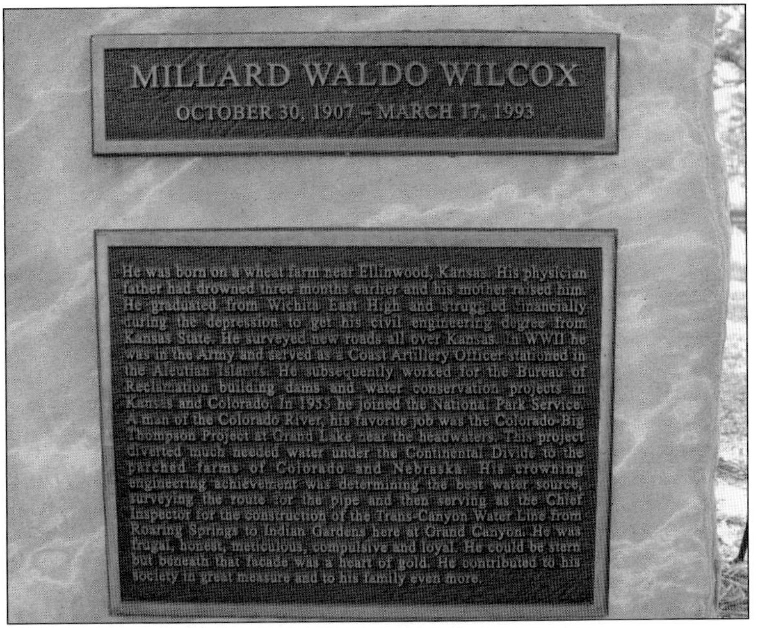

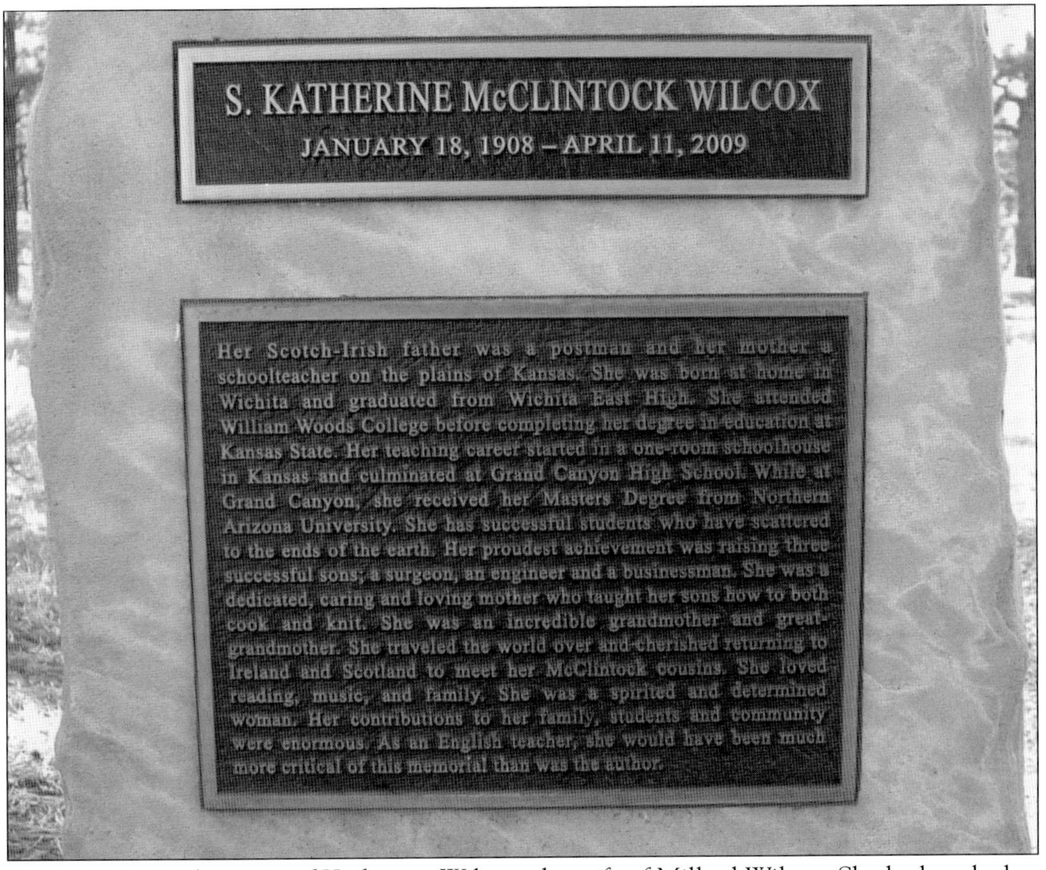

Pictured here is the grave of Katherine Wilcox, the wife of Millard Wilcox. She had worked as an English teacher in the Grand Canyon school system. (David Schmittinger.)

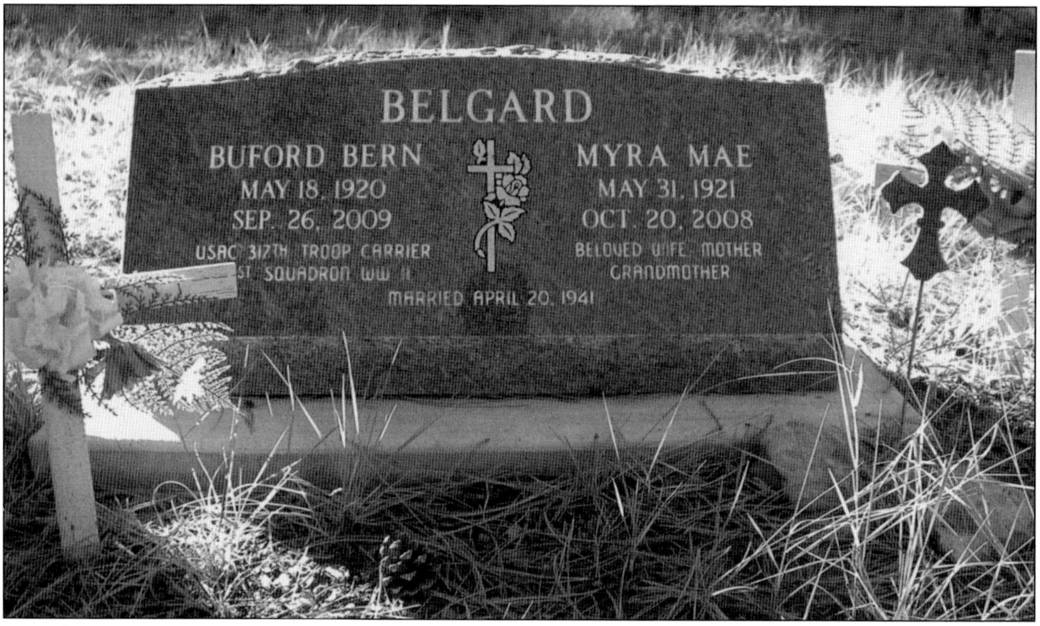

Seen here are the graves of Buford Belgard and his wife, Myra. He came to the Grand Canyon in 1937 and became manager of the laundry and dry cleaning plant for the Grand Canyon hotels. He also served as post commander for the American Legion, John Ivens Post No. 42, from 1950 to 1951. Among other accomplishments, he served on the Williams City Council in the 1970s and was a 52-year member of the Masonic Lodge. (David Schmittinger.)

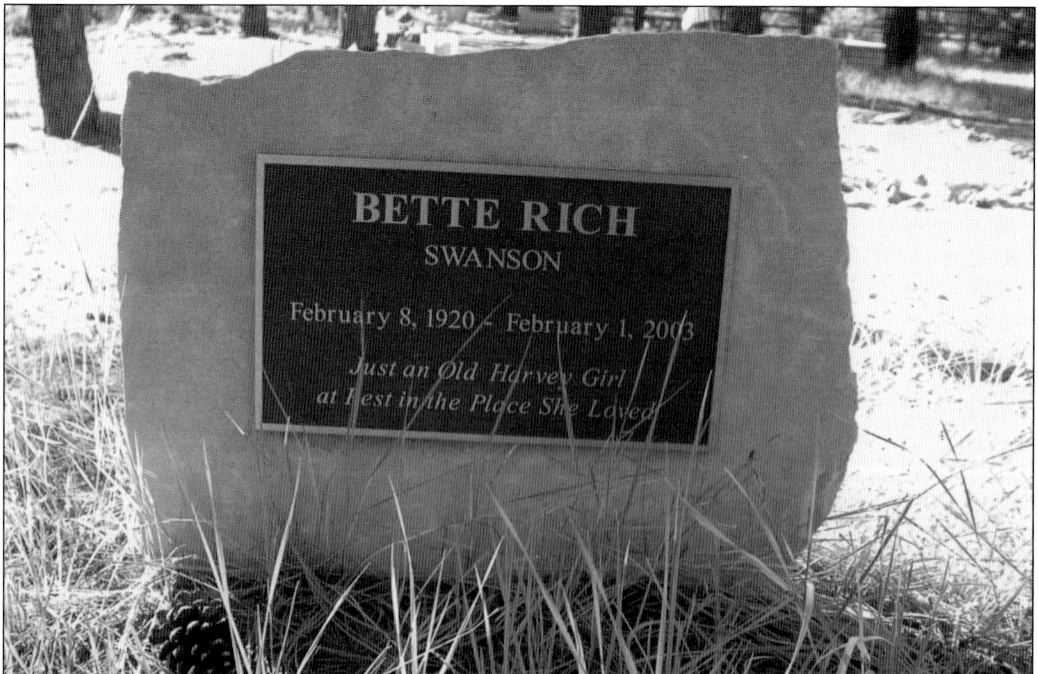

This is the grave of Bette Rich, whose story is simply but eloquently told on her tombstone—she was a Harvey Girl. (David Schmittinger.)

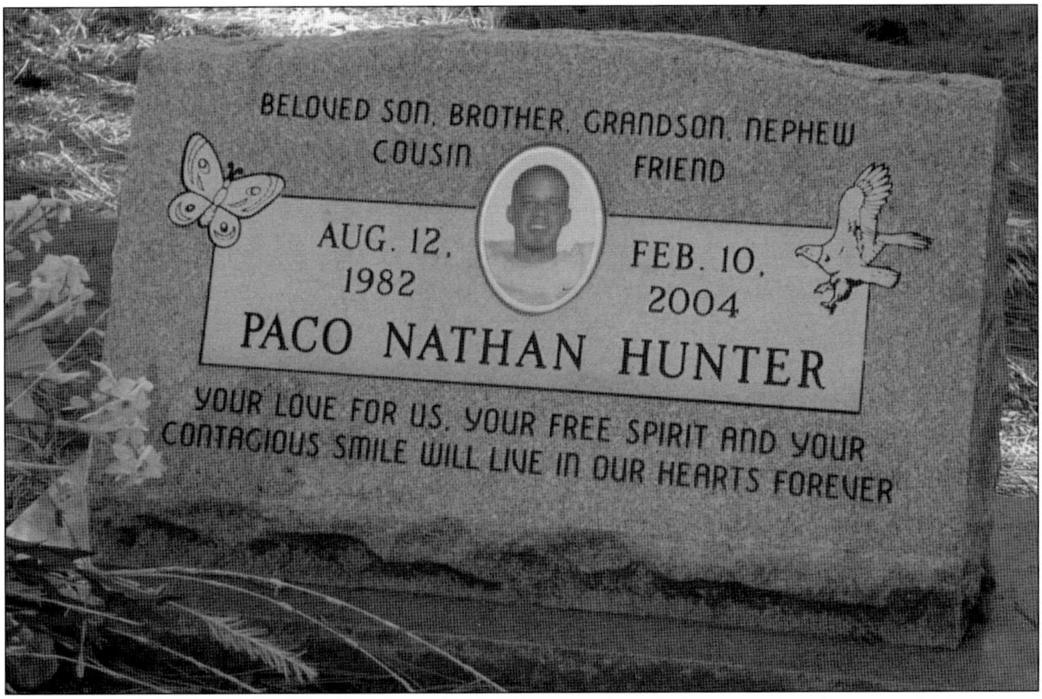

A tragic story of two young people, the children of two Grand Canyon families were killed in an auto accident on Highway 69 near Prescott Valley, Arizona. Paco Hunter and Jessica Cochran are buried side by side in the Grand Canyon Pioneer Cemetery. (Both, David Schmittinger.)

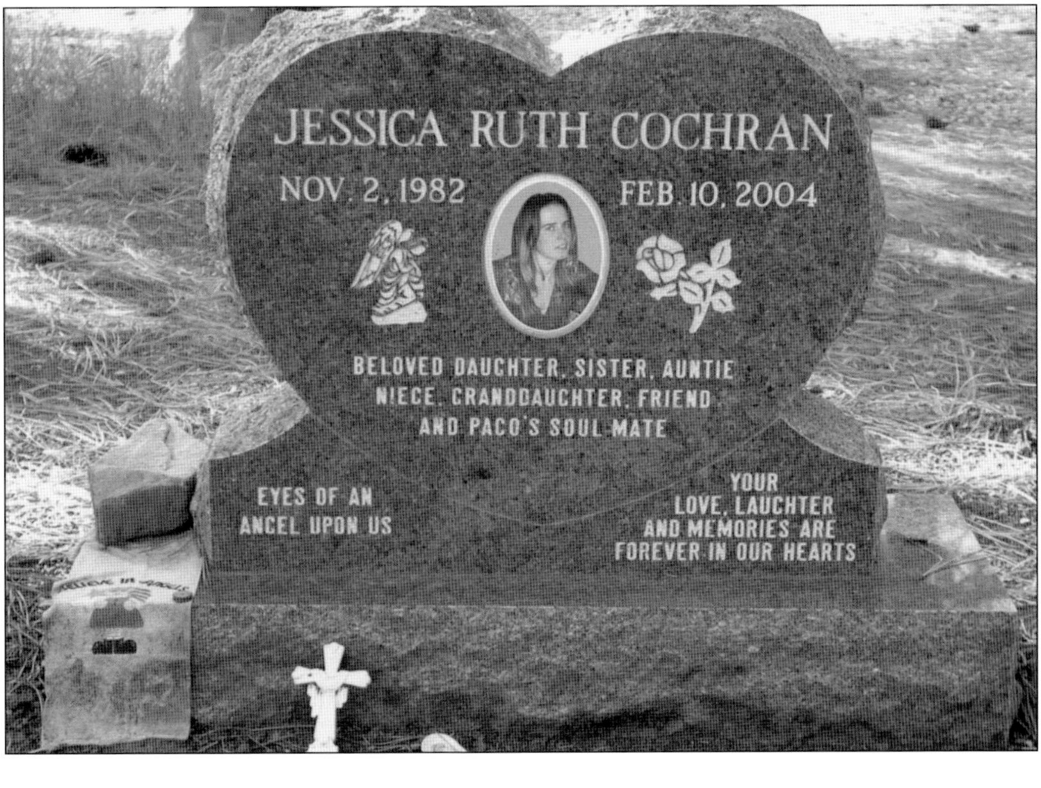

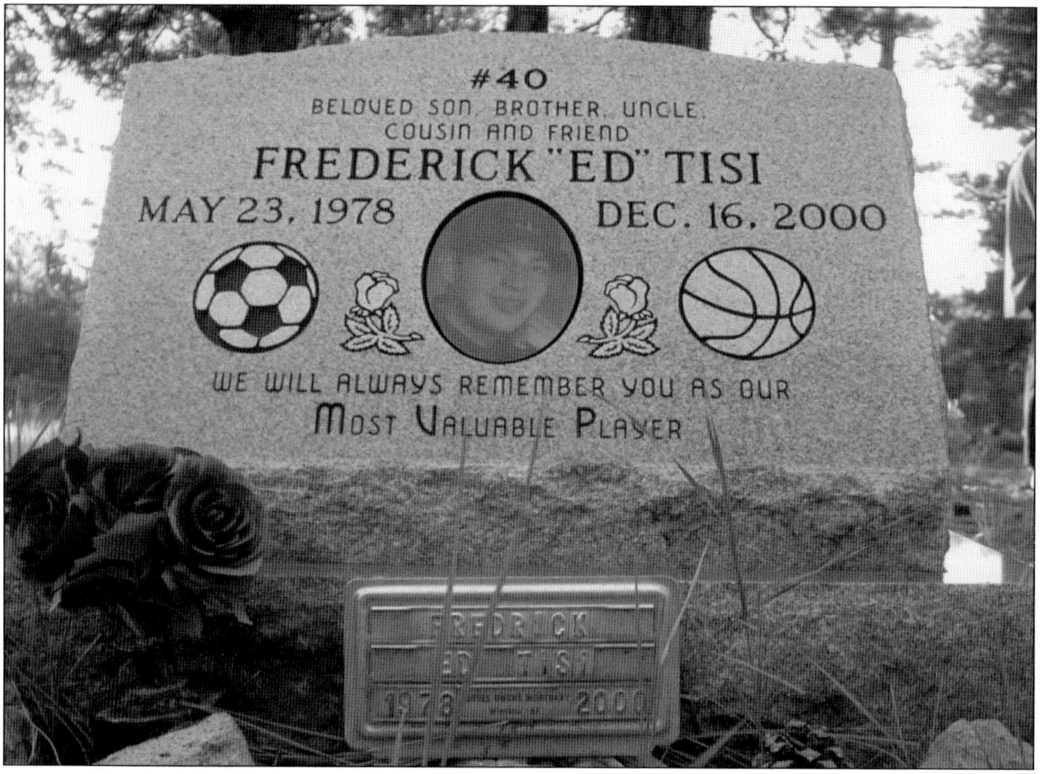

A reminder of another man from the Grand Canyon who died far too young—Frederick Tisi passed away at the age of 22. (David Schmittinger.)

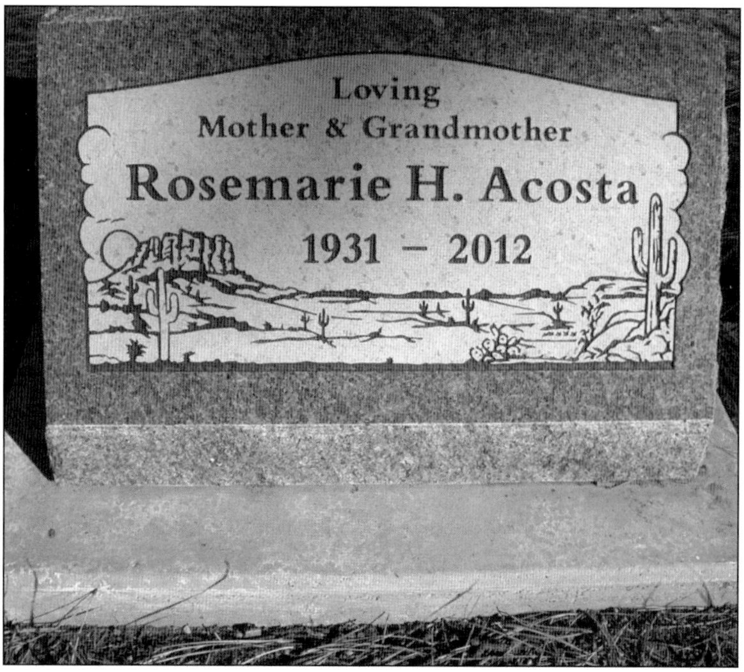

Rosemarie H. Acosta (1931–2012) emigrated from Germany aboard the *Queen Mary* in 1956 and became a Harvey Girl at the Grand Canyon. She later worked at Tusayan, near the canyon. (David Schmittinger.)

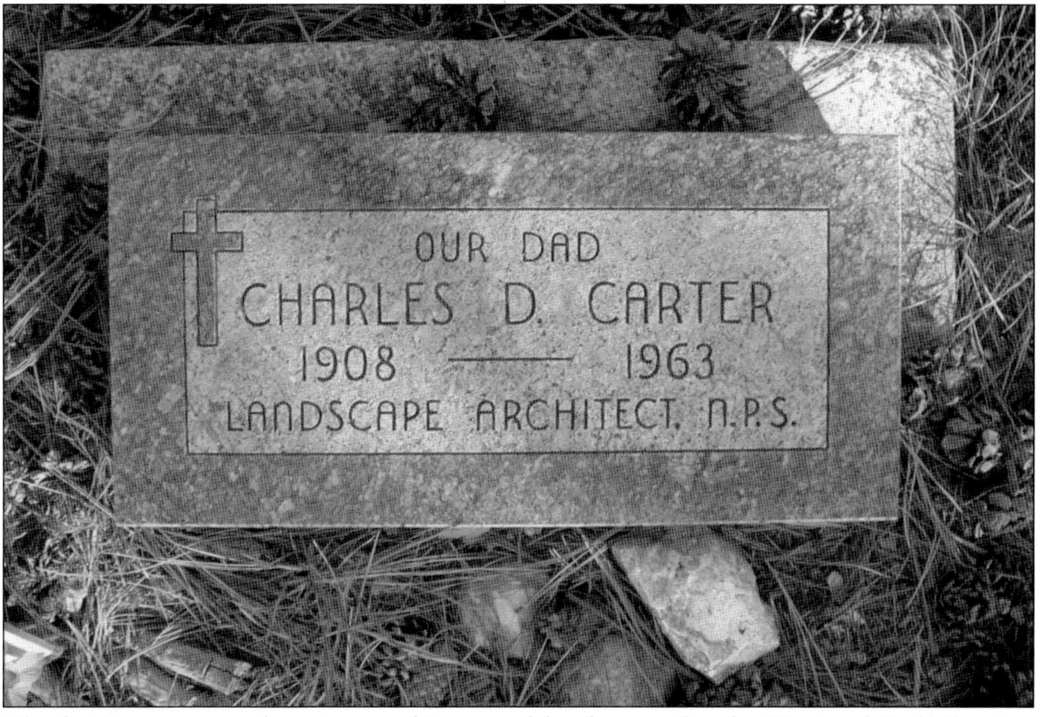

Charles Carter was a longtime architect and landscaper for the National Park Service. (David Schmittinger.)

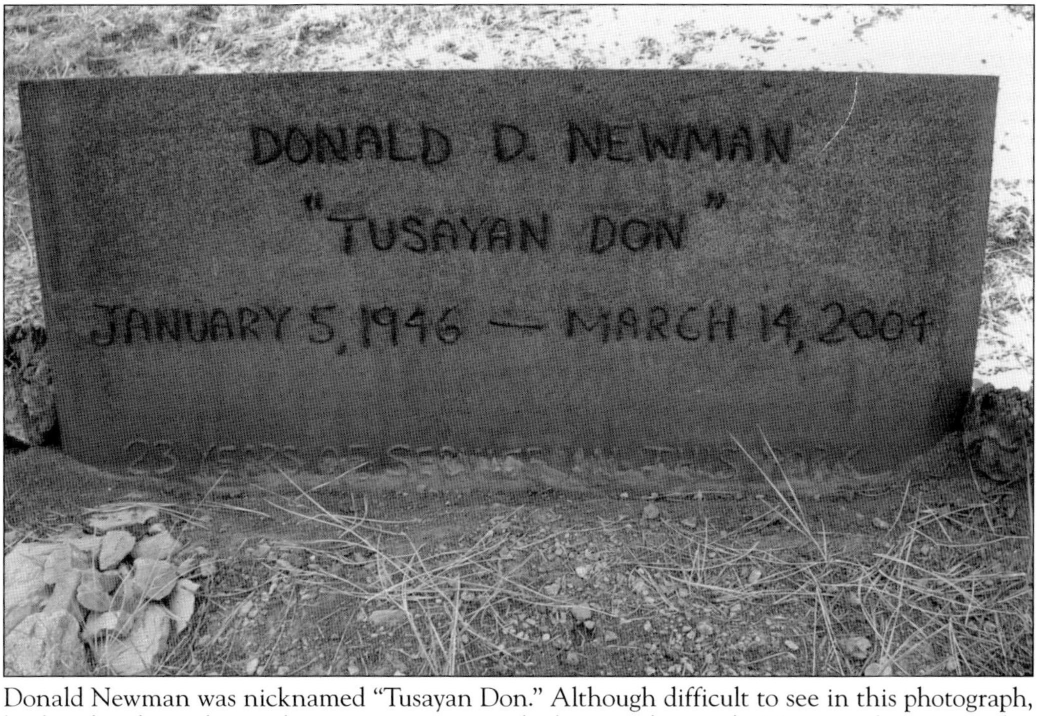

Donald Newman was nicknamed "Tusayan Don." Although difficult to see in this photograph, his handmade tombstone has an inscription at the bottom that reads "23 years of service in this park." He was a carpenter for the Fred Harvey Company. (David Schmittinger.)

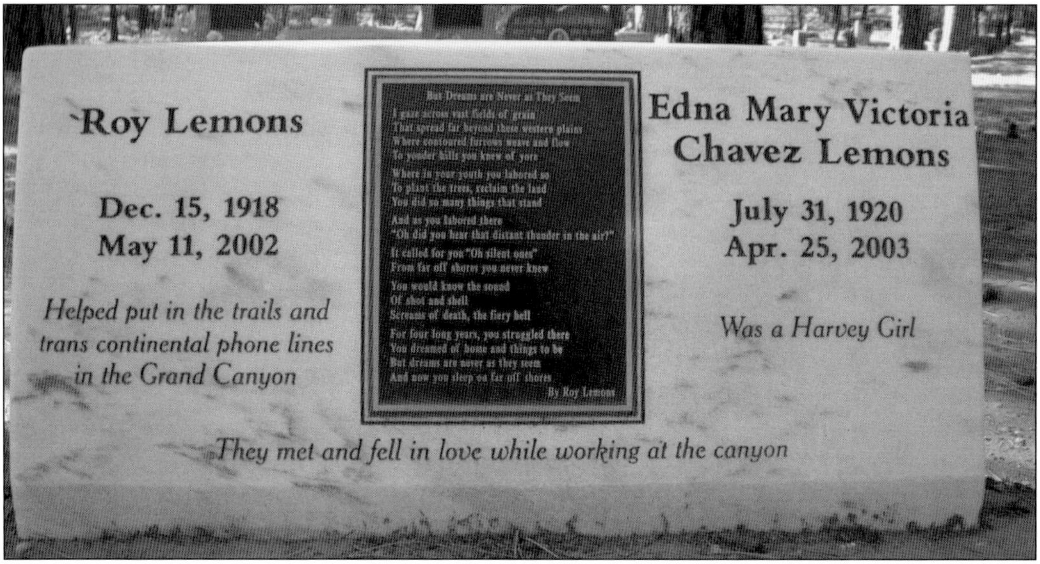

As the tombstone says, Roy Lemons helped put in the trails and transcontinental phone lines in the Grand Canyon. Here, he met and married his wife, Edna (also buried here), who was working as a Harvey Girl. In the center of their tombstone is inscribed a poem Roy wrote. (David Schmittinger.)

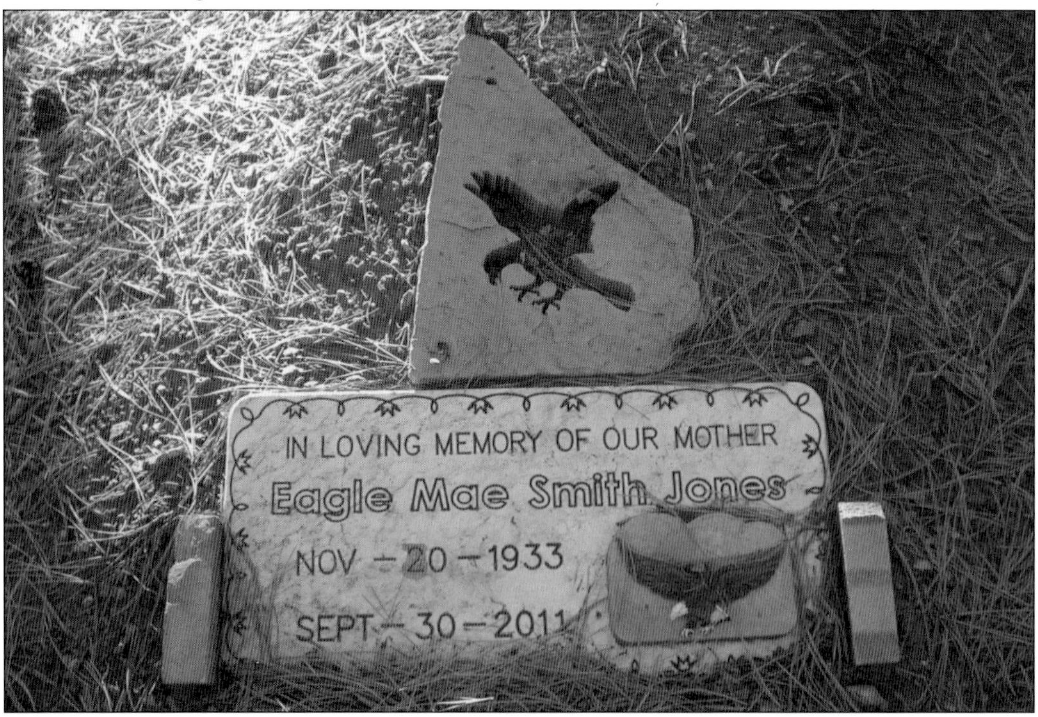

Eagle Mae Jones was employed by Mountain Bell as a telephone operator at the Grand Canyon from 1955 to 1961, and she was on duty when the 1956 Grand Canyon air crash occurred (see chapter 7). She later worked for the Fred Harvey Company, Verkamp's curio store, and also at the Valley National Bank branch at the Grand Canyon where, according to her obituary, she was Emery Kolb's favorite teller. (David Schmittinger.)

Nine

Burials Outside the Cemetery

Not all of the graves in the Grand Canyon are in the Pioneer Cemetery. There are known to be many throughout the canyon, and quite a few of these have had any trace of them obliterated by time and the elements. Also, the Havasupai Indians buried their dead at the bottom of the canyon for thousands of years, and even today, Supai Village maintains its own cemetery.

Prior to the creation of the Grand Canyon Cemetery in 1919, deaths in the canyon were handled in different ways among the early white settlers and businessmen. If someone died at the canyon, they were usually sent into Flagstaff for burial (as it was for Niles J. Cameron, Ralph's brother and partner) or back to wherever they came from.

Others were sometimes buried on the spot where they died, if they happened to be killed in a fall or some other kind of accident. A small number of these graves are still visible in the canyon, while all traces of others have vanished with time.

This chapter examines a small number of such burials in the Grand Canyon, which are located not in the cemetery, but at various locations around the canyon.

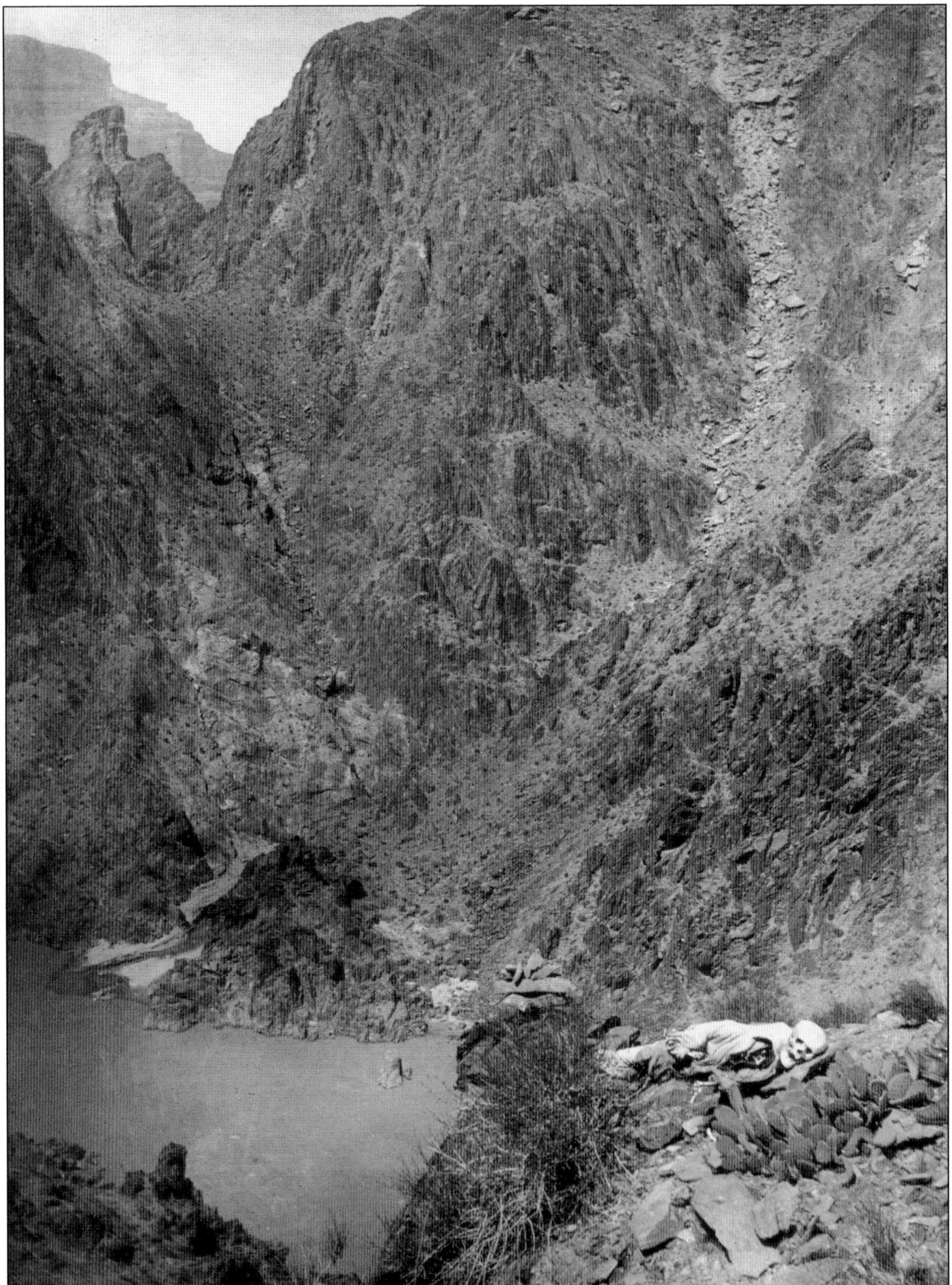

This famous photograph of a sun-bleached skeleton was taken by Emery Kolb in 1906, shortly after the unidentified body was discovered. He had papers in his pockets dating to 1900, indicating he had been dead for six years before he was found. The unidentified man was reportedly buried near this site, but the exact location of the grave is no longer known. (Grand Canyon NPS Museum Collection No. 17199.)

In 1921, Emery Kolb took this photograph of a marker somewhere in the Grand Canyon that reads, "C.F. Welch—Fell In Action," indicating that the deceased man fell to his death. The passing years have obliterated all traces of this grave, and at this time, no one knows for sure where in the canyon this photograph was taken or who C.F. Welch was. (Northern Arizona University-Cline Library Special Collections.)

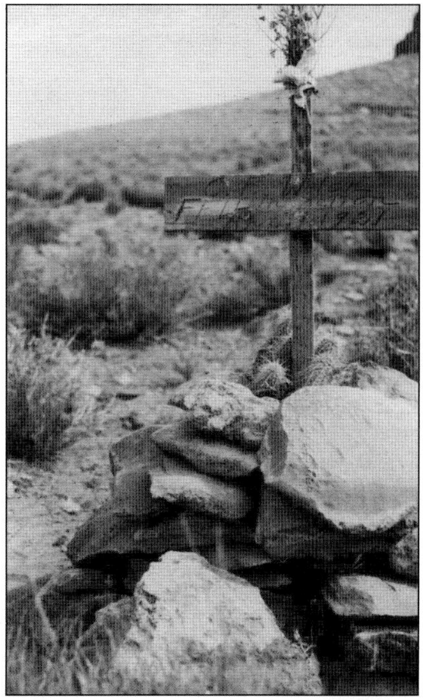

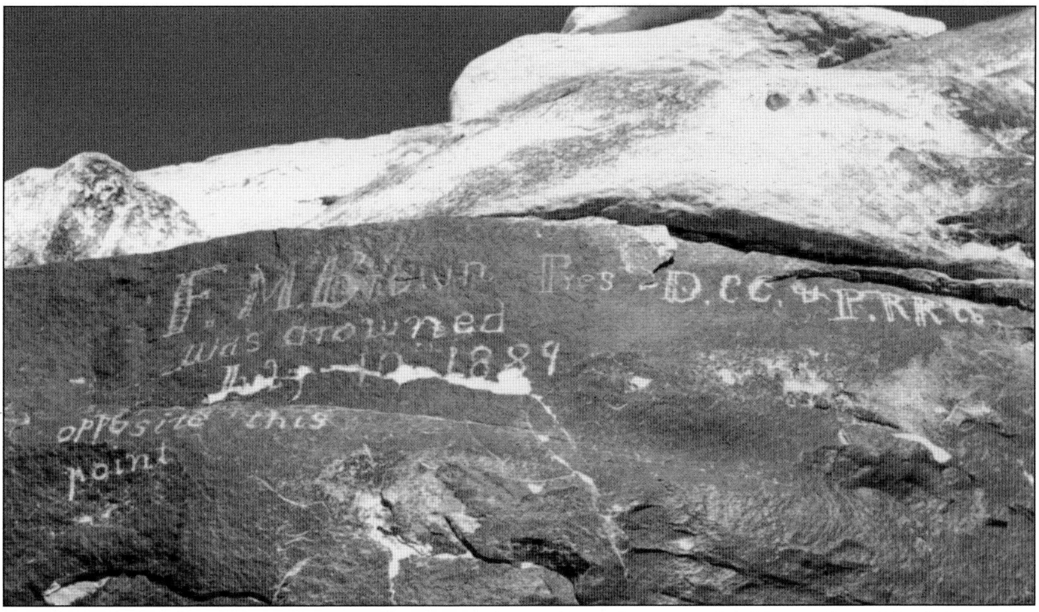

In 1889, businessman Frank Mason Brown devised a scheme to build a railroad bed from the Colorado Rocky Mountains to San Diego, California, with much of the track following the Colorado River. Brown formed the Denver, Colorado Canon & Pacific Railroad (DCC & PRR Co.) and launched a surveying party with chief surveyor Robert Brewster Stanton. The trip turned tragic on July 10, 1889, when Brown's canoe flipped and he drowned at River Mile 11.9. His body was not recovered, but party member Peter M. Hansbrough carved this inscription on a rock opposite where Brown died. This photograph was taken on July 5, 1978. (Photograph by Robert C. Euler; Grand Canyon NP Museum Collection No. 06544.)

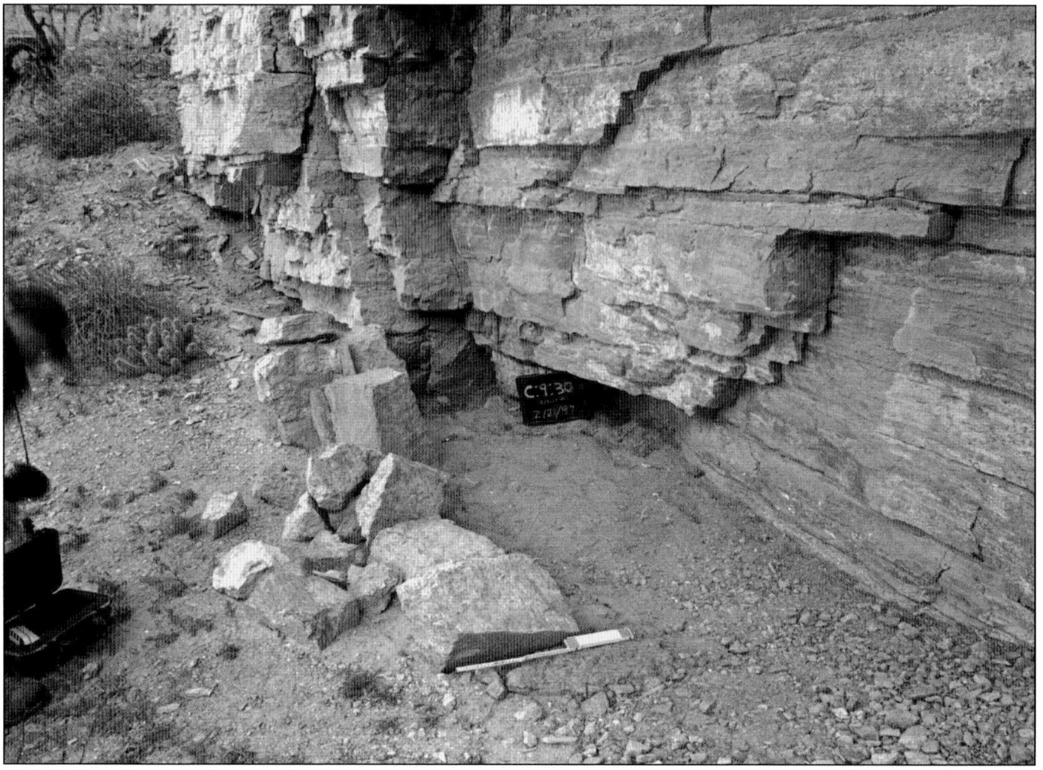

Despite the death of their leader, F.M. Brown, the Brown/Stanton surveying trip decided to continue their journey. On July 15, 1889, five days following Brown's drowning, a boat carrying oarsmen Peter M. Hansbrough and Henry C. Richards flipped over. Both men drowned. Richards's body was never found, but Hansbrough was buried on the shore opposite where he drowned at the 25 Mile Rapid. These two photographs of the site are from February 21, 1997. (Grand Canyon NP Museum Collection No. 08472; below, Grand Canyon NP Museum Collection No. 08470.)

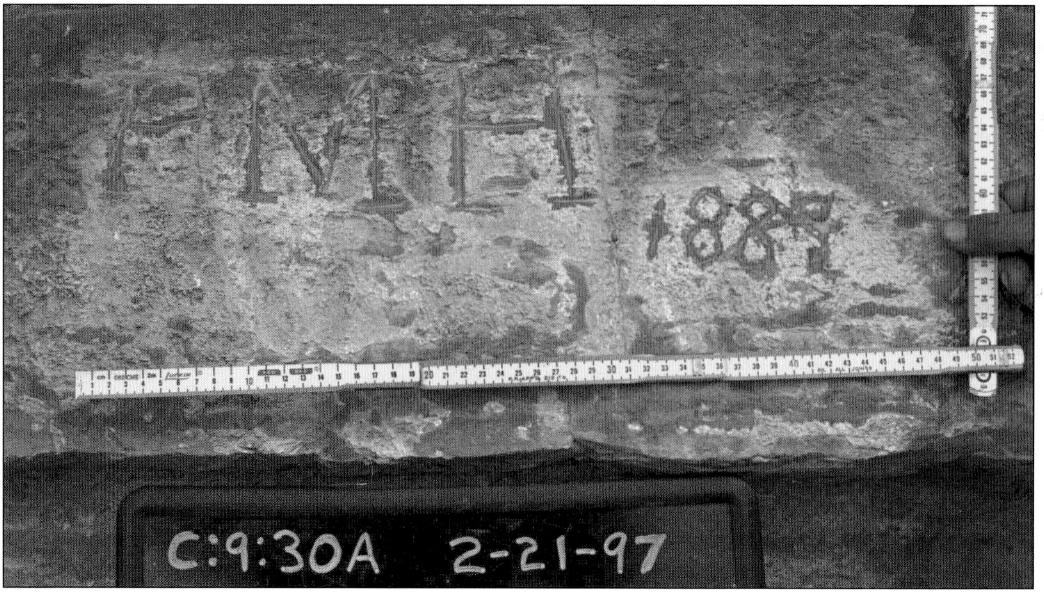

Rees B. Griffiths was a construction foreman working on the South Kaibab Trail in 1922. He was killed by a falling boulder that was loosened by dynamite his crew had set off. He was buried near the place where he fell. This photograph was taken in 1935, and he is still there. (Grand Canyon NP Museum Collection No. 00575.)

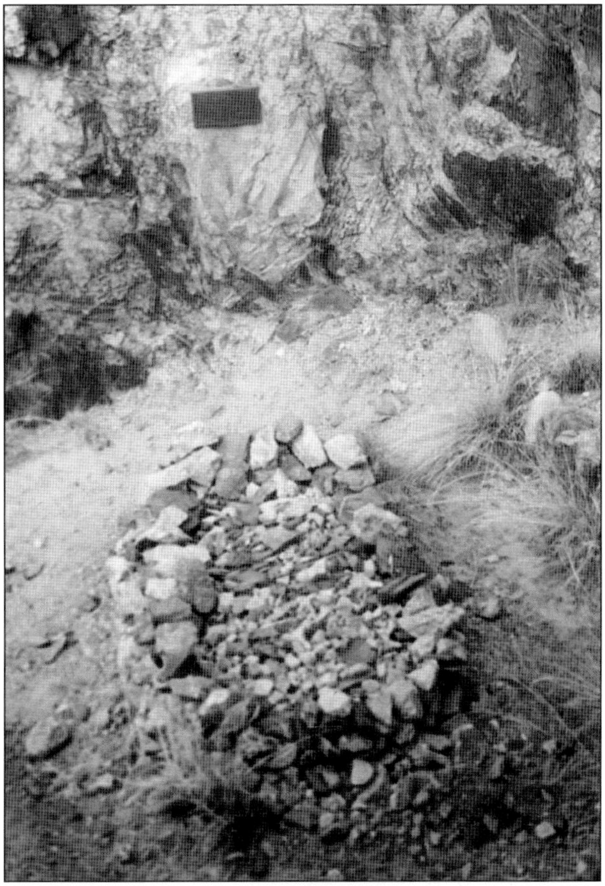

This photograph, taken on July 20, 1985, shows the detail of Rees B. Griffiths's grave marker on the South Kaibab Trail. In recent years, people have taken to leaving various ornaments on his grave. His family is buried in Fredonia, Arizona. (Grand Canyon NP Museum Collection No. 11726.)

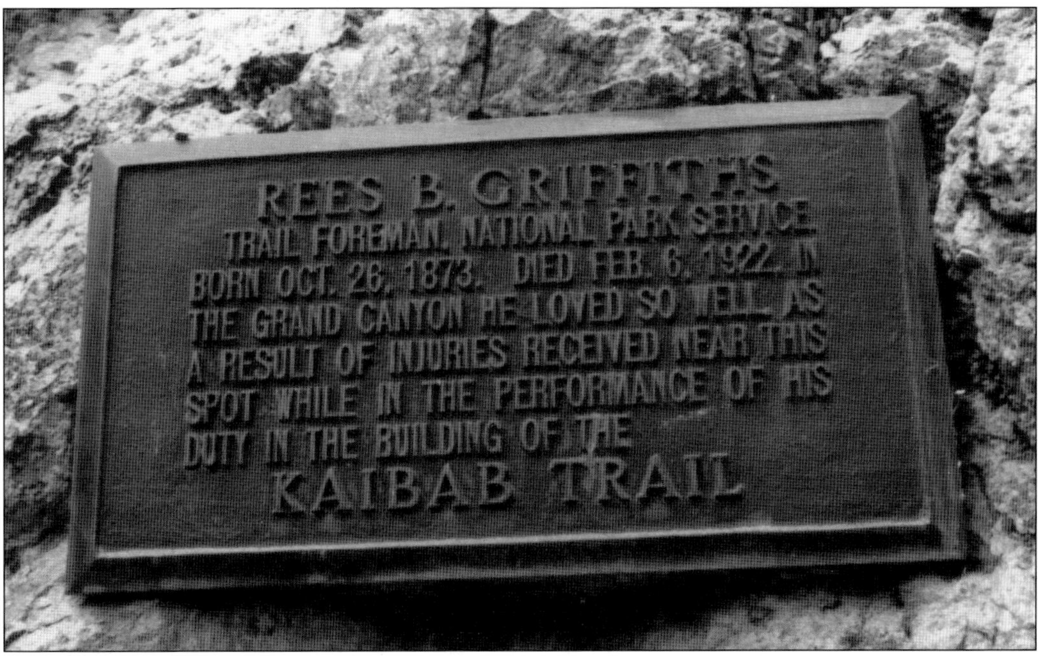

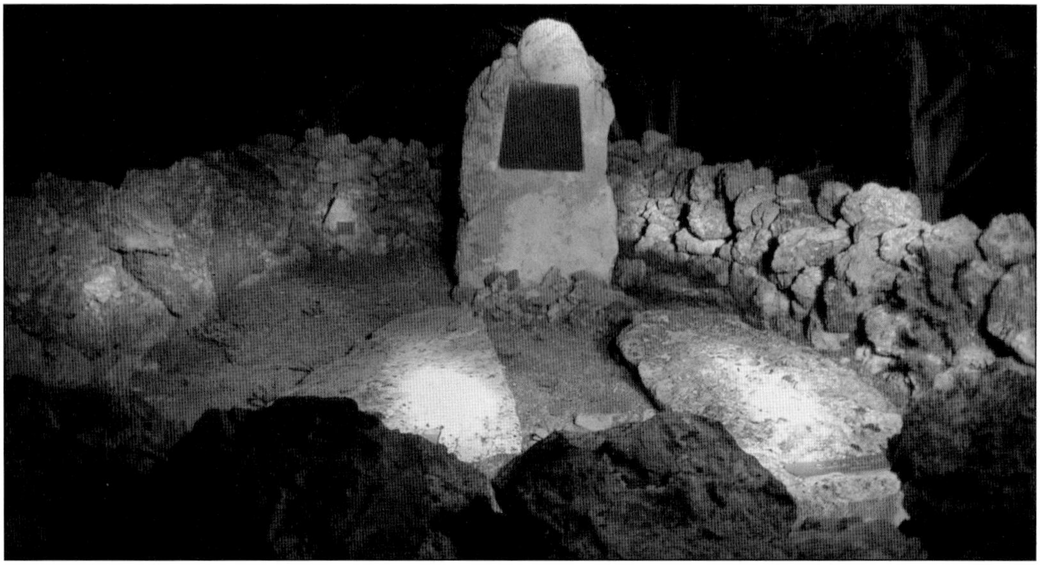

Charles Brant and his wife, Olga, managers of the El Tovar Hotel, made arrangements with the newly formed Grand Canyon National Park administration to be buried within sight of their facility. Today, their graves are difficult to find, located off the Rim Trail from the Hermit's Rest interchange near the worship center. There is no clear trail to these gravesites, but they can be found with some exploring. The above photograph, which is quite striking, was taken of the site at 9:28 p.m. on March 15, 2014, under a full moon. To the left in the photograph above is a tiny marker for the Brants' beloved dog, Razzle Dazzle, who died in 1928 and was buried in this plot. Pictured below is detail of the marker on the isolated graves of Charles and Olga Brant. (Both, David Schmittinger.)

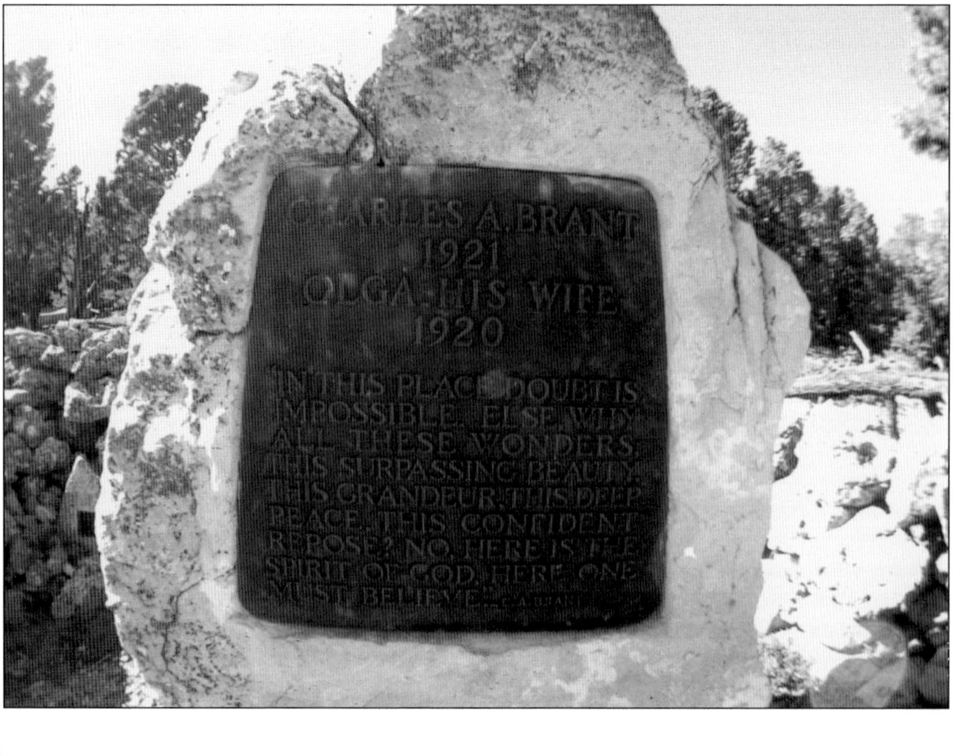

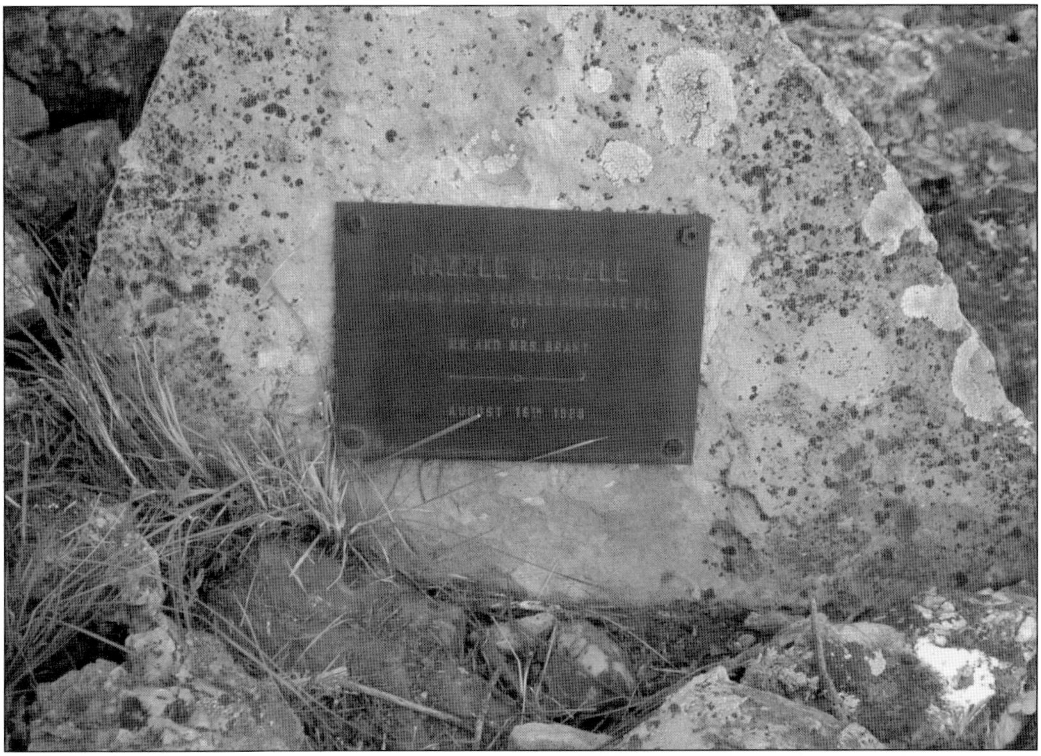

Charles and Olga Brant's dog, Razzle Dazzle, was interred at this gravesite with them upon his death in 1928, complete with a small marker in the corner of the plot. (David Schmittinger.)

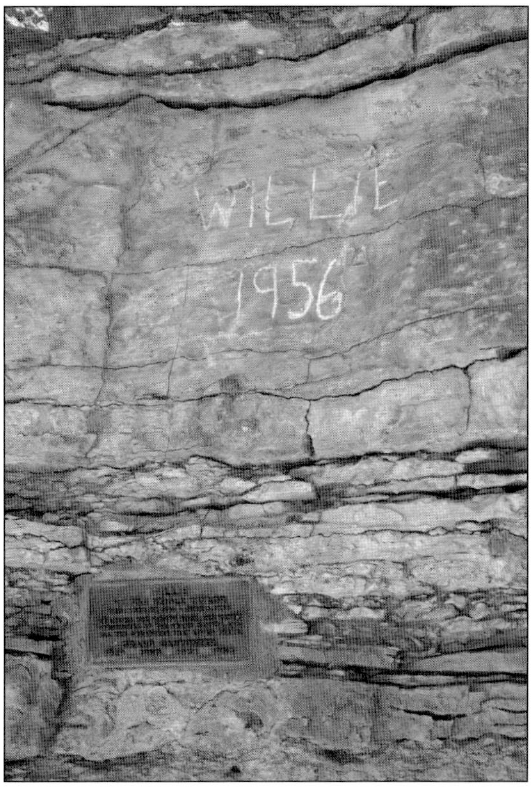

Wilson "Willie" Beigle Taylor was a river runner who died of massive cardiac arrest on June 6, 1956, near River Mile 44.5 on the Colorado River. His companions buried him on the spot without consulting the National Park Service, and he is still there. This photograph of his marker was taken on June 7, 2006. Taylor was also a small-time folk musician, friend of folk singer Katie Lee, and member of the Bohemian Club (Bohemian Grove) in San Francisco, California. (Jeff Shaw.)

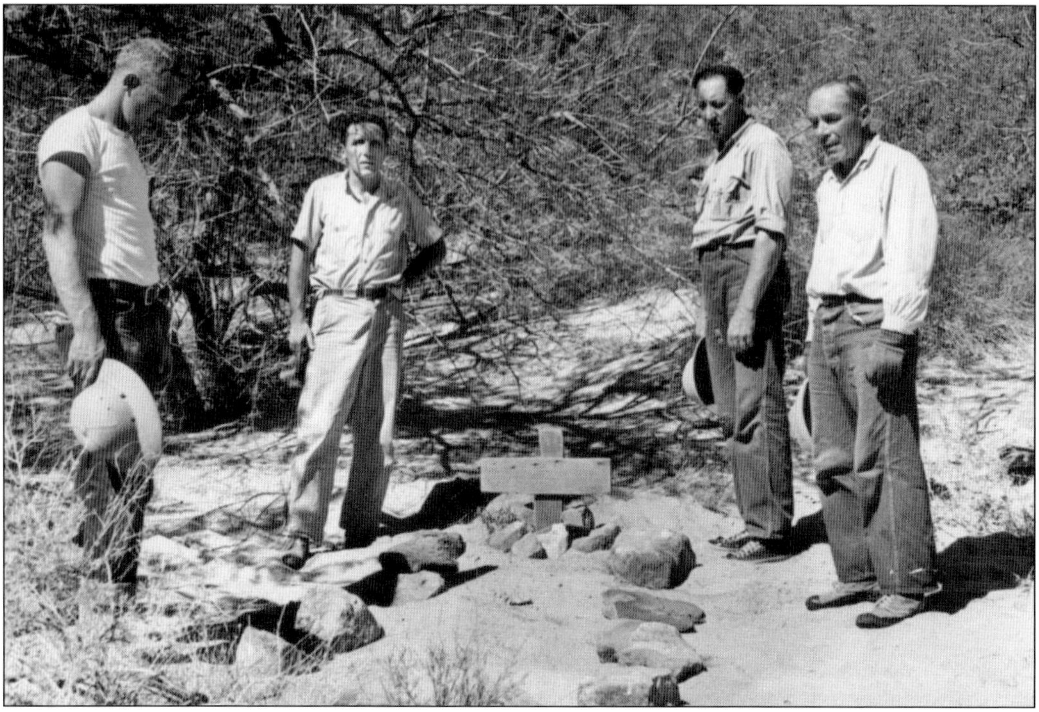

This undated photograph (probably mid-1950s) shows four unidentified men standing around the grave of David Quigley, a young Boy Scout who drowned in the Colorado River on June 26, 1951, at Rincon in Glen Canyon. His body was found five years later, washed downriver, at River Mile 44.5 near where Wilson Beigle Taylor drowned in the Grand Canyon. Quigley was buried on shore and is still there. (Photograph by Emery Kolb; Northern Arizona University-Cline Library Special Collections.)

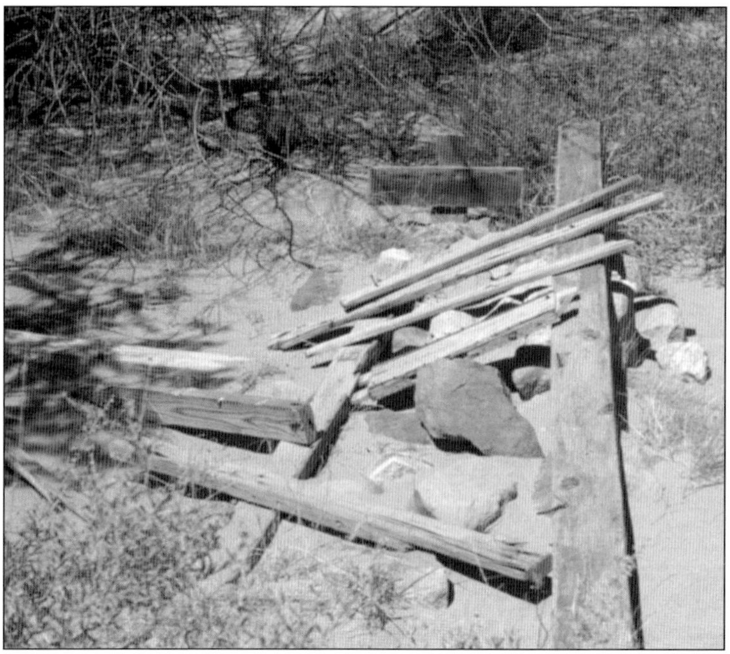

Another 1956 photograph shows the grave of David Quigley, probably shortly after burial. The pile of lumber in this photograph is unexplained, possibly the remains of a grave fence destroyed by a rising current. As Quigley died in Glen Canyon, he is generally not counted among the Grand Canyon's fatalities, even though he is buried here. (Northern Arizona University-Cline Library Special Collections.)

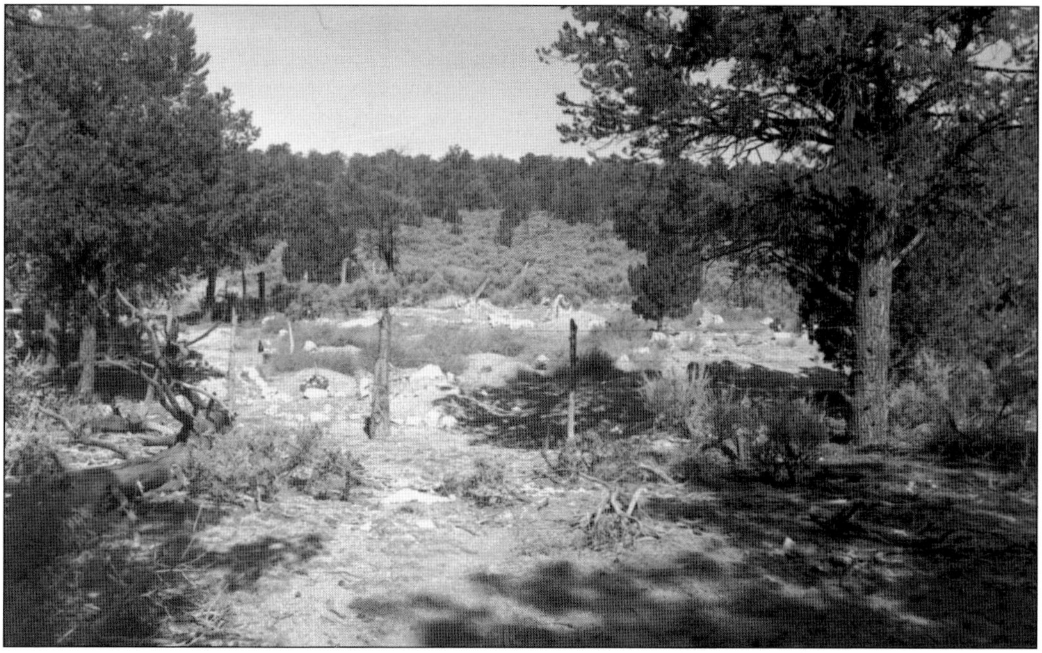

The Drift Fence Cemetery at Supai village on the Havasupai Indian Reservation at the bottom of the Grand Canyon is still active. This photograph, taken March 31, 1953, gives an overview of the tribal cemetery where generations of Havasupai are buried. (Photograph by Steve Leding; Grand Canyon NP Museum Collection No. 02491.)

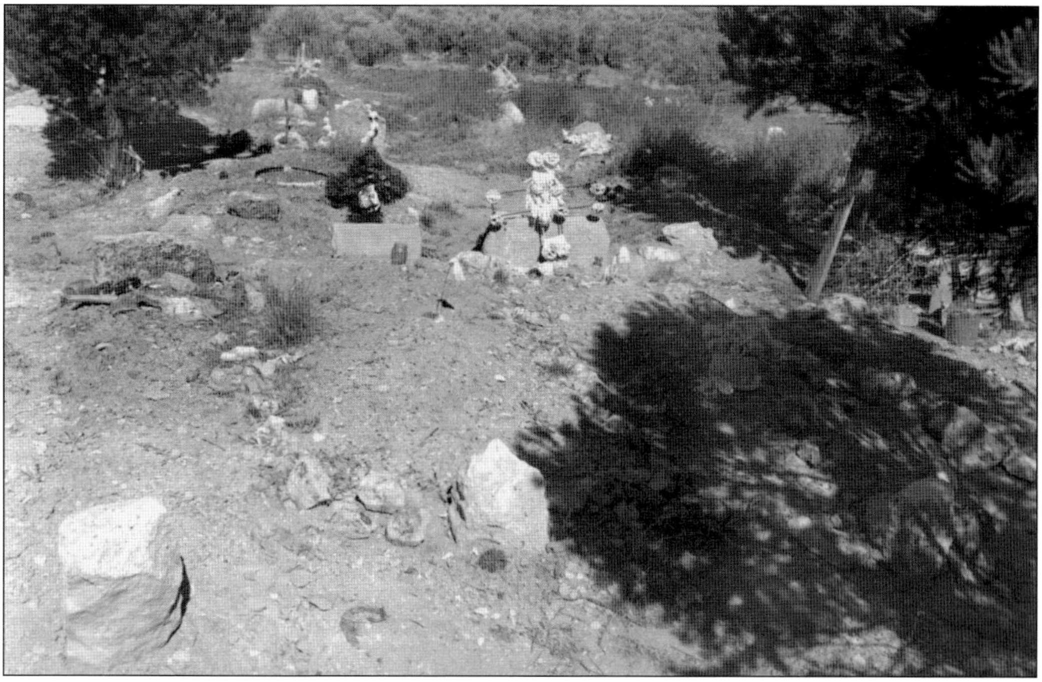

In the center of this photograph of the Drift Fence Cemetery at Supai is the grave of Rose Wescogame, who died in 1935. This photograph was also taken on March 31, 1953. (Photograph by Steve Leding; Grand Canyon NP Museum Collection No. 02489.)

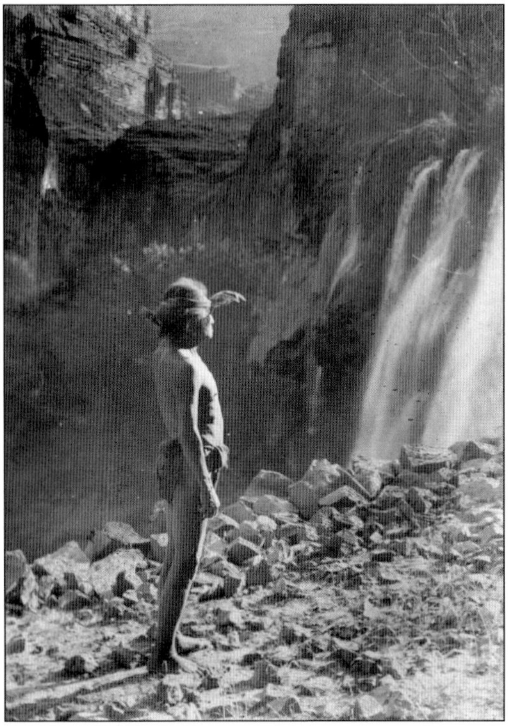

Billy Burro, seen in this 1913 photograph, is a significant figure in Havasupai tribal history. He is remembered as a hero for refusing to vacate his farm near Indian Gardens when the Grand Canyon became a national park. He was forcibly repatriated by rangers to the Havasupai Reservation. (Photograph by Emery Kolb; Grand Canyon NP Museum Collection No. 05546.)

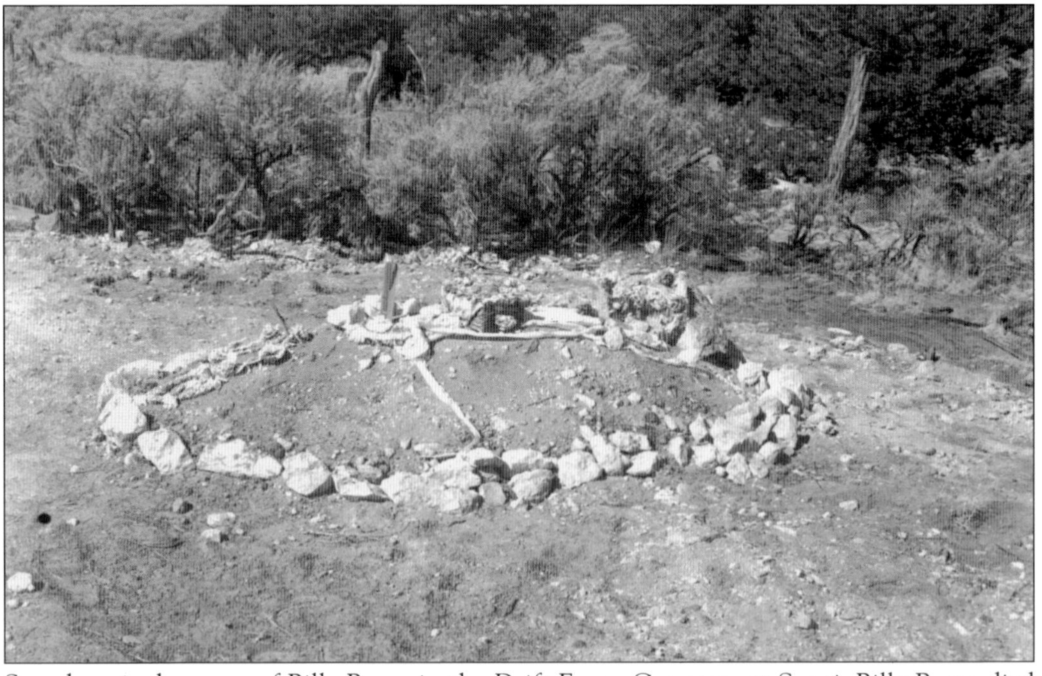

Seen here is the grave of Billy Burro in the Drift Fence Cemetery at Supai. Billy Burro died February 16, 1953, at the Phoenix Indian Hospital at the age of 92. Photographs of Native American burial grounds are rare. The three photographs of the Havasupai cemetery in this chapter were all taken on March 31, 1953. (Photograph by Steve Leding; Grand Canyon NP Museum Collection No. 02490.)

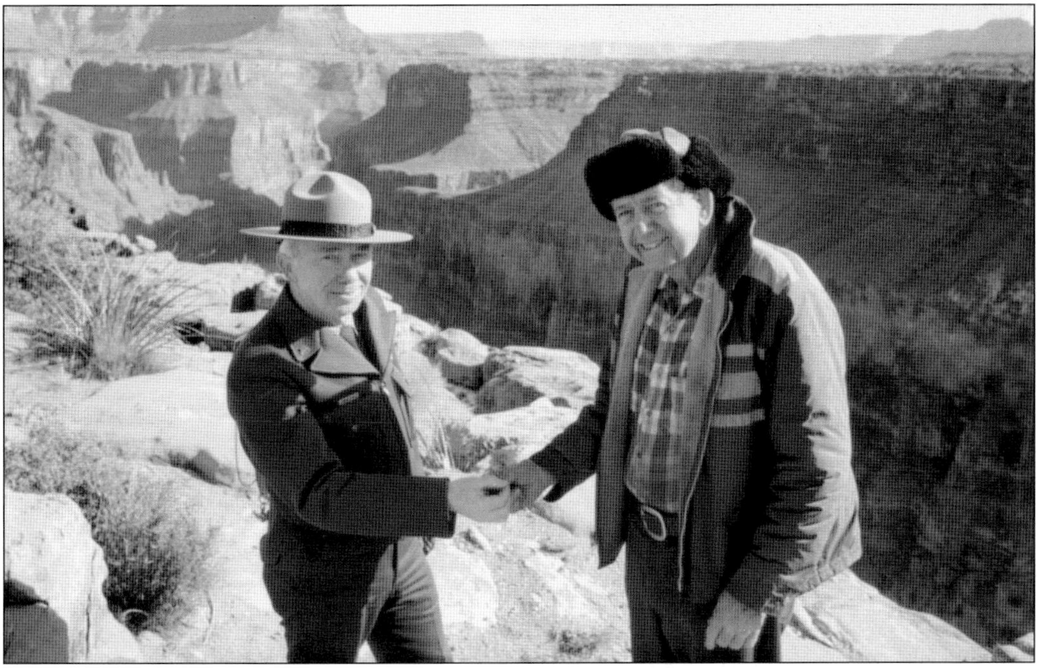

John Riffey (right) was a Grand Canyon park ranger for over 40 years, spent mostly at the Tuweep Ranger Station at the North Rim. This photograph, taken January 26, 1980, shows park superintendent Merle Stitt (left, see page 108) posing with Riffey on the occasion of Riffey receiving his 40-year pin. That may be a Masonic Lodge brotherly handshake they are sharing. This was Stitt's last day before he retired. (Grand Canyon NP Museum Collection No. 05718B.)

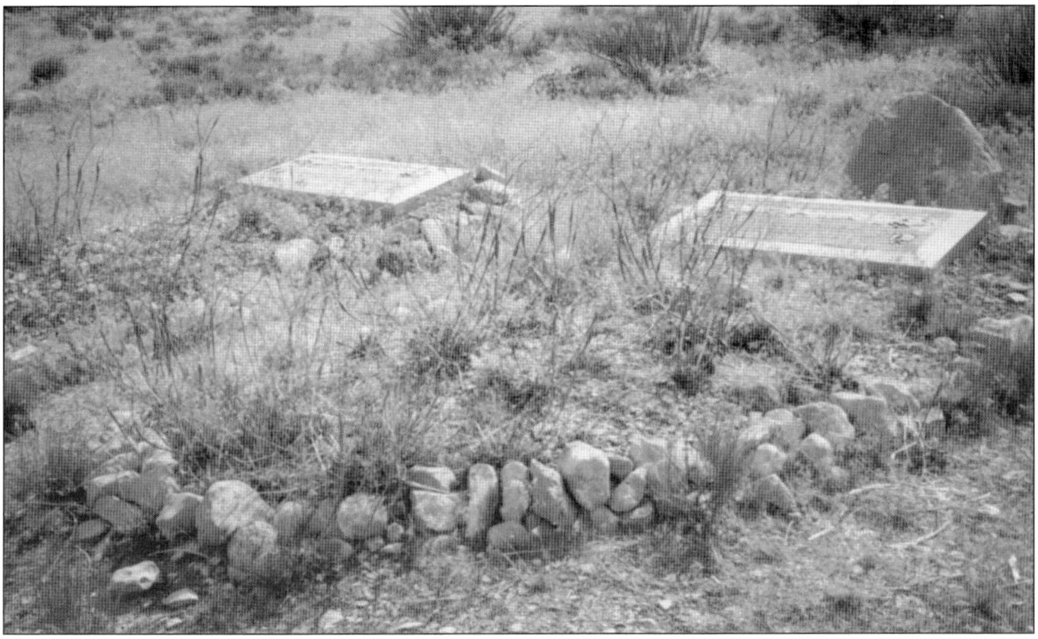

Per their wishes, ranger John Riffey and his wife, Merribeth, are buried near the Tuweep Ranger Station on the North Rim of the Grand Canyon. This photograph shows an overview of their gravesites. (Grand Canyon NP Museum Collection: Cemetery Files.)

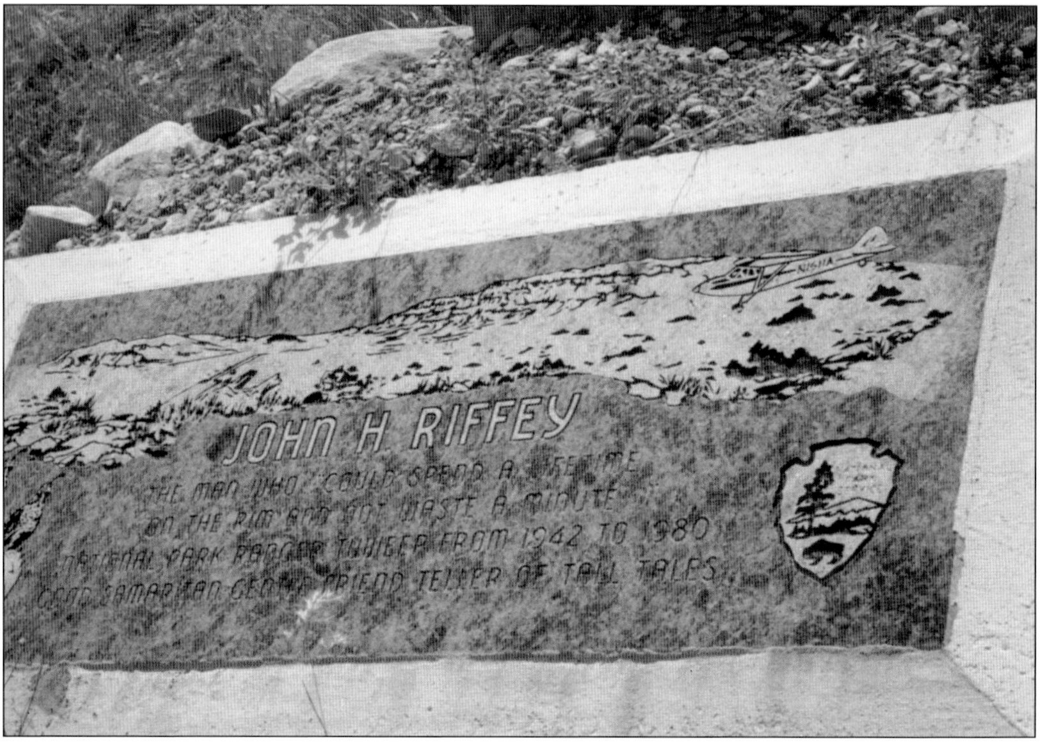

These are the tombstones of John and Merribeth Riffey, near the Tuweep Ranger Station on the North Rim where they wished to be buried. The North Rim does not receive as many visitors as the South Rim. (Both, Grand Canyon NP Museum Collection: Cemetery Files.)

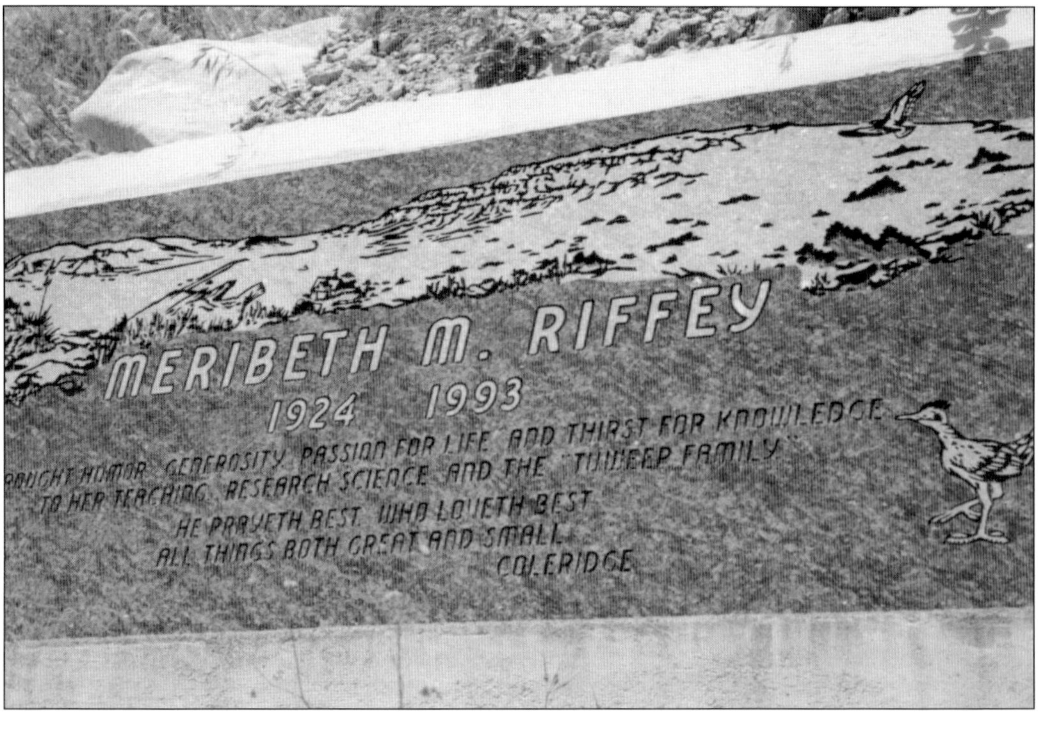

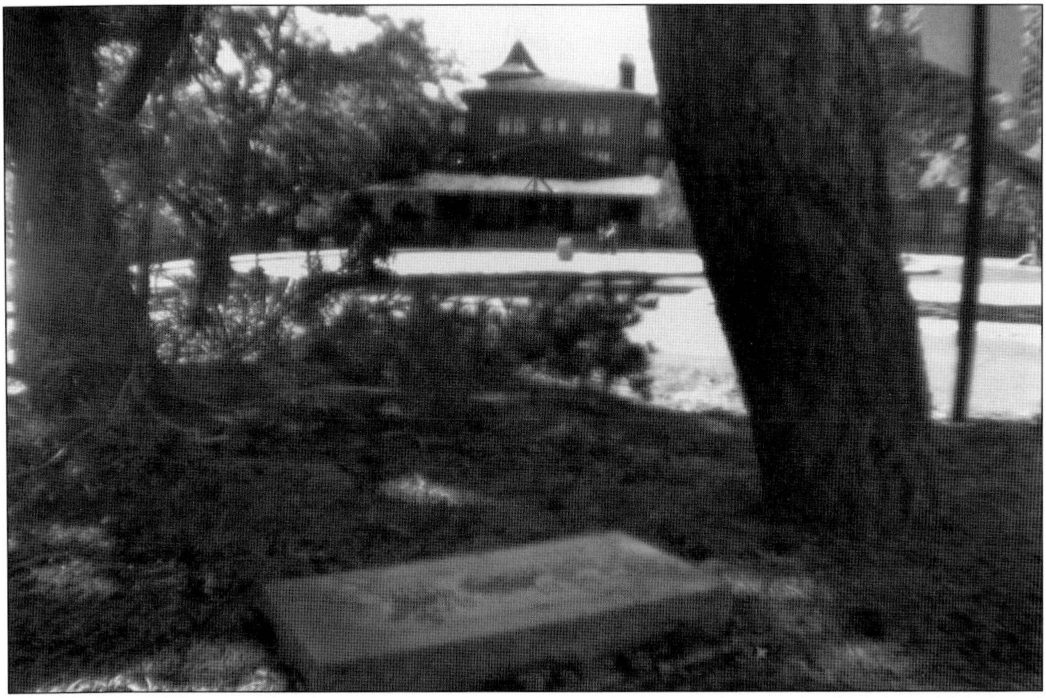

When is a grave not a grave? Pirl Ward was a construction contractor who helped build the El Tovar Hotel. When he died in 1934 and was buried in Artesia, California, the El Tovar placed this marker in his honor just off their parking lot. It is odd placement, and the fact that it so resembles a tombstone has given rise to folklore. The most common (but nevertheless untrue) story contends that Pirl Ward was a Harvey Girl who came to a bad end. When confronted with the truth about this marker, folklorists respond by accusing the National Park Service of a cover up. (Both, David Schmittinger.)

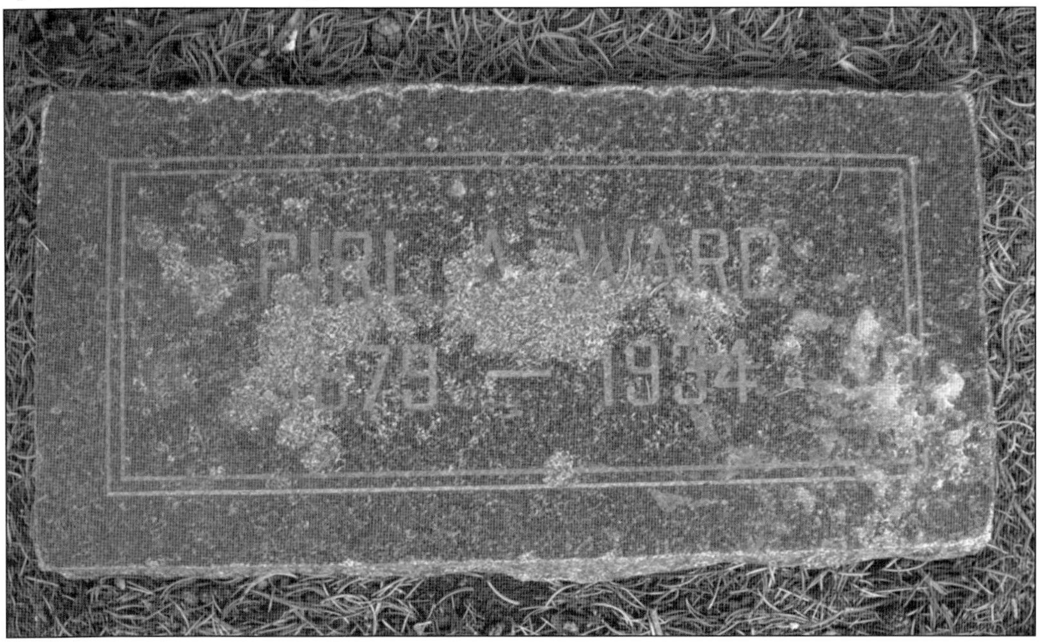

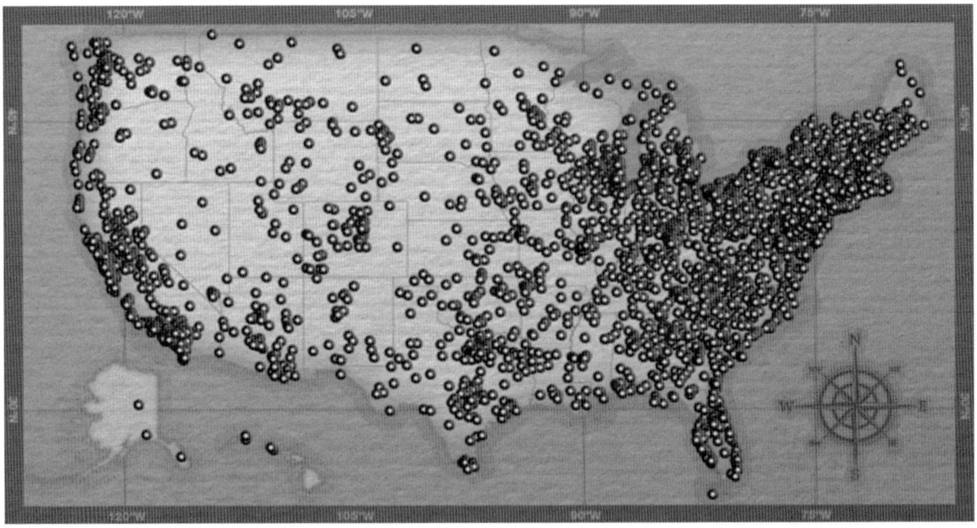